Coalition

The Politics and Personalities of
Coalition Government from 1850

By Mark Oaten

To Belinda with love

HARRIMAN HOUSE LTD

3A Penns Road
Petersfield
Hampshire
GU32 2EW
GREAT BRITAIN

Tel: +44 (0)1730 233870
Fax: +44 (0)1730 233880
Email: enquiries@harriman-house.com
Website: www.harriman-house.com

First published in Great Britain in 2007
Copyright © Harriman House Ltd

The right of Mark Oaten to be identified as Author has been asserted
in accordance with the Copyright, Design and Patents Act 1988.

ISBN: 1-905641-28-1
ISBN 13: 978-1905641-28-4

British Library Cataloguing in Publication Data
A CIP catalogue record for this book can be obtained from the British Library.

Printed and bound by Biddles Ltd, Kings Lynn, Norfolk

Contents

Biography

Mark Oaten was managing director of Westminster Public Relations before standing as Member of Parliament for Winchester in 1997. Mark's two-vote victory in the May election was challenged but he won the subsequent by-election with a majority of 21,556. In the following ten years he served as PPS to Charles Kennedy, Chairman of the Liberal Democrats and the party's Shadow Home Secretary. He currently lectures in politics and is a Trustee for Unlock, the prison reform group. He lives in Winchester with his wife Belinda and two children.

Preface

Forewords and prefaces seem to be a chance for the author to get in before the critics and justify certain stances. So, firstly this book is not designed to be a comprehensive historical record of the events that took place between 1846 and the present day. I have deliberately focused on the periods when significant party co-operation took place and during those periods examined the elements surrounding coalitions more than the events taking place at the same time.

Secondly, I have excluded writing about all the European coalitions and left both Ireland and Israel out as they have very particular sectarian circumstances that set them aside from the normal process.

Thirdly, I picked Scotland rather than Wales because of the strong Scottish links between the Liberals and Labour at Westminster.

Finally, some important thanks. This book would not have been possible without three key people; Celine Tricard worked on the First and Second World War chapters and was infallible and I am enormously grateful for her commitment to accuracy. To Gill Kilmartin and Lyn Anderson I owe a great deal. They have struggled with my handwriting and hundreds of drafts, without a single word of complaint. I must thank Iain Dale for suggesting my publisher, Harriman House. To Myles Hunt at Harriman House for agreeing to take on the project and Suzanne Anderson for editing the book. Thanks to the House of Commons Library for their patience on overdue books. A large number of people agreed to be interviewed: I would particularly like to thank David Steel and Paddy Ashdown for their frankness and Tom McNally for the ability to talk about politics covering four decades with such enthusiasm.

When you write a book you also need people to offer encouragement and ideas, thanks go to Matt Grimshaw, Adam Cohen, and Rhys Williams for this.

This book has helped me recover from a rough time. I will not forget the people who have helped me write it – their support means a great deal.

PS Alice and Milly – thank you for letting daddy hide in his office. Yes, it's now finished!

1

A Stormy Start

A Stormy Start

The night of 15th December 1852 was wild as a storm raged and thunder clapped above the Palace of Westminster. Inside, exhausted Members of Parliament had to wait until 1 a.m. before Chancellor Disraeli wound up the debate on his budget. Knowing he was facing certain defeat from a combination of opposition MPs he launched his now famous attack on coalitions:

> *But coalitions, though successful have always found this, that their triumph has been brief. This too I know, that England does not love coalitions.*[1]

So was he right? This book attempts to answer that question. The story starts with the events that led up to that night and ends looking ahead to what may happen at the next election.

In between there have been various pacts, arrangements and coalitions in Britain, but we remain a country more used to one party power. Coalitions have been created to solve problems. Some during times of national crisis such as the two Great Wars at the start of the last century, others are formed as a result of economic crisis, like the National Government established in the 1930s. There are also those created due to political crisis, such as in the 1970s when Labour had a wafer thin majority, or a political realignment similar to the circumstances Disraeli found himself in after the Conservatives split over the Corn Laws. All very different cases, but with a common trend involving crisis and instability.

With the next election looking like a photo finish, I wanted to write a book that looks back so we can look forward. To see what, if any, lessons can be learnt from history and the rest of Europe.

But it's not just a book about process. I was keen to explore the way in which personalities and trust are key to coalitions. How do politicians from different sides come together and bury the hatchet? Does it lead to incredible friction and tension, or are the politicians behind the scenes able to work effectively together? Personalities drive politics and when egos are forced together in coalition it can lead to fireworks.

Palmerston, Gladstone and Russell ended their period of co-operation in total disarray and mistrust. The Liberals Asquith and Lloyd George even ended up as arch rivals, destroying their party whilst the country was at war. Then there are the odd couples; Edward Heath and Jeremy Thorpe spent an odd weekend trying to form a pact between the Conservatives and Liberals, but never really hit it off.

Sometimes great friendships and partnerships are created and each coalition depends on the personal chemistry working between two leaders. Stanley Baldwin served under Ramsay MacDonald in the National Government of 1931 even though the Baldwin Conservatives had over 400 seats and MacDonald had no party.

Paddy Ashdown and Tony Blair created a friendship that imagined a realignment beyond the comprehension of their two parties. David Steel and Jim Callaghan built trust and loyalty within weeks when the young Liberal leader helped the Labour Prime Minister remain in office. Donald Dewar and Jim Wallace brought power sharing to Scotland for the first time.

Then there are the personalities that end up turning their backs on party politics; MacDonald, Peel, Lloyd George and Churchill all ended up as Prime Ministers without a party.

Most coalitions are formed through a combination of a large party and a small party. This book examines the impact that this has on both partners involved. Do the smaller parties end up benefiting from the arrangement, or suffering through association with a larger party? Will they lose their party identity or grow as a result of power sharing? Particularly relevant is the 1970s arrangement that David Steel and Jim Callaghan put in place and David Steel's interview with me was helpful in understanding the risks involved for the Liberals at the time.

Hung parliaments and coalitions also throw up a number of constitutional issues. In particular the precedent that allows the sitting Prime Minister the first opportunity to form a government even though he may have lost the election and have the least number of seats in parliament. Is this really democratic or does tradition serve us best in terms of uncertainty? The role of the current monarch is very limited compared to her predecessors. King George V played a key role in deciding who should lead the 1930s government. Decades earlier Queen Victoria was exasperated at her attempts to try and find a Prime Minister following the collapse of the Aberdeen coalition.

I have also decided to look at the mechanics of putting a coalition together and the length and type of agreements that parties work to.

Britain is, yet again, out of sync with the rest of Europe. So I visited Italy, Germany and Austria to see how these countries cope with the consequences of a proportional election system which delivers regular coalition governments.

Some of the examples in Europe have been quite helpful and I spent time looking at the various processes, particularly those that were set up during the Grand Coalition in Germany which binds the parties together. Similarly the Scottish agreement is a useful model closer to home.

Beyond these process issues is the very important issue of whether coalition governments actually provide the country with good government. Coming as they do at times of crisis, coalitions are often by their very nature asked to take on demanding and challenging tasks. So it would be unfair to judge them alongside normal political periods, but I wanted to see whether they are able to deliver the challenges they are set and what the impact is when politicians come together in this way.

Does coalition lead to government by committee? Do politicians work together to create dynamic ideas or a fudge based on the lowest common denominator?

My final chapter plays 'what if' and looks ahead to the next election. How will the polls translate into seats? What will each of the three parties do if there is a hung parliament and for the Liberal Democrats (a party I have been part of for half my life) will the opportunity to gain electoral reform slip away yet again, or finally be won?

The story starts over 150 years ago; I am not sure where it will end, but it has been a fascinating journey and has completely changed my opinion on what is best for the country at the next election.

References

1. Hansard, 15 Dec 1852

2

A Coalition Of Egos

A Coalition Of Egos

In the present cabinet are five or six first-rate men of equal, or nearly equal, pretensions, none of them likely to acknowledge the superiority or defer to the opinions of any other, and every one of these five or six considering himself abler and more important than their premier.

Charles Greville

The cast of politicians involved in the political turmoil of the mid nineteenth century reads like a list from the Who's Who of great parliamentarians. Gladstone, Disraeli, Palmerston and Peel all played key parts in a drama that included party splits, the Queen in despair, war with Russia and a coalition government.

Sir Robert Peel though stands out. His decision as Conservative Prime Minister to repeal the Corn Laws created turmoil in his party and led to the formation of a new political movement in his name. The Peelites' influence on politics lasted beyond his death and it was their decision to join ranks with the Whigs that created the coalition led by Lord Aberdeen and eventually the foundation of the Liberal Party.

Abolishing the Corn Laws in 1946 has become a turning point in the political history of the Conservative Party. The measure challenged the party and the long held landed interest of many of its MPs. They regarded the laws as the protection of society and despite party loyalty it was a decision they would fight, creating bitterness and division.

The two leading opponents of Peel's measures were odd bedfellows. Lord Stanley was ultra loyal to the party and held in high regard. Lord George Bentinck was a maverick, more a landowner than Conservative. He was outraged at the attack on his livelihood and did not hold back from public criticism of Peel:

> *I told him I thought Sir Robert Peel and his colleagues were no better than common cheats and ought to be dealt with as such. I believe the punishment in the good old times for an offence of this kind used to be cropping the ears and putting the vagabonds in the pillory.*[1]

Colourful language from a character who was not a stranger to spats that often landed him in court.

As the Conservatives began to divide on the Corn Laws issue, Bentinck emerged as the unofficial leader of the Protectionist wing of the party, leading a large rebel group that was soon to sit in a separate block in the Commons. Lord Stanley was a less willing rebel; always hopeful that the split would be temporary, he held back from the more provocative language used by his allies, but felt strongly enough over the issue to take on the leadership of the Protectionists in the Lords. The Protectionists remained smaller in number than Peel's official Conservatives and lacked strong leadership. Bentinck was not a great parliamentary performer, having sat in eight parliaments without giving a major speech; he was prone to bouts of nerves before he spoke. The real emerging talent was the young Disraeli. He was growing in influence and chose to work with the Protectionist group, forming a bond with Bentinck (a lover of horse racing) that gave them the nickname of "The Jockey and the Jew".

Despite these relative weaknesses the Protectionists were a major problem for Peel, leaving him with a much reduced parliamentary majority and his fate in the hands of the rebels. Even those loyal to Peel were uneasy at his leadership, growing increasingly anxious at the division it was creating in the party. They feared Peel was on a mission over free trade that would damage the party. He was regarded by colleagues as aloof and overbearing, and his single-minded approach to the Corn Laws issue was creating turmoil. However, Peel had been convinced that after the shocking potato harvest and blight in Ireland the removal of restrictions on food and clothing was essential. As Wellington put it:

> The dammed rain wasted away the Corn Laws, wasted away also the Conservative Party that Peel had built.[2]

Critics accuse Peel of looking for a fight with his party and in particular the Tory squires. They argue that he could have found less controversial ways of helping with the Irish famine, by temporarily suspending the Corn Laws he could have achieved the same aim. I think that after five years as Prime Minister he rather enjoyed the impression that he was above party politics. It is a tendency that can affect many leaders and one that Disraeli was quick to pick up on:

> He is so vain that he wants to figure in history as the setter of all the great quotations, but a parliamentary constitution is not favourable to

such ambitions – things must be done by parties, not by persons using parties as tools.[3]

Increasingly both sides became more and more determined that they were representing the true interests of the Conservative Party and the division grew more hostile.

The Protectionists were determined to make Peel's parliamentary life a nightmare, seeking out opportunities to defeat him, and time after time it was only the vote of the Whigs that saved him.

When eventually the Commons moved to debate the Corn Laws there was little love lost between Peel and Disraeli. Speaking for two hours Peel spoke of the benefit free trade could bring and lectured his party on the need to put public interest ahead of self-interest:

I will only hold that office upon the condition of being unshackled by any other obligations than those of consulting the public interests.[4]

When Disraeli rose from the benches behind Peel, he mocked him, accusing him of having few original ideas, chasing public opinion and destroying the country. The debate was bitter and personal; its impact was to last for years as both sides would find it harder and harder to forgive. The actual vote itself showed just how divided the Conservatives had become. The Bill was passed in the Commons on the 15th May by 327/229 votes. The Peel majority contained over 200 Whigs and the opposition was made up of 222 Protectionist Conservatives. Although he had won the vote Peel had lost the party and was now totally dependant on the votes of Whigs.

The vote marked the final stage of the Conservative split, and the Protectionists very quickly organised themselves into a more formal structure. By the end of March 1846 they had elected Whips, formalised Bentinck's position and set themselves the objective of bringing down Peel. Bentinck was a pretty determined character set on revenge:

One of those rare political figures who placed prejudices or principles before everything else including it seemed party unity.[5]

Meanwhile the Whigs were only supporting Peel as long as they needed him to get the Corn Laws passed. Their only hesitation in defeating him was to do it in a way that would not damage future relations with the Peelites.

Peel's great ally, Lord Aberdeen, with wise foresight, had warned the Whigs they:

> had better take care that he did not turn them out in such a fashion as to make it impossible for them to support him afterwards.[6]

Both sides did not wait long for revenge. Within a few months the Commons were debating the Irish Protection of Life Bill, designed to protect life and property against a rise in crime in Ireland. Initially both Whigs and Protectionists voted for it, but within weeks it became regarded as a vote of no confidence in Peel, as its timing came as the Lords were passing the Corn Laws legislation. On the 25th June, Whigs and Protectionists planned careful co-ordination between debates in the Lords and Commons. The Corn Bill received its third reading in the Lords, becoming law with Whig support. Then a few hours later the Whigs joined with the Protectionists to defeat Peel on the Irish Bill in the Commons.

Peel, for his part, seemed to have shown little fight over the final defeat. Exhausted after the Corn Laws experience, he could have worked harder to obtain support in the Irish vote, but seemed resigned to his fate. He immediately resigned and the Queen summoned the Whig Lord John Russell to become Prime Minister. Peel was defeated, but his influence was far from over.

Three-Party Politics

Three-party politics was now in place and it struggled to fit into the Commons' system, with arguments about seating arrangements and party names. The normal order was thrown into chaos and it would take over a decade for the party politics system to settle down.

> In fact between Peel's resignation in 1846 and the Second Reform Bill in 1867 there were nine administrations, several of which had no stable parliamentary majority.[7]

A general election quickly followed in 1847, but did little to provide stability. The Peelites and Protectionists did manage to avoid standing against each other in most cases although there were ten direct fights. The major significance in the result was a reversal of power between the two groups. The election left the Protectionists with 243 MPs and the Peelites with 89. It was at least now clear who the main opposition were, but not who led them. By December 1847, Bentinck had resigned as the Protectionists' leader after yet another bitter internal row, this time over the position of various rights for Jewish people. A new leader, Lord Granby, was appointed but lasted just three days. The vacuum at the top of the Protectionists was complete when Bentinck then died the following September. The obvious choice to lead the party was Disraeli, without doubt the most talented MP they had, but he was not a popular choice:

> *There can be no doubt that there is a very strong feeling amongst Conservatives in the House of Commons against him. They are puzzled and alarmed by his mysterious manner which has much the foreigner about it and are incapable of understanding and appreciating the great ability which certainly underlies and as it were are concealed by his mask.*[8]

In the end the party turned to the Upper House for its leader and Lord Stanley (soon to become Lord Derby) emerged as the compromise candidate. He would lead working closely with Disraeli for the next few years, although theirs was not an easy relationship, Stanley was always nervous that his association with Disraeli would make any reunion with the Peelites much harder – describing him as:

> *The most powerful repellent we could offer to any repentant or hesitating Peelites.*[9]

It is true that Disraeli was a major barrier to reunion. I think that without his influence, Stanley might have been able to hold an olive branch out to the key Peelites, Aberdeen and Gladstone. He certainly needed these men of talent as the opposition was struggling and too dependant on Disraeli.

However, despite Stanley's wishes I could see little realistic hope of a reunion taking place at this point. The damage had been done; the bitter words and personality clashes were still too fresh in people's minds. If there was to be a coming together then Peel's death in 1850 could have been a trigger. Unexpected death often brings old allies together, but after Peel's death, a few days after a riding accident, there was no reconciliation. Even in death the bitterness continued and while the nation mourned, some Protectionists could not resist describing him as a class traitor.

Throughout all of this, the Whigs governed without much effective opposition and with little impact.

It is the duty of a government to govern and not merely to administer then Russell's Ministry was not a government.[10]

He lacked real leadership and the government was run rather like one long select committee meeting. His more talented Ministers, Lord Palmerston and Earl Grey, were mavericks with little regard for the Cabinet. The administration staggered from session to session dependent on occasional Peelites support and a divided opposition. In particular the Whigs had depended on the talents of Peel and his death left Lord Russell in a perilous position. Peel himself had been determined to keep Lord Russell in office, without any formal pact, or coalition, he preferred to act as a grand advisor. He also knew that any formal arrangement with the Whigs at this stage might have pushed his followers too far. After all, only a few years ago they had all been Conservatives. Sir John Young summed up the view of many Peelites:

He told Peel that the men who held the balance in the House, Conservatives who favoured free trade, had no sympathy with and no confidence in the present government. They are with you, not with Lord Russell, they will not make sacrifices and risk their seats night after night and year after year for those whom they cannot help regarding as political opponents.[11]

Eventually, without any formal arrangement in place, the Russell administration ran into serious trouble. The Whigs were defeated in the Commons early in the 1851 parliamentary sessions over a proposal to change county and borough franchises. It was clear that his parliamentary majority was very unstable and Russell resigned suggesting to Queen Victoria that Lord Stanley should try to establish a Conservative administration.

It is not clear if Russell seriously thought he should resign, or was calling the Conservatives' bluff. Either way it worked and Lord Stanley spent the next few days being humiliated as he tried to form a government.

The Conservatives had little to offer and were out of favour at the court. The Queen and Prince Albert were more sympathetic to the Peelites and distrusted Disraeli. Stanley struggled to find able ministers he could present to the Queen and eventually abandoned his attempts.

Disraeli was furious that the chance for office, now within his grasp, was to slip away. The experience left him restless and he became determined to create another opportunity to eject the Whigs as soon as possible.

For his part Russell returned as Prime Minister, secure at least in the knowledge that the Conservatives remained, for the moment, unfit to replace his government.

Although his position remained weak, the resignation episode had also shown him that the Peelites were not prepared to reunite with the Conservatives. It was an important indicator of where future loyalty would lie. With this in mind Russell and his Whig colleagues became more and more aware of the need to develop strong links with the Peelites. They knew that next time they lost a key vote the Conservatives might be in a better position to snatch power. For the Whigs the Peelites represented an important insurance policy and the start of negotiations between the parties seemed to emerge at about this time.

Russell calculated that if any deal had to be done then the question would be how Peelites and Whigs could work together. Would it be a merger, pact, or coalition? For his part Russell was keen to see a merger, but the Peelites were determined to avoid absorption. They were not Whigs and did not want to throw away their independence. Queen Victoria used her influence to stress this point to Russell explaining, in her opinion that:

> *He was unlikely to affect the absorption of the Peelites into the Whigs government though she believed (a little prematurely) that they were quite ready for a fusion.*[12]

The steps towards coalition were underway, but there was to be a further drama before any arrangements were set in place.

Palmerston had remained a loose cannon in the Whigs' administration. Above collective responsibility, he was a risk taker and robust Foreign Secretary. He eventually overstepped the mark when he decided to issue a note congratulating Napoleon III on his tough crackdown on French radicals. The Queen was not a fan of the French President and was furious that her Foreign Secretary had written without her approval. Russell was left with little option than to sack him, creating a time bomb on the backbenches.

Palmerston now found himself out of office and out of favour with the Whigs. He was in no mood to retire and sought revenge at the earliest opportunity. His chance came a few months later when Lord Russell introduced a bill to set up local militia. Palmerston saw his chance and moved an amendment ridiculing the idea of locally based organisations and calling for a national body that could stand up to a foreign invader. The Conservatives supported it and Russell was defeated by thirteen votes.

> *The Palmerstons were jubilant. This was their revenge for*
> *Palmerston's dismissal from the Foreign Office. Two months after*
> *Palmerston's fall he had shown the government could not survive.*[13]

Russell resigned yet again and once again the Queen called for Lord Stanley, now Lord Derby. Desperate to avoid the embarrassment of his previous failed attempt to take power, Derby quickly sought out new allies. He immediately turned to Palmerston and offered him the Chancellorship. Despite his bitterness towards Russell, Palmerston was not prepared to join the Conservatives and he turned down the offer, preferring to take his position as the grand elder statesman that all parties sought to get on side.

Derby did not give in so easily this time and despite the lack of high profile names was able to form an administration. Its lack of star quality gained it the nickname of the 'who who administration'. The story goes that the deaf Duke of Wellington muttered 'Who? Who?' as the list of Ministers was read out to him. The Queen remained doubtful about the Cabinet – in a letter to her Uncle Leopold she said that Lord Derby had a 'very sorry Cabinet. I believe, however, that it is quite necessary they should have a trial and then have done with it'.[14]

The "trial" was to last for most of 1852, but the administration managed to survive on a day-to-day basis. The big success for the Conservatives was the Chancellorship of Disraeli. He gained public and critical acclaim; this in the *Edinburgh Review* was typical:

> *His appointment to this post was one of the most startling domestic*
> *events which have occurred in our time. People seemed never tired of*
> *talking and speculating on it. He glittered in the political horizon as a*
> *star of the first magnitude.*[15]

Even his royal critics had cause to reconsider their opinions. Prince Albert had two long meetings with Disraeli and declared him:

One of the best educated men, indeed over educated, something of a
pedant and a theorist, but a man of talent nevertheless.[16]

With things going well by the summer of 1852 Derby felt confident enough
to call a general election. The result did little to clear things up. As with the
previous election no party had a clear majority. The Conservatives rose in
number to 290, the Peelites on 43 and Whigs on 319.

Derby formed a new minority government, but was quickly to be tested on
the old sore of free trade. The Conservatives had come to the view that they
should abandon their policy of reintroducing protectionism, but rather than
gracefully accepting the conversion the Whigs and Peelites were irritated at
the U turn and immediately put the government on the spot with a vote of
censure on the issue.

The opposition's anger was shared by Queen Victoria:

When Lord Derby told the Queen in June 1852 that he considered
protection 'quite gone' she wrote somewhat wearily that it was a pity
he had not found this out a little sooner. 'It would have saved so much
annoyance, so much difficulty.' [17]

It was left to Palmerston to use his new-found independent status to step in
and suggest a compromise amendment that welcomed the government's
adoption of free trade. His intervention saved Derby and Disraeli and they
lived to fight another day. Encouraged by Palmerston's intervention they
made another attempt to get him to join them, but again he refused. He
could see that the Derby ship was clearly starting to take on water and was
not about to clamber aboard at such a late stage. Derby was in a near
impossible situation. He had no majority and was dependant on either
Peelite or Whig support, without any formal arrangement with either group.
It was remarkable that his administration had lasted so long, but its days
were numbered as the opposition looked for the next big confidence vote.
That day came with the budget due in December 1852. It was now clear
that the government would stand, or fall, on its contents and Disraeli's
ability to take the House with him.

The key budget issue was over the way in which earned and non-earned
incomes were to be taxed. This was part of a long list of complex measures
that Disraeli planned to help reform the tax system. He also proposed new
forms of relief to help industries that had lost out due to the end of

protection. Realistically though as the days built up to the budget it became clear that Whigs and Peelites were now sufficiently organised and motivated to turn this into a vote of no confidence, irrespective of the merits of his proposals.

The night of the 16th December 1852 was a foul one. Outside the Palace of Westminster a storm raged with thunder and lightening creating a dramatic backdrop to the final days of the budget debate and vote. Disraeli, knowing that his budget was set for defeat, launched an attack on coalitions:

> *Yes, I know what I have to face. I have to face a coalition. The combination may be successful. A coalition before this has been successful but coalitions although successful, have always found this, that their triumph has been brief.*

Then after a pause and with a thump of the hand he concluded:

> *This too, I know that England does not love coalitions.*[18]

His great rival Gladstone responded, infuriating Disraeli with stinging remarks and a line-by-line demolishment of the budget.

Exhausted MPs then divided at 3 a.m. The government lost by nineteen votes with Whigs, Peelites, radicals and the Irish all streaming into the opposition lobby. The drama and the government were over.

What happened next was to present politicians and the monarch with a major headache.

Horse Trading With Victoria

The Whigs could not return to power with Lord Russell, as Palmerston and his supporters would not join following the row the year before. An alternative Whig leader was needed.

So when Derby resigned on the 17th December he advised the Queen to send for the Whig, Lord Lansdowne, an elderly statesman and safe pair of hands who had served as Chancellor of the Exchequer forty years before.

Derby had also mentioned to the Queen that he was aware of talks between Whigs and Peelites about a joint administration under Lord Aberdeen.

In the end the Queen and Prince Albert decided to call both Lansdowne and Aberdeen to find out what the various options were. Russell remained out in the cold! However, Lansdowne was unable to travel due to a severe attack of gout and Aberdeen was reluctant to go until he had a plan in place.

Aberdeen had wanted to see a fusion between the Peelites and Whigs. He believed that a realignment could take place and wanted a new party called the Liberal Conservative Party created from a merger between Peelites and Whig principles.

In the past he had hoped that the Conservative Party would be reunited, but the failure to heal those wounds led him to believe a merger with the Whigs was the best route to create political stability. He was determined that any merger would be of equals – not with Whigs dominating. For this reason, on a temporary basis at least, he felt he, rather than Russell, should lead the coalition.

He had been involved in preliminary discussions with fellow Peelites and Whigs before Derby's government was defeated; now with only hours before he was due to see the Queen, the talks stepped up a gear. The first step in creating the coalition was Lansdowne. When Aberdeen called on him he said he was not prepared to become Prime Minister, arguing that he would find it hard to get Peelites to serve under him and telling Aberdeen he would make a better Prime Minister. A trickier meeting was to follow with Russell when the two men bumped into each other in Hyde Park. Aberdeen left that meeting believing that Russell had agreed to serve under him as long as he was made Foreign Secretary. It was a conversation Russell was to dispute later, but as Aberdeen left for the Queen on Sunday 19th December, he believed he had support to form a coalition from the two leading Whigs, Lansdowne and Russell.

Aberdeen told the royal couple that he had an agreement in place, but that:

> *The new government should not be a revival of the old Whig Cabinet with the addition of some Peelites, but should be a Liberal/ Conservative government in the sense of that of Sir Robert Peel.*[19]

Queen Victoria was content. The deal was done. Aberdeen left having kissed hands as Prime Minister. By Sunday evening the embryonic coalition was already in trouble.

The day after agreeing to serve as Foreign Secretary, Russell changed his mind. Historians have argued that Russell was persuaded by his wife and friends that it was demeaning to serve under Aberdeen. He told Aberdeen that he would 'support the coalition from outside, while advising his friends to accept office'.[20]

Within a few days Russell changed his mind again and agreed to take on the Foreign Office. What remains unclear is if Aberdeen also promised him that he would shortly step down as Prime Minister in favour of Russell. Aberdeen denies any deal took place, but equally he'd never made any secret that he regarded himself as the creator of the coalition and did not plan to lead forever.

Deal or no deal, this relationship was to be a troublesome one throughout the coalition. Russell was to cause endless problems for Aberdeen. His behaviour was outrageous giving Aberdeen conflicting messages, threatening the whole coalition and still holding his own ambitions to be Prime Minister. I think Aberdeen should have accepted Russell's first refusal; by allowing him to change his mind he was left with a Foreign Secretary that would undermine his leadership.

Russell seemed to have an ability to provoke strong opinions on all sides and at various times those who refused to serve under him included Palmerston, Peelites and many in his own party.

> He possessed, despite his oddities, his eccentricity and his tiresome second wife, a prestige which made him an indispensable member of the coalition. But he was thin-skinned, sensitive about loss of status and fussy about his honour.[21]

It was now four days since Derby had resigned and Aberdeen was still trying to pull together his coalition team. With the monarch and Russell now on board he turned his attention to the next big political prize. Palmerston and Aberdeen met on the 21st December. Palmerston's first instinct was to stay out of the coalition.

> They had stood so long in hostile array one against the other that it was too late now to join and the combination would not be acceptable to either party.[22]

He also warned that he would find parliamentary reform a tricky issue. It was a warning that Aberdeen should have paid more attention to.

Like Russell days before, it was now Palmerston's turn to change his mind. The next day he told Aberdeen he would serve as Home Secretary. On 31st December, Palmerston wrote to his brother-in-law, Sullivan, and explained why he had changed his mind:

> *I have for the last twelve months been acting the part of a very distinguished tight-rope dancer and much astonishing the public by individual performances and feats…So far, so well; but even Madame Sacqui, when she had mounted her rope and flourished among her rockets, never thought of making the rope her perch, but prudently came down again to avoid a dangerous fall.*[23]

Aberdeen now found himself with two rather reluctant and indecisive bedfellows. By agreeing to include both Russell and Palmerston in the government he was asking for trouble. That said, by Christmas week the Cabinet list that he was able to present to the Queen was much more a 'Who's Who of Politics' than Derby's 'who who' administration. The proposed Cabinet included seven Peelites, five Whigs and one radical. Palmerston, Russell and Gladstone held the major offices of State. Graham summed up the team:

> *It's a powerful team, but it will require good driving. There are some odd tempers and queer ways amongst them, but on the whole they are gentlemen, and they have a perfect gentleman at their head, who is honest and direct and who will not brook insincerity in others.*[24]

For Aberdeen there was to be one more drama before he could enjoy Christmas. Russell was furious at the allocation of Cabinet places. He argued that the Peelites were far too dominant compared to the number of seats they had in parliament. In fairness he had a point and suggested adding extra Whigs to the Cabinet to balance things out. Desperate to resolve the issue Aberdeen agreed and on Christmas Eve the final Cabinet was agreed. The four key offices of State were evenly divided:

- Prime Minister: Earl of Aberdeen (Peelite)

- Chancellor of the Exchequer: W E Gladstone (Peelite)

- Home Secretary: Lord Palmerston (Whig)

- Foreign Secretary: Lord John Russell (Whig)

The talent in the coalition was without question – the bitterness, however, was never to disappear; the distrust between Russell and Aberdeen was like a cancer in the coalition. Aberdeen's reluctance to be Prime Minister did not help, but despite this he had shown enormous patience in dealing with the egos of both Russell and Palmerston. I have tended to regard him as more of a diplomat than a leader, but Disraeli described him in less than glowing terms:

> *His manner, arrogant and yet timid – his words insolent and yet obscure – offend even his political supporters.*[25]

He managed to create a Cabinet that gave major positions to the Peelites despite their smaller strength. They were happy at the outcome and with good reason; as the smallest of the three parties they had secured the posts of Prime Minister and Chancellor. The Whigs had less reason to welcome the outcome. Although Russell was Foreign Secretary, many Whigs felt they had thrown away an opportunity to dominate events. Queen Victoria was delighted at the turn of events. Writing to update her Uncle Leopold, she wrote:

> *The success of our excellent Aberdeen's arduous task and the formation of so brilliant and strong a Cabinet is the realisation of the country's and our most ardent wishes and it deserves and will, I think, command great support.*[26]

'It Will Require Good Driving'

So Britain found itself with a coalition government. So often a coalition needs a direct focus and challenge to draw parties together, but this time there was no war, or economic crisis for it to solve. The challenge for this coalition was to provide a period of political stability. There had been little progress on domestic issues since the Corn Laws had been repealed six years before. Aberdeen did not have a great reforming programme in mind when he drew together his coalition. He had the goodwill of the monarch and he had a talented, if temperamental, team, but he lacked strong leadership. He was not a great speaker, or powerful leader, his skill was diplomacy and bringing a team together.

The first big challenge for the coalition was the economic situation. There was no crisis, but after years of instability the country needed a clear budget and direction.

It had been Aberdeen's wish that the coalition should draw its direction from his old ally Peel – with a pro-free trade financial system. The task for the first budget fell to Gladstone who was to emerge as one of the great successes of the coalition. His 1853 budget was radical and sought to reduce, and then scrap income tax over a seven-year period.

Income tax was seen as an unfair source of revenue as it targeted earned, rather than unearned, sources of income.

He also achieved a long held Peel ambition by abolishing 123 articles from the tariff list and reducing levels on a further 135. Amongst the tariff changes was the reduction of duty on tea, newspapers and soap.

The budget reviews made great reading for Gladstone and the coalition. Colleagues heaped praise on him, even Russell who had a difficult relationship with the Chancellor described the budget as:

One of the most powerful financial speeches ever made[27]

The budget was an important start for the coalition giving it much needed confidence early in its life and helped extend its predicted life expectancy.

Other domestic policies were to follow, notably education funding. The grant was increased by £250,000 per year. This was to be matched with a plan to create local education authorities. The measure, however, was delayed following pressure from religious groups and then ran out of parliamentary time. Other reforms also fell for lack of time including reform of the Civil Service.

Meanwhile Russell remained desperate for a role in the coalition. Still ambitious to replace Aberdeen and envious of Gladstone he decided to make his mark with a Reform Bill. During the recess of 1853, he drafted plans which would modernise the election process and try to reduce corruption. His measures also sought to change the franchise with the reform of voting rights and systems. He proposed to abolish small parliamentary seats and reduce the number of MPs that could represent small boroughs. In all, 66 seats would face some sort of re-distribution. The effect of the measure would be to increase the vote for working class urban areas.

It was a brave attempt by Russell to make the system fairer in representation, but it was a political hot potato. Any measure to change boundaries and representation is guaranteed to be unpopular in Westminster – Russell's was no exception! By the end of November 1853, Aberdeen began to realise that the coalition may struggle to pass the Bill. These fears were realised when Palmerston made it clear he regarded this as a resignation issue. When he joined the coalition he had expressed concern at working with Russell and his dislike of a Reform Bill; now both had combined and he was 'not prepared to be dragged thought the dirt by John Russell'.[28]

Faced with his resignation, Aberdeen, as so often in the past, turned to the Queen for guidance. Not surprisingly she and Prince Albert were keen to finally see the back of Palmerston and urged Aberdeen to sack him before he could resign.

> *The Queen very much advises Lord Aberdeen to let him go at once.*
> *He will be a source of mischief for the country as long as he lives, but*
> *the Queen has now had ample and varied experiences that the*
> *mischief he is able to do in office exceeds any he can do in*
> *opposition.*[29]

The next few days were followed by the now all too familiar indecisiveness on all sides. Aberdeen sought to obtain a resignation from Palmerston, who in turn kept changing his mind. Eventually on the 16th December 1853, the resignation came and the first blow was landed on a now weakening coalition.

Russell continued with his Reform Bill into the Spring of 1854, but Palmerston's resignation had created widespread opposition. Seeing the writing on the wall, Russell was keen to withdraw the Bill until a later date. He felt bruised by the criticism and did not have the heart for a long parliamentary battle for a Bill that looked doomed. Despite several attempts to abandon the Bill and then resign, Aberdeen did all he could to keep Russell in the Cabinet. Although they had an uneasy relationship he believed that the reforming measures were important for the country and he was frustrated that yet another domestic reform was to fail. He was also unwilling to lose Russell so soon after Palmerston had quit. Bluntly the coalition was looking fragile and although Russell was not a popular member, to lose another Whig at this stage was unhelpful.

In the end the decision was taken out of both men's hands as the coalition was rocked by an event that would mark the beginning of the end for both of them.

War By Committee

A war sixty years later would lead to the creation of a coalition government, but in 1854 the Crimean War was to end one. I actually think in part that the divisions and weaknesses of the coalition actually helped create the war.

For the purpose of this book I will not record the details of the war with Russia. Its interest to me relates to the way a coalition government had to compromise and helped create an unnecessary war.

Russia's decision to occupy parts of Turkey had created a diplomatic crisis. The French and British governments' declaration of war against Russia was drawn out until on the 27th February 1854 the two allies finally sent an ultimatum to Russia to withdraw from the principalities within a month. There was no response from the Tsar and on the 28th March war was declared.

One reason for the delay in resolving the crisis was a serious Cabinet split on the best approach to take. The Whigs' view can best be summarised as a more aggressive stance, they would have issued tougher and earlier warnings to Russia. The Peelites on the whole tended to favour a more softly, softly diplomatic approach. Aberdeen himself was opposed to the war. He felt that the crisis could be resolved through diplomacy. The resulting compromise was, however, the worst option displaying indirection, confusion and a drift into war. If coalitions can be accused of policy by committee then this was surely an example where the policy was poorer for compromise. The position did not even have the merit of creating a united Cabinet as both sides felt uneasy at the approach. As events got out of control, both, with justification, could argue that their preferred route would have avoided the worsening situation.

After war was declared Aberdeen had no clear strategy for war and the Army was badly lacking in equipment and resources. It was a disaster in the making and month by month, battle by battle, events spiralled out of control. Unlike previous wars this was the first to get in-depth and detailed media coverage. *The Times* sent a journalist, William Henry Russell, to the

Crimea, who became the first war correspondent to join an army. His reports on the horrors he saw had a major impact on public opinion.

Of the 30,000 troops sent to the Crimea, 6,000 had died and 8,000 were injured or sick within the first seven weeks. Politicians, and now the public, became concerned over reports that troops had poor equipment, no tents, and a lack of food and medical supplies. Florence Nightingale's mission to the Crimea caught the public's imagination and for the first time people saw the horrific, rather than glorious, side of war.

Aberdeen had misjudged public opinion and faced with a hostile media his style of laidback leadership was ill-fitted to the demands. The cold winter of 1854/55 brought increased pain for the troops, but it was the disaster of the Charge of the Light Brigade that became the final symbol of government failure.

On the 13th December Russell raised the event at the Cabinet, calling on the Secretary of State for War, Newcastle, to resign and for Palmerston, his old enemy, to be put in charge. The Cabinet united to save Newcastle, and once again Russell was left isolated.

Colleagues were suspicious that Russell was again putting his own ambitions ahead of unity, but in fairness to him, he had raised these concerns months before. In May 1854 he wrote to Aberdeen:

> *Had I full confidence in the administration of which you are the head, I should not scruple to take office under you. But the late meeting of the Cabinet has shown so much indecision that there is so much reluctance to adopt those measures which would force the Emperor of Russia to consent to a speedy peace, that I can feel no such confidence.*[30]

Whether fired by ambition, or genuine concern at the war, Russell was not going to let the issue die.

On the 23rd January 1855, parliament returned after the Christmas break and immediately ran into a political crisis over the war. A radical, Yorkshire MP, John Arthur Roebuck, had tabled a motion calling for a parliamentary Committee of Inquiry into the conduct of the war. It was in effect a vote of confidence in the coalition's handling of events in the Crimea.

Russell had little doubt that he should strike again – he immediately resigned from the Cabinet and made it clear that he would support the Roebuck motion. Aberdeen initially felt it was yet another of Russell's resignation threats and doubted he would vote to bring down the government. In doing so he misjudged the level to which Russell was prepared to go. Still bitter at Aberdeen's failure to honour the so-called agreement to step down as Prime Minister, Russell saw a chance to tap into public opinion over the war and defeat Aberdeen.

On 25th January Roebuck moved his resolution and the combined support of the Conservatives, Radicals and Russell defeated the government by 305 to 148.

'I Can't Resign, I Sometimes Wish I Could'

Aberdeen, defeated by a combination of war, disloyalty and poor leadership, immediately resigned and watched as the battle to replace him turned into a farce.

> *The uncertainty which resulted from the fall of the Aberdeen coalition was extreme even by the standards of instability which marked the whole period between the end of the Peel government in 1846.*[31]

The Queen had four potential Prime Ministers in waiting: Palmerston who she was reluctant to ask; Russell who had little support; Lansdowne who was too old; and Derby the official leader of the opposition, who she turned to first.

Derby had been in this position a number of times and knew he needed to get non-Conservatives on board if he was to stand any chance of forming a stable administration. Yet again he turned to Palmerston and for the third time in five years, he declined. His condition for joining was the appointment of his Whig ally, Clarendon, as part of another coalition government, but Derby and Clarendon did not get on and it was clear the dynamics would not work. Derby had again failed to form a government so the Queen now asked Lansdowne, who declined on grounds of age, then Clarendon who also refused.

Still determined to avoid turning to Palmerston she was running out of options. Step forward, Russell. Keen as ever to serve, he mounted a campaign to create a Cabinet at the monarch's request. Russell soon found that his past lack of loyalty had created strong feelings of resentment towards him. One by one key MPs refused to serve and he could, 'get no man worth getting'.[32]

Clarendon summed up Russell's problem in a note to the Queen:

> He could do no good in joining Lord John, his government would be 'a stillborn government' which the country would tread under foot the first day.[33]

The Queen was desperate for a solution and irritated that senior politicians were proving to be a bunch of prima donnas:

> Lord John Russell may resign and Lord Aberdeen may resign, but I can't resign. I sometimes wish I could.[34]

Eventually on the 4th February 1855, Palmerston got the inevitable summons and was invited to form a government.

The drama, or comedy, was still not over. Forming the Cabinet presented Palmerston with just as many problems as the Queen had in finding a Prime Minister in the first place.

Palmerston set about recreating the coalition, this time without Aberdeen and Newcastle. Both felt shattered at the attacks over the war and Aberdeen felt:

> That it would be a degradation to which I would never submit, I would rather die than do so.[35]

The other Peelites, including Gladstone, also initially refused out of loyalty to Aberdeen. They felt uneasy at forming a government without him:

> Our most noble victim struck down and we set to feast over the remains.[36]

Their minds changed within forty-eight hours when Aberdeen announced that although he would not join Palmerston he would endorse the government. The little band of Peelites now felt able to join and Gladstone was reappointed as Chancellor, James Graham as First Lord and Sidney Herbert as Colonial Secretary.

It had been an embarrassing and very public episode, but worse was to follow. Although Roebuck had helped defeat the government over the war he was still determined to have a full inquiry into the war. He would not back down:

> The change of government, he said, had not meant a complete change of ministers; Palmerston was still surrounded by guilty men.[37]

When Palmerston agreed to the inquiry it was a step too far for the Peelites, and having been sworn in as Ministers at Windsor Castle on the 8th February the Peelites then resigned on the 21st. Roy Jenkins also makes the case that Gladstone was also unhappy at his first few Cabinet meetings.[38] A view confirmed by Palmerston's own words to Gladstone:

> To speak plainly and frankly you distrust my views and intentions.[39]

The coalition was over, but it was not clear what had replaced it. Palmerston was leading the Whig dominated administration with a few Peelites. It was not a coalition, Whig, or Liberal administration. I think it's best to describe it as a Palmerston government with Whig dominance. Disraeli, as ever, had a more colourful description:

> We have replaced a cabinet of all talents by a cabinet of all the mediocrities.[40]

Two-party politics was almost back, but the realignment was not complete. The obvious amalgamation of Whigs and Peelites had failed to take place. Peelites entered the Aberdeen coalition as a group and left the Palmerston government still as a separate body. Creating a Liberal Party would take a few more years yet; meanwhile Palmerston went on to be Prime Minister for almost all of the next decade.

A Missed Opportunity

The Aberdeen coalition goes down in history as a missed opportunity. It had plenty going for it when the final Cabinet was agreed on Christmas Eve 1852. Unlike other coalitions it was not born out of war, or economic crisis. In fact this period was one of the most prosperous there had been. The country felt confident in itself and had just celebrated the half century with a Great Exhibition at Crystal Palace. Queen Victoria was bemused at the political failings against this strong background:

Altogether it is very vexatious and will give us trouble. It is the more provoking, as this country is so very prosperous.[41]

The individuals that joined were some of the most able nineteenth century politicians and the monarchy was extremely supportive throughout its period in office. Despite these advantages the government failed to deliver major domestic reform. Plans to restructure education and introduce progressive franchise reform and methods to prevent electoral fraud were all announced, but then abandoned in the face of opposition. The one unqualified success was Gladstone's first budget, which introduced tax reforms and removed protectionist tariffs on a range of goods. The ultimate failure lay in foreign policy with a lack of clear direction on how to deal with Russia's aggression towards Turkey. The indecisiveness led to an unnecessary war and a string of embarrassing military disasters and the death of thousands of troops.

As well as these policy disasters the coalition also failed to resolve the political instability that had been created after Peel split the Conservatives over the Corn Laws. The creation of three parties had thrown parliament into turmoil and some form of readjustment was needed. The Peelites were either going to reunite with the Conservatives, or a realignment with the Whigs would take place. It was clear after the attacks between Conservative and Peelites that a reunification of these parties was unlikely. The merger of Whigs and Peelites to create a Conservative/Liberal Party seemed inevitable after Peel's death in 1850. This realignment was unnecessarily drawn out because of the egos involved. Russell and Palmerston must shoulder some of the blame for letting personal ambition get in the way of this logical next step. When, eventually the coalition brought the parties together they then split again afterwards, creating a further step backwards for the forces of progressive politics. It took another four years before the Peelites eventually joined forces with the Whigs and Radicals. This was the birth of the Liberal Party, but it had been a very long gestation from 1846 to 1860.

Leaders must also take their blame, Aberdeen had shown great patience in creating the coalition and it is very unlikely that anybody else at the time could have managed the egos and tantrums as well as he did. His relationship with Victoria and Albert was central to his ability to pull in the key figures he needed to give his government credibility. For him the frustration was that these same talented individuals that he sought were also to be the very people a stronger Prime Minister might have dismissed. But Aberdeen allowed both Russell and Palmerston to change their minds too often over joining the government. There is a fine line between demonstrating patience and being undermined. In the end his tolerance of Russell was an embarrassment:

> *Russell had threatened resignation so often that Prince Albert kept a special file marked in his own hand concerning the part which Lord Russell took in breaking up Lord Aberdeen's government.*[42]

Aberdeen lacked the dominance and control that any modern day Prime Minister needs to run an effective government. It would, however, have been tough to create the coalition without these two men, but once in place firmer leadership should have been the order of the day. This indecisiveness came to a head over the strategy for dealing with Russia. Trying to walk a tightrope between diplomacy and aggression was a recipe for disaster. Aberdeen lacked the qualities to lead a war and his hesitation was to have disastrous consequences. When the Roebuck Inquiry finally reported, it was highly critical of the administration.

Many of the problems of Aberdeen's government were because it was a coalition. Trying to keep sides together, dealing with mistrust and a lack of collective spirit were the characteristics of this coalition. Rather than a fusion of great ideas and people it was a clash of personalities.

A non-coalition government would have been able to deal with the likes of Russell by sacking him. A non-coalition government would have established a clearer strategy on Russia. A well run coalition should have fused the Whigs and Peelites forever. It was in my view a failure. Back on that stormy December night Disraeli had been right.

References

Opening quote from Charles Greville, Clerk to the Privy Council, Lord Aberdeen, Muriel Chamberlain

1. *The Conservative Party from Peel to Thatcher*, Robert Blake

2. *The Passing of the Whigs, 1832-1886*, Donald Southgate

3. Disraeli letter to Lord John Morris, from *Disraeli* by Sarah Bradford

4. Hansard, 22 January 1844

5. *The Conservative Party from Peel to Thatcher*, Robert Blake

6. *Sir Robert Peel: The life of Sir Robert Peel after 1830*, Norman Gash

7. *England in the Nineteenth Century: 1815-1914*, David Thomson

8. Lord Malmesbury's diary, *Memoirs of an Ex Minister, Volume 1*, James Howard Harris Malmesbury

9. *Disraeli*, Sarah Bradford

10. *The Passing of the Whigs, 1832-1886*, Donald Southgate

11. *Ibid.*

12. *Lord Aberdeen: A Political Biography*, Muriel E. Chamberlain

13. *Lord Palmerston*, Jasper Ridley

14. *Disraeli*, Robert Blake

15. *Ibid.*

16. *Disraeli, Derby and the Conservative Party: Journals and Memoirs of Edward Henry, Lord Stanley, 1849-1869*, John Vincent

17. *Victorian People: A Reassessment of Persons and Themes, 1851-67*, Asa Briggs

18. *Disraeli*, Robert Blake

19. *Lord Aberdeen: A Political Biography*, Muriel E. Chamberlain

20. *Ibid.*

21. *Coalitions in British Politics*, David Butler

22. *Lord Palmerston*, Jasper Ridley

23. *Ibid.*

24. *Lord Aberdeen: A Political Biography*, Muriel E. Chamberlain

25. *Disraeli*, Robert Blake

26. *Lord Aberdeen: A Political Biography*, Muriel E. Chamberlain

27. *Gladstone*, Roy Jenkins

28. *Lord Palmerston*, Jasper Ridley

29. *Lord Aberdeen: A Political Biography*, Muriel E. Chamberlain

30. *The Passing of the Whigs, 1832-1886*, Donald Southgate

31. *Gladstone*, Roy Jenkins

32. *The Passing of the Whigs, 1832-1886*, Donald Southgate

33. *Ibid.*

34. *Lord Palmerston*, Jasper Ridley

35. Aberdeen Letter to Sidney Herbert, from *Coalitions in British Politics*, David Butler

36. *The Passing of the Whigs, 1832-1886*, Donald Southgate

37. *Victorian People: A Reassessment of Persons and Themes, 1851-67*, Asa Briggs

38. *Gladstone*, Roy Jenkins

39. *The Passing of the Whigs, 1832-1886*, Donald Southgate

40. *Victorian People: A Reassessment of Persons and Themes, 1851-67*, Asa Briggs

41. *Ibid.*

42. *Ibid.*

3

Fighting At Home
And Abroad

Fighting At Home And Abroad

National unity alone can save Britain, can save Europe, can save the world.

Kenneth Morgan

At the start of the new century, British politics had settled down into a pattern of two-party politics. The Conservatives and Liberals dominated the system and although the Labour Party had just been created, it could not yet be considered as a national contestant in parliament. The two main parties were heavily divided on the major issues of the day; Lords reform, Welsh disestablishment, and in particular Ireland. Many of these differences came to a head in 1909 with the so-called "People's Budget" that attempted to redistribute wealth from the rich to a much wider group. The Liberal Chancellor, Lloyd George, sought to introduce new taxes and a radical welfare programme. The measures plunged the country and political parties into a constitutional deadlock and it required two general elections, nicknamed 'Peers v People', before the measures were finally accepted in the Parliament Act of 1911.

Against this backdrop, no one could have predicted that the political parties would undergo a national reconciliation, let alone form a coalition. In the end, though, as the country faced war, a quite unique and complicated phenomenon took place and government moved from extreme division to a period of coalition that was to last for almost eight years.

War Breaks Out

When war was declared in 1914, the Liberal government, under the leadership of Asquith, decided to govern alone. Although the party was divided over the war, the majority of Liberals backed their leader, and even Lloyd George, who had advocated peace, gave his support. The only real mention of coalition was used by Asquith to frighten doubtful backbenchers into supporting his position.

Relations between the two main parties remained poor; a truce had been agreed so that by-elections would not be contested, but it was an uneasy arrangement that had to be renewed every couple of months. Asquith did not go out of his way to please the Conservatives and insisted on forcing the controversial issues of home rule and the Welsh Church Bills through parliament. In response the Conservatives complained that the measures were 'bound to revive party controversy',[1] and Bonar Law, their leader, even marched his party out of the Commons in protest on one occasion.

The first stages of the war were handled with remarkable skill and success and there was a mood of optimism amongst the population as people felt the war could be over within months. The government managed to implement plans which had been devised in previous years to prevent panic taking over the country and to enable 'business as usual' to continue.[2]

However, by the end of the year, cracks were starting to appear. Lloyd George was profoundly dissatisfied with the way his colleagues were conducting the war and more than ready to make this known to the Conservative opposition. Other Cabinet members began to see that the situation was getting increasingly difficult to handle. Fellow Liberal Walter Runciman said, 'the political truce is wearing thin'[3] and away from Westminster the media began to question the lack of progress, complaining that the 'war is not being taken seriously'.[4]

Towards Coalition

In the spring of 1915, a number of events went against the government, leaving Asquith to face considerable opposition in parliament.

Firstly, an article and accompanying editorial appeared in the *Times*, 'Shells and the Great Battle', which blamed the defeat at the Battle of Neuve Chapelle on a lack of shells. Known as the 'shells scandal', the thrust of the article was that the military blamed the politicians for the lack of resources and defeat, a criticism that would occur a number of times throughout the war. Indeed, Lord Kitchener, responsible for the War Office, had been warned of this problem a number of times, especially by Lloyd George.

Secondly, after weeks of arguing over the Dardanelles Campaign, Lord Fisher resigned as First Sea Lord under Winston Churchill at the Admiralty.

Taken together it began to look like the military problems were more to do with political failure than the armed forces.[5] The media picked up on the events and used them as part of a long and heated campaign against Asquith. For his part he had never made a great effort with the press and now paid the price for ignoring them. Against this hostile backdrop Asquith also faced the prospect of an election. Under the 1911 Parliament Act, the life of parliament had been reduced to five years. This meant Asquith would have to dissolve parliament and hold a general election at the very latest in January 1916. The idea of an election must have haunted the Prime Minister as the dissolution of parliament could break the already shaky spirit of national reconciliation and unity. He was also concerned that the Conservatives had a strong chance of triumphing in a wartime election. They were not yet tainted by defeat and were traditionally seen as the patriotic party, and therefore more appropriate for a wartime government. Despite this, few Liberal MPs were advocating a coalition and the Conservative backbenchers were not particularly eager to share the responsibility for running a war with their political adversaries, especially since there seemed to be a good chance of the Conservatives gaining office themselves.[6]

However, the 'shells scandal', hostile public opinion and a looming general election finally combined to convince Asquith to seek a coalition with the Conservatives. For the opposition, Bonar Law accepted the offer as he shrank from the prospect of governing the country in wartime with a purely Conservative majority.[7]

Opinions differ on the main reason for the coalition's formation. Some historians, such as Martin D. Pugh,[8] stress the threat of a looming general election and Conservative uneasiness at governing the country alone, whilst others, like Roy Jenkins,[9] believe that the shell shortage and in particular the resignation of Fisher at the Admiralty are responsible. Even Asquith's account remains bland and insufficient to explain his change of direction.[10] In any case, it is certain that the various "crisis" issues all helped trigger this new direction; ultimately though, the coalition arose as the product of desperate efforts for both Asquith and Bonar Law[11] to maintain credibility as party leaders. In the end the coalition formed in May 1915 did not come from the parties' desire to unite to win the war, but through crises and fear of facing the voters.

Within the Liberal Party, a backbench revolt, led by usually faithful MPs, erupted after the announcement. Charles Trevelyan, a Liberal backbencher, said:

This is the end of the Liberal Party, now all Liberalism will be
abandoned and we shall live under conscription and martial law.[12]

A meeting was held on 19th May when Asquith faced a gathering of MPs and it took his greatest oratory skills to restore order. The Conservatives were equally unenthusiastic about the arrangement. Walter Long, who was offered the Local Government Board, was very negative despite his inclusion:

I loathe the very idea of our good fellows sitting with these double-
dyed traitors; but of course I shall support our leaders and the
government.[13]

The media were quick to pick up on the lack of unity and consensus. On 23rd May, James Louis Garvin, editor of *The Observer*, commented that the country faced a choice between 'Coalition – Chaos – or Dictatorship' and regretted the way in which the new administration had come into existence, feeling that it did:

not answer in all respects to the theoretical or even to the practical
idea of a Ministry of all the Talents, with every statesman among its
members in his right place.[14]

In many respects, Garvin was right; the Cabinet continued to be dominated by the Liberal Party and the Conservatives did not get a very good deal. All the main Cabinet positions were given to the Liberals. Bonar Law himself was only offered the Colonial Office, a disappointing position for a party leader. In the end Asquith only had to sacrifice two Liberals, Haldane and Churchill, as the Conservatives refused to serve alongside them. The Labour Party was included, although it was only a token gesture on Asquith's behalf. When Asquith announced the coalition government, twelve posts were attributed to Liberals, eight to Conservatives, one to Labour and one to Lord Kitchener. Historians have widely picked up on this lack of unity within the new government, as John Ramsden said:

Asquith's 1915 government was only halfway to coalition…it was in
fact a coalition of parties rather than a coalition of men, and it was
run so as to maximise continuity.[15]

This was never a coalition that blended together and although the lines of fracture blurred during these eighteen months, it remained the case that Liberal principles were confronted with Conservative ones and victory could only be understood as one triumphing over the other, rather than a merging of the two.

It was clear that only a superficial spirit of reconciliation would exist within the coalition. In fact, for a month or more, ministers from the two principal parties usually sat in separate groups in the House of Commons and often when a minister from one party addressed the House, no ministers from the other party were present to hear him.[16] Although the party truce continued, many issues continued to test the coalition and the Cabinet continued to stumble along, failing to truly come together and resolve urgent issues. Considering that a war was raging just outside Britain's borders, it is amazing that the Cabinet members were incapable of putting their parties, or worse their personal ambitions, aside.

From the beginning, Asquith recognised that some changes were needed to the previous government. Firstly, he set up the Dardanelles Committee to replace the War Council, consisting of eleven members, five of whom were Conservatives. Secondly, the Liberal members of the Cabinet understood that some of their Liberal principles, especially on free trade, would need to be discarded temporarily, something which they had refused up until now: for example, Reginald McKenna introduced new duties in 1915 on imported luxury goods. Finally, and most importantly, Asquith agreed to create the Ministry of Munitions, headed by Lloyd George. This is by far Asquith's greatest achievement during the First World War, and built up as a formidable 'businessman's organisation'.[17]

The Conscription And Home Rule Battles

We do not have enough space to discuss all of the coalition's failures in this chapter so let us focus on two of them: conscription and home rule, which both exemplify the blurring of party divisions, the role of personalities, and the importance of strong leadership. Conscription produced perhaps the most far-reaching effects on political relationships. Although everyone recognised the need for some form of compulsion, both parties, in particular the Liberals, were divided on the extent of it. Some, including Asquith, continued to cling on to their pre-war principles arguing for various forms of voluntary conscription. He wrote to Arthur Balfour, First Lord of the Admiralty, in September 1915:

the voluntary system has stood the ordeal of fiery experiment with marvellous success...[18]

Not only were Cabinet members heavily divided on the issue, so was parliament. On 6th January 1916, 35 Liberal MPs voted against the government on the conscription of single men, in the Military Service Bill. But, a week later, the *Times* reported the formation of the Liberal War Committee of about 40 MPs, dedicated to a more vigorous prosecution of the war.[19]

Despite these divisions, the coalition started to face up to the problem when by June 1915 it became clear that if the generals continued to engage in frontal attacks on heavily fortified positions, more troops would be needed. During the debates on the Registration Bill over the summer, the King wrote to Asquith:

I fear recruiting for the Army is by no means as brisk as it was a fortnight ago. I earnestly trust that the Cabinet will agree without delay to registration being carried out as no-one would object to that. I trust we shall not be obliged to compulsion; but I am interested to know it has been advocated in the House of Commons this evening by one of your late whips who has been at the front for ten months![20]

Asquith felt that the gradual approach to conscription was the best solution to allow time for all those against to come around to the idea, but it showed him to be indecisive and even devious with his fellow Liberals. By finding half-solutions, he angered both the conscription and anti-conscription supporters.

There certainly was cause for concern that conscription would bring the country to the 'verge of revolution' but Asquith had also lost valuable time by procrastinating over taking the decision. In the summer of 1915 alone, the British lost 60,000 troops and by the end of the year, the front had not moved by more than three miles, a major military failure.[21]

Throughout the controversy, Asquith was at fault in overestimating the level of opposition in the country to the idea. Even most of the Labour MPs, and probably many of their supporters, would have accepted military conscription as a means of enforcing equality of sacrifice. When he introduced a new mediocre conscription bill to parliament, the House was disappointed, reacted violently and eventually convinced Asquith to introduce a new, stricter measure. This revised bill met with little opposition and was through all its stages in three weeks during May 1916.[22]

The other coalition crisis concerned the issue of home rule. Here, the disagreements were much more clearly defined along party lines. In May, Asquith asked Lloyd George to take on the problem after the outbreak of the Easter Rebellion. The task given to Lloyd George was certainly not an easy one; he needed to suppress the revolt sufficiently firmly without alienating the Irish Nationalists or opinion abroad, as well as transform Ireland's system of government.

Working with John Redmond, the leader of the Irish Nationalists, and Edward Carson, leader of the Irish Conservatives, he was able to draw up a comprehensive agreement by June. However, the Conservatives objected and once more, the coalition seemed on the point of break-up. The seriousness of the problem prompted Asquith to issue a firm call for unity and remind all sides of the need for National Government. This appeal was enough to get the Cabinet to reluctantly agree to Lloyd George's solution and the Tories abandoned their threat of resignation. The agreement did not last long and a couple of days later Lord Lansdowne finally killed off the measure when he spoke against it in the Lords. Cabinet unity was tested again, but this time it was decided to bury the Irish question. In the face of criticism Lloyd George found Asquith less than supportive and the episode was to mark a worsening in their relations. For his part Asquith had tried to solve the Irish problem but the prejudices of some of his Conservative colleagues were too great and his authority over them too small for the opportunity to be taken.

It is hard to know whether, if Asquith had chosen to wholeheartedly support Lloyd George in this event, the agreement could have worked. Once more, political calculations were at the heart of the problem. If Asquith had insisted that the Conservative Cabinet members stand by their approval of a home rule it could have split the Conservatives, and risked their backbenchers voting against Bonar Law and forcing a general election. The crisis demonstrated that Bonar Law was a weak leader and did not have overall control of his party. He had been a compromise candidate for the leadership in 1911 and had never sat in the Cabinet until Asquith gave him the Colonial Office in 1915. In the end Asquith was obliged to abandon home rule agreement as he discovered that Bonar Law could not command his own party.[23] Paying off those who threatened Bonar Law's position became the price for coalition and the hoped-for consensus.

A Cabinet At War

Personalities and egos within the Cabinet go a long way in explaining the coalition's failures. It is particularly revealing that the leaders of the two parties themselves never worked well together. From the very beginning, Asquith went to great lengths to avoid giving Bonar Law an important position in the Cabinet, finally relegating him to the Colonial Office. The two had an awkward and uneven relationship, which is neatly illustrated by the fact that all Bonar Law's letters began with a stiff 'Dear Mr. Asquith' and all Asquith's with a gracious 'My dear Bonar Law'. This lack of communication was as much Bonar Law's fault as it was Asquith's. If he had behaved like an equal, the Prime Minister would have been more likely to treat him as one. Conversely, Asquith would have been a better Prime Minister if he had responded by deliberately according a special consideration to the leader of the Conservative Party.[24]

Other members of the Cabinet also refused to work together. As secretary of the War Office, Lord Kitchener only accepted the creation of the Ministry of Munitions when it was finally forced upon him. Lloyd George and he constantly fought and by October 1915, Lloyd George believed that nothing could work so long as Kitchener remained in the War Office. His abilities were clearly flagging, and when the Germans entered Belgrade, Kitchener was not even aware that the War Office had known for 20 hours and he was accused of not reading his telegrams properly, or forwarding them on time.[25] His position was, however, secure as his reputation with the public was still very high and he was the greatest recruiting sergeant.

Lloyd George fought with most of the Cabinet members during this period and in doing so gained a reputation for acting out of pure ambition. Churchill even blamed him later for his 'Machiavellian cleverness'[26] in carrying through the first coalition, let alone the second. That said, even if he was an ambitious character, he was also truly devoted to winning the war. Despite having resisted intervention in August 1914, his approach was not half-hearted once Britain was involved:

it was not "my war"... But being in it, I realised that the only safe
way out was through the gates of victory, and that victory was only to
be won by concentrating all thought and energy on the making of the
war.[27]

It is true that he fell out with a number of Cabinet members and he certainly destabilised the government with his constant resignation threats and bartering with Asquith. However, by threatening to resign, he also enabled certain measures to be enacted and effectively put an end to both conscription crises as Asquith realised he had no choice but to agree to the measures himself.

Ultimately, the coalition failed as a result of Asquith's weak leadership. He was far too indecisive when making decisions. For example, it took him nearly three weeks to appoint a new Secretary of State for War after the death of Lord Kitchener. It seems absurd and completely incompetent to have waited for such a long time. He also strongly believed that military decisions should be left to the experts, refusing to criticise decisions made by army chiefs, even if he did not agree with them. Most importantly, he lost control of his Cabinet members. When he was taken ill in autumn 1915, the War Cabinet ordered him to set up a new War Committee. In effect, they took the opportunity of his sick leave to override his authority. On his return, not only was he obliged to implement this decision, he also had to negotiate with several resilient and stubborn members as to the Committee's size and membership. By this point, Asquith had lost much of his original prestige and was disappointing his party and failing to stamp his authority on the new coalition Cabinet.

The press also played their part in undermining his leadership. During 1914 and 1915, press attacks against Asquith had been relentless. He had hoped that by bringing the Conservatives into the government, it would moderate their attacks.[28] However, he could not have been more mistaken; in fact, the press attacks intensified in the months following the formation of the coalition. In April 1916, the *Observer* portrayed the War Office's efforts as an example of 'How Not To Do It'.[29] Not only did the media attack Asquith, they increasingly began to favour Lloyd George as a potential leader. By mid-1916, even the *Nation*, usually severely critical of him, admitted that he was:

a true personality of the hour. It has made him; his audacities of manipulation excite and please, and even inspire men with hope.[30]

The coalition and Asquith's premiership might have been saved if a major breakthrough on the war front had been made. However, by December 1916, the war was going extremely badly, only made worse by the 'Suvla inquiry' into the failed Dardanelles Campaign. Nothing could save Asquith now and events slowly started to move against him.

Beginning Of The End

It was to be a military issue, the Battle of the Somme, which was the first sign that Asquith could fall. This was not a bigger defeat than the other disappointing campaigns but it did have momentous consequences for the conduct of the war. The politicians and the country now understood that the war would be a long, drawn-out affair. The 1916 offensive had been intended to bring about an early victory and in order to achieve this, the government had gambled by knowingly weakening the civilian economy and hugely increasing Britain's overseas debt. But the plans had failed, and Britain was heading towards bankruptcy and a serious shortage of manpower. It became clear that in financial terms the war allies would be completely dependent on the United States by June 1917 and fighting would have to go on until at least 1918 and possibly longer. For the first time since the outbreak of the war, the Cabinet was obliged to contemplate the possibility of failure. They also faced the prospect of industrial unrest as workers grew restless at the growing demands placed on them. On 16th November 1916, the first signs of disquiet appeared when fitters in Sheffield went on strike over the case of Leonard Hargreaves, a skilled worker who had been conscripted. The government managed to solve the problem in two days but it was a warning of further industrial problems to follow.

Meanwhile, during the Allied Conference in Paris in November 1916, Lloyd George and Maurice Hankey, Secretary of the War Council, discussed plans for a new War Committee which would be headed up by Lloyd George. Under the scheme Asquith would take a less hands-on approach and occupy a more presidential role in the background. Many have believed that this plan was devised to ensure that the Prime Minister would turn it down and resign but the evidence is not as clear-cut as this. I don't think we will ever be able to uncover Lloyd George's true motives but, in my opinion, it does seem as if he genuinely desired a more efficient system of government rather than the role of Prime Minister itself. Lloyd George admired Asquith for his great qualities of mind and speech, but increasingly believed that Asquith was losing the war and that he himself could do better if he was given executive control as chairman of a small war committee.

At the same time the Conservatives were becoming restless. In November, Bonar Law performed badly in the House of Commons over an unimportant debate on the issue of the disposal of enemy property in Nigeria. One of his leading backbenchers, Carson, attacked him particularly ferociously, and the government was only sustained thanks to Liberal votes. Sixty-five Conservatives voted with Carson, seventy-five with Bonar Law and nearly 150 abstained or were absent. This internal disagreement destabilised the government even more and convinced a weakened Bonar Law to search for a better ally among the Liberals.

The atmosphere of mutual distrust and recrimination was to increase with the arrival of the Lansdowne Memorandum. It was submitted after Asquith invited the Cabinet members to give their view about the prospects for the next phase of the war. Lord Lansdowne's submission, circulated on the 13th November 1916, was long and extremely pessimistic, favouring immediate peace. Within days, the document had become public property and hostile critics outside used it as 'a stick with which to beat most of the government and Asquith in particular'.[31]

The media further inflamed the situation. Some newspapers were coming out openly in favour of Lloyd George: the *Daily Chronicle*[32] favoured him over Asquith and soon made public his idea of creating a new War Committee. H. A. Gwynne, editor of the *Morning Post*, wrote a strong leader at Carson's inspiration and praised Lloyd George as a potential 'saviour'.[33] Not only did this weaken Asquith's position, it also alerted public opinion to the serious problems and challenges he faced. By now the public, media and politicians were all moving in favour of establishing a War Cabinet. Asquith, however, remained opposed. It was left to Bonar Law and the Conservatives to turn up the pressure. They issued a resolution for immediate transmission to Asquith:

> *we therefore urge the Prime Minister to tender the resignation of the government. If he feels unable to take that step, we authorise Mr. Bonar Law to tender our resignation.*[34]

Bonar Law took the resolution immediately to Asquith, and although he never actually showed it to him, Asquith realised that the Conservative ministers had swung into a position of complete hostility towards him. Asquith felt trapped and obliged to accept that there should be a small War Committee under Lloyd George's chairmanship. A couple of issues remained to be resolved, but the principle of the idea was accepted by Asquith on 3rd December, and it seemed that the crisis was coming to an end.

Events took a further twist. The next day, the *Times* published an article which had obviously been written or inspired by someone who was privy to the previous afternoon's discussions.[35] The article angered Asquith as it implied that he had accepted he was ineffective as a war leader and had made a complete surrender of power to Lloyd George. He believed that Lloyd George was responsible for the article and dramatically announced he was going back on his agreement. This was the final straw: after a series of meetings with both Liberals and Conservatives, and a final meeting at Buckingham Palace to discuss the situation, Asquith finally understood that he had lost the authority to remain as Prime Minister, and resigned. He did this only after receiving the order from the King to dissolve the government and form a new one under his leadership. But, when it became clear the Conservatives wanted to join Lloyd George he finally accepted defeat. It was a bitter end and throughout the rest of the war he refused offers to join the government.

The events surrounding the fall of Asquith and formation of the Lloyd George coalition are, at best, mildly confusing, and at worst, completely mind-boggling. Within three weeks, the government had completely changed; the Liberal Party was all but thrown out of mainstream politics and the Conservatives had reconciled their differences with Lloyd George. And yet it is hard to find a real trigger to explain the political crisis of December 1916 and the fall of Asquith. The new coalition was created more as a result of an accumulation of several problems and finally culminated with Asquith's refusal to accept Lloyd George's plan to establish a War Cabinet. Many of the primary accounts themselves disagree on the sequence of events. It has even been suggested that Lord Beaverbrook, who wrote a very comprehensive account of the coalition government, even made up certain meetings in his account. Historians themselves are divided on the subject and most have felt obliged to recount the political coup day by day, and even hour by hour. But none are quite sure of the motives behind Lloyd

George and Bonar Law's plan. In my opinion, it is not enough merely to represent the leaders of the Asquith coalition as a pack of squabbling children, or as men struggling for office, even if at times they really do give us that impression. In the end it was a sequence of events that caused the downfall of Asquith and led to Lloyd George becoming the new leader of the coalition.

Lloyd George To The Rescue

Few expected the new Lloyd George coalition to survive for more than a couple of months. And yet, during the war at least, it was one of the very few truly successful coalitions in British history. It resembled a real National Government, encompassing all the parties (even if it was dominated by the Conservatives), and was strongly led by the Welshman. The coalition's main aim was to win the war and Lloyd George was clearly prepared to go to great lengths to achieve this. In effect, the Cabinet and the State were successfully transformed for the duration of the war and Lloyd George led the country back to peace.

Lloyd George's position on his arrival to the premiership was nevertheless extremely awkward. He was obliged to rely on others for support as he effectively became a leader without a party. He was guaranteed the support of the Conservatives through Bonar Law and Carson, and on the Liberal side, Christopher Addison remained loyal and tried to recruit further Liberals to his cause. Initially, Addison claimed that 135 Liberal MPs supported the Prime Minister, but in reality this was closer to 50, with a large contingency coming from the Liberal War Committee. The rest of the Liberals had followed Asquith and now formed the official opposition.

The coalition itself met with difficulties from the very beginning. In fact, many assumed that this would not be the last wartime government and also expected another to follow within a couple of months. Lloyd George was very aware that he was being given an opportunity to prove himself, and he quickly set about creating unity. He was obliged to compromise with both the Conservatives and the Labour Party for their inclusion in the Cabinet, leaving him slightly restrained during the rest of the war. With such strong signs of industrial unrest, Lloyd George could not ignore the concerns of the Labour Party anymore and he sacrificed labour conscription (which was ready to be implemented) to win their support. To keep the Conservatives happy, and particularly to get Lord Curzon to accept the offer of a Cabinet position, he promised to keep Haig at the military High Command, a decision he soon came to regret. In addition, he promised Austen Chamberlain that he would not offer a ministry to Churchill or Lord Northcliffe. It was like a game of chess but these various appointments were testament to Lloyd George's skill and ability at bringing everyone together.

From the very beginning, Lloyd George understood that the current system of government needed complete overhauling for the country to win the war. He set about creating a small War Cabinet of only five members, all of whom were freed from departmental responsibilities. Not only did it meet almost every day, but for the first time ever, an agenda was circulated before each sitting and minutes were kept. He also created a Cabinet Secretariat and his own small team of advisers, nicknamed the 'Garden Suburb'. It is debatable as to how effective this new machinery really was. Lloyd George had misjudged the failures of the Asquith government, assuming that the delays he experienced were inherent in the relationship between the full Cabinet and the Asquithian War Cabinet. In reality, these delays had been caused by clashes of personalities and politics rather than by the institutional framework within which they operated.

As part of the government's revamp, Lloyd George created a number of new ministries in an effort to mobilise British resources more effectively. The Ministries of Pensions and Labour were set up in an effort to control the industrial workforce more efficiently. A Shipping Controller and Food Controller were appointed as well as a Director of National Service. Most of these ministries were headed by non-partisan businessmen, which was a first for a government.

Lloyd George's first major challenge was the economy as Britain looked like it was heading for bankruptcy. In December, the Federal Reserve Board warned American investors to be careful about buying Allied bonds. For the next couple of months, the British credit faced temporary destruction in the United States. Fortunately, the Finance Division for the Treasury proved flexible enough to carve out a new division, the 'A' Division, which became wholly responsible for overseas finance, especially for the raising of funds in the USA and the loaning of money to the Allies. With the entrance of America into the war in April 1917, the problem of finance was finally resolved and British credit regained at least some of its reputation.[36]

Food Or Troops

A particularly striking example of the fight over manpower is the Corn Production Bill introduced into the Commons in 1917. The agricultural problem had already surfaced at the outbreak of the war as most produce was now imported. Pre-war discussions had assumed that the superiority of the British Navy over the Germans would enable corn to continue to be imported but plans had to be revised due to German attempts to block transportation. Asquith had successfully detected the problem but only took piecemeal measures to deal with it by creating a Royal Commission on the Wheat Supply and the Sugar Supply. His effort remained half-hearted and he rejected all the recommendations made by Lord Selborne's Committee on Food Production. By the end of 1916, the situation had become far more urgent when a poor harvest and the success of the German blockade campaign began to hit home. Lloyd George immediately decided to take a more vigorous approach to the problem, establishing a Food Controller, who, after a long time, produced a rationing policy. It was hoped that control could eliminate the risk of food queues and potential food riots. This was a constant source of anxieties for the War Cabinet and although some trouble did occur in July 1917, the most common grievances were about food profiteering.

In early 1917, Lord Prothero, President of the Board of Agriculture, announced that an extensive tillage campaign had become a political necessity to encourage home food production. The Board created a Food Production Department and prepared the Corn Production Bill. The Board also issued an order requiring farmers to cultivate derelict land and in some instances to plough up pasture for grain crops. The decision was to create enormous tension in rural communities and between government departments as they faced a battle finding the men and petrol to plough up fields.

The government's new policy was immediately blown off course in January 1917 when the War Office declared that it would be necessary to take another 30,000 men out of agriculture for the war effort. This created even more disquiet and in the end the War Cabinet set up a committee to resolve the differences between the War Office and the Board of Agriculture. Eventually the War Office reluctantly agreed to provide 15,000 Home Office reservists to work on the land but the tension remained.

The situation became more serious when the Corn Production Bill was introduced into parliament and the internal disharmony turned into a public embarrassment. The introduction of the Bill came at a difficult time in the relationship between the government and opposition Liberals. Lloyd George was feeling particularly vulnerable in the Commons and looked to Asquith for more support on the issue. On the other hand, leading Liberals like McKenna and Runciman were looking for an opportunity to score a parliamentary triumph over Lloyd George. They found their opportunity in the Corn Production Bill.

> A good many things are making the government unpopular, and
> Asquith and Co may think they see their chance.[37]

Asquith remained relatively quiet while the Bill went through its committee stages, but his ex-Cabinet colleagues took offence at the government's policies and gradually the combativeness of the Liberal front bench increased. Eventually, the Bill only passed through thanks to governmental pressure on pro-war Labour members.

At the end of the day, the Corn Production Act received the Cabinet unity that it had needed as they united against a common political enemy after witnessing Runciman's venomous attack on it. The Corn Production Bill destabilised the government but not just because the battle was fought with the Liberals. The government disagreed as to how to redistribute the available resources as there were simply not enough to go around. The issue was not fully resolved and within the Cabinet, the pressure from the War Office to recruit men from agriculture did not let up.

Not only did the Corn Production Bill create serious tensions and disagreement within the Cabinet, it also acted as a focus for disappointment and opposition within the House of Commons. Lloyd George never quite understood the importance of the parliament. Even if within his government, party politics had nearly disappeared, it was still very much present in the Commons. As the editor of the Times wrote in June 1917:

> On the whole I think that the government remains fairly strong in the
> country, and that it deserves to be strong on its record in the war and
> in foreign affairs. No doubt Lloyd George has proved himself a great
> diplomatist and stands very high in France and Italy. It is in domestic
> questions that he is likely to come to grief, and I put this down very

largely to Bonar Law's incurable nervousness of the House of Commons.[38]

To try to calm the parliamentary unrest Lloyd George and Bonar Law set about a reshuffle. It took six weeks of discussion between them as they attempted to create new junior ministerial posts for some of the restless backbenchers. In particular the danger of having Churchill as a parliamentary critic made it important to bring him into the administration and he was given the job of Minister of Munitions.

At the same time, Arthur Henderson was forced to resign after advocating that the Labour Party attend a Socialist peace conference in Stockholm. His loss had come at a heavy cost, and the risk of losing the support of the Labour Party was a problem for the coalition.

With the loss of Labour and the re-invigoration of the Asquithian Liberals, the coalition abandoned a small part of its claim to be a National Government even if the Labour Party and the trade unions essentially continued to support the government until the end of the war. Despite the reshuffle, the new government had begun to understand that a parliamentary majority was extremely hard to balance. It was also becoming impossible to satisfy military and civilian demands at the same time and it had become too demanding to coerce an industrial population into limitless improvements in productivity. This dawning realisation was coupled with the military collapse and America's hesitation to enter the war. These were complex problems, but also marked a turning point as Lloyd George responded by deciding to take greater control of both the political and military process.

Once the financial crisis was resolved he then started to focus on the two major areas that he would need to tackle: military strategy and manpower. Manpower was needed on two fronts. Abroad, Haig needed troops to prepare for a new attack in Flanders. At home, industry and agriculture were crying out for more men. Manpower became an issue between the civilian and military world, the Home Front and the war effort, the businessmen and the generals, and a battle between government departments as they tried to get as many men as they could.

To help reduce the problem, Lloyd George set up the Ministry of Labour and the Department of National Service. The Ministry of Labour's principal asset was the Labour Exchange Network, which offered a ready-made national organisation for controlling labour supply. Meanwhile the task of forming a policy for the better use of civilian labour was given instead to the Department of National Service. Neville Chamberlain was in charge of this department but he had limited powers and was rather inept. He was also restrained by Lloyd George's promise to halt industrial conscription. With hindsight it was a mistake to try to split the task between two departments and it was further complicated by allowing the War Cabinet to allocate labour between military and civilian uses. At the end of April 1917, the War Cabinet decided to introduce the new Schedule of Protected Occupations to replace the Trade Card scheme (voluntary conscription). This sparked the widespread 'May Strikes', which became the focus of a number of grievances, including wages and food prices, as well as conscription. The strikes at least conveyed to the military leaders that an industrial society could not be drained of too much skilled manpower without the total collapse of the country. When linked to the collapse of the Tsarist regime in Russia, the strikes were also proof that Lloyd George was right to be fearful of the political consequences of a limitless land war on the Western Front. They show how finely balanced Lloyd George's policies needed to be. The war could not be won without more soldiers but to win the war the soldiers needed the supplies. In many ways the problems encountered by the government were no longer ones related to parties but the very willingness of the working class to accept their leadership.

Taking On The Military

Lloyd George was particularly successful in an area which Asquith had chosen to leave untouched: civil-military relations. He eventually managed to stamp his authority on the military and rid himself of his enemy, William Robertson, Chief of Imperial General staff.

Control over the Admiralty was surprisingly easy to obtain: in April 1917, he forced the introduction of the convoy system upon the reluctant First Sea Lord, Lord Jellicoe, to combat the menace of the U-Boat. This was a momentous victory for Lloyd George as he swept aside centuries of protocol by almost single-handedly taking over the Admiralty.[39]

Imposing his will on the army was to take a lot longer. Relations between Lloyd George and the military leaders had always been difficult and by

March 1917, the Prime Minister was already looking for ways to rid himself of Haig.

The first test of nerve came when Haig announced he wanted to launch a new offensive in Flanders. A War Policy Committee was set up in June 1917 to discuss the idea. Lloyd George opposed Haig, but after six weeks of discussion the War Cabinet agreed to the attack. In the end Lloyd George had been unwilling, at this stage, to overrule the army. As Clive Wigram, the King's Equerry, reported:

HM thinks the War Cabinet is afraid of Haig.[40]

When the Flanders offensive failed with over 300,000 British casualties, it resulted in major disputes between the politicians and generals over the inquest into what want wrong. Relations worsened when the military then decided to move further resources into the Western Front after the collapse of the Russian army. The military argued that it was essential to bolster the front to ensure the Germans kept most of their troops there, instead of sending them eastwards.

Lloyd George was not convinced and he continued to meet with British and French politicians to discuss alternative strategies, in particular the possibilities of a negotiated peace with Austria and the creation of a Central Staff to control overall military strategy. This put him on a collision course with the Chief of the Imperial General Staff. The relationship between the two men is rather well summarised by Robertson:

Lloyd George being keen on the Italian project for the time being and knowing that I am against it and the French are for it, and the French keep rubbing in that it is necessary to have a Central Staff at Paris, I can see Lloyd George in future wanting to agree to some such organisation so as to put the matter in French hands and to take it out of mine. However, we shall see about this.[41]

Robertson was completely out of hand by this point, only concerned by his own quest for power and authority rather than choosing the best path for British military strategy. This was a new era for him; not only had Britain never experienced such total warfare before, but it was also the first time that his authority was seriously challenged by a politician and he was clearly finding it difficult to adjust.

However, his actions needed to be curbed by Lloyd George and the civilian control of strategy became the issue of the moment. The generals continued to push the coalition further and further and started to give the politicians misleading information to try and make their case. One example came over a plan Lloyd George supported which involved attacking Turkey in Palestine. Despite having an actual 5 to 1 numerical advantage over the Turks, the military misled the Cabinet by claiming they needed an extra thirteen divisions. It was a key turning point in relations and showed the War Cabinet they could not trust the army for unbiased military advice.

To take control Lloyd George started to draw up plans to create a new military system with centralised staff for the whole allied military effort. In effect he was moving control of the army into the hands of the politicians. The plans met with support from his War Cabinet, but faced opposition from a peculiar alliance of Asquith, backbench Conservatives and the army. He also had to face a hostile media who had been worked up by Robertson and Haig to oppose the plans. Asquith's opposition was drawn from his belief that politicians should leave war to the experts, but he was also mistrustful of Lloyd George taking even more power for himself.

In the end, the unity of the War Cabinet was enough to win through and the Conservatives agreed, putting the future of the coalition ahead of their concerns. Not all could agree and a splinter group of Conservatives created a National Party led by Henry Page Croft in opposition to Lloyd George's proposals.

Although the coalition's position in the Commons was less secure than it had been in early 1917, opinion was gradually coming round to support Lloyd George's quest against the generals but only as long as the Prime Minister played his cards right. Eventually things came to a head and in March 1918 a complete collapse of trust occurred between the War Cabinet and the General Staff over the allocation of manpower between the military and civilian war effort. Lloyd George responded by creating a Manpower Committee. Then, with the Cabinet behind him, he went on to split up Haig and Robertson. In February, Robertson was sent to Versailles as Deputy Chief of the Imperial General Staff, a position for which he held particular contempt and disdain. For much of the rest of the war, supreme strategy was essentially directed by the so-called 'X Committee' consisting of Lloyd George, Henry Wilson (Robertson's replacement) and the independent minded Alfred Milner. Lloyd George had finally won his battle for control.

Working As A Team

Lloyd George's relationship with the rest of the Cabinet and the reaction of the opposition were the key to the coalition's eventual success. He made a very strong and persuasive War Leader and, contrary to Asquith, the relationship between Lloyd George and Bonar Law remained generally harmonious. Lloyd George made a point of bestowing important positions on the leader of the Conservatives. Not only was he a member of the exclusive War Cabinet, he was also Chancellor of the Exchequer and leader of the Commons. During the war, the last two positions were actually not that important, as most of the Treasury's responsibilities were transferred to the Prime Minister, but still it was important for Bonar Law to be recognised as a party leader and an equal to the Prime Minister. Bonar Law supported him because he believed that there was no possible alternative Prime Minister and never felt up to the job himself. In the end, Bonar Law and Lloyd George worked remarkably well as a double act. They met almost every day and the Prime Minister would use him as a sounding board. Conversely, Lloyd George left most of the conduct of parliament's routine business in Bonar Law's hands.

Lloyd George's relations with the rest of the Cabinet were a lot smoother than under Asquith. He did not hold the same contempt for Conservatives as Asquith and chose his ministers for their level of expertise and usefulness rather than out of obligation. For example, he placed Arthur Balfour (Asquith's ally during the conscription crises) at the Foreign Office because Lloyd George recognised his political value as the last Conservative Prime Minister and he had a genuine regard for his intellect and pliability. Of course, disagreements did exist within the government and Lloyd George had bitter arguments with some of them. The difference between Lloyd George's and Asquith's governments is that these arguments were not simply over policy and between political parties, they tended more towards issues and efficiency.

On the whole, the government functioned far better as a unit than under Asquith. This was partly due to the fact that troublesome personalities such as McKenna and Runciman had been removed and replaced by non-partisan businessmen. But having the new War Cabinet also helped as it reduced the number of people involved in making essential decisions.

As leader of the opposition, Asquith gave general support to the government and mostly refrained from all but the most moderate criticism. In fact, for the rest of the war the Asquithian Liberals remained in a sort of limbo, undecided as to whether they supported or opposed the government. All that really united them was a distrust of Lloyd George and it soon became evident that this was not enough to make either a policy or a position.

From the beginning, Asquith announced that he was not an opposition leader and would give the government 'support, organised support'.[42] In fact, very early on, Asquith disappointed his own supporters. In May 1917, the government introduced a form of tariff protection for the Indian cotton industry. Naturally, Asquith was expected to resist this but the furthest he would go was to propose a compromise resolution, acceptable to and probably pre-arranged with the government, affirming that the matter should be considered afresh after the war. A year later he again supported the government when Lloyd George attempted to extend conscription to Ireland in April 1918. The Liberal MPs were much more forthright in opposing Irish conscription than their leader; Asquith even went so far as telling the House that he disliked the measure but would not do anything to oppose the government at this time. It seems as if Asquith had abruptly moved from one extreme to another. Unable to rid himself of his Liberal principles when he was Prime Minister, he had now resigned himself and abandoned his beliefs in favour of a National Government.

Interestingly, the only issue which stirred Asquith into action was the raging conflict between Lloyd George and the military leaders of the nation. Asquith might have been expected to side with the politicians against the soldiers but he saw this not as a struggle between civilians and the military but as another manifestation of Lloyd George's lust for power.[43] This came to a head over the Maurice Affair in May 1918. General Sir Frederick Maurice publicly accused Lloyd George of being responsible for the shortage of troops in France and thus the reverses during the early days of the German offensive. He specifically blamed the Prime Minister and Bonar Law of misleading parliament and the public on a number of military issues, including the Allies' rifle strength in France at the beginning of 1918, and the War Cabinet's responsibility for forcing Haig to extend his line in January 1918. This had been an ongoing theme throughout Lloyd George's premiership when the military were convinced that he was deliberately limiting the number of troops for military offensives. So strongly did Asquith feel about the subject that he called for an inquiry into Maurice's charges and pressed the motion to a division after Lloyd George had characterised it as a vote of censure. The *Times* even called the division, 'the *début* of an organised opposition.'[44] Asquith lost the vote and the whole affair ended up branding him as a 'conspirator against the government at the most critical moment of the country's fortunes.'[45]

Lloyd George was now in total control. Asquith and the Liberal Party were defeated. Bonar Law and the Conservatives were weak but loyal coalition partners. The military had finally succumbed to political control and the media were generally supportive of his leadership. He now sought to take even greater control of the political situation.

Towards A Coupon Election

Whilst Lloyd George's main aim was to win the war, he was keen to consider more long-term peace and reconstruction plans. As he declared in March 1917:

> the nation now is in a molten condition: it is malleable now, and will continue to be so for a short time after the war, but not for long.[46]

He was given an opportunity to put his ideas into practice when he reshuffled the Cabinet in August 1917 after Henderson's departure, by creating the Ministry of Reconstruction. The portfolio had existed under Asquith as a junior department but Lloyd George elevated the position and put Addison, his most loyal supporter, in charge of it.

The Ministry's obvious concern was planning for the transition to peace and dealing with new, upcoming issues such as the demobilisation of soldiers. More ambitiously, the Ministry soon began to devise ways in which the wartime machinery of the State could be employed after the Armistice for the purpose of modernising industry and improving the living conditions of the British people. In May 1918, an outbreak of strikes in the engineering industry put pressure on the department to bring forward reforms to help control militant class-conscious elements that had been behind the unrest. As John Turner writes:

*slowly and unselfconsciously, the Lloyd George coalition began to
make itself a counter-revolutionary government.*[47]

Under Addison, the Ministry of Reconstruction maintained a strong sense
of optimism and it was seen as a real opportunity for carrying out reforms
to transform the social conditions of the people and ensure that the unity,
forged in the war, would continue into peace. For example, housing issues
and the creation of the Ministry of Health were seen as national rather than
party issues. In October, the War Cabinet circulated a report chronicling the
coalition's achievements and laying down guidelines for a future
reconstruction programme. These were the early signs that politicians were
thinking seriously about a post-war coalition government under Lloyd
George's leadership.

Not only was there a lot of work to be done to ease the country back into
peace, but the coalitionist supporters quickly understood that substantial
steps needed to be taken to ensure that the government would survive in
the post-war era. The Prime Minister still had no party basis, since the
Liberal machinery and constituency organisation were in the hands of
Asquith. To try and fill the vacuum Lloyd George had set up policy
discussions with his closest advisers, Milner, Addison and Fisher: Addison
wrote in his diary, 'Lloyd George's chief weakness at present [was] that he
ha[d] no organisation' but he also felt that there would be:

*no difficulty in having a really comprehensive programme which
would carry a large mass of the Tory Party as well as of Labour and of
Liberals since a good many old distinctions are dim these days and the
country is ready for a bold move forward under State inspiration.*[48]

By May of the following year these discussions had led to the establishment
of a 'Coalition Liberal' organisation created under Guest (Lloyd George's
Chief Whip). This was the first necessary step towards a viable peacetime
coalition and, as Kenneth Morgan writes, meant that:

*Lloyd George was no longer a lonely hostage to the Conservative
majority and now he could bargain with the Conservative Whips on
something like equal terms.*[49]

The rise of Coalition Liberalism offered a prospect of translating Lloyd
George's wartime ascendancy into something more durable.[50] As things
stood Lloyd George's future remained shrouded in uncertainty; even after

the Maurice Affair, he still had little idea of how much support he actually commanded in the House. Lloyd George was very much aware that opting for a close co-operation with the Conservatives rather than his own party 'would bring about an absolute and definite split' in Liberal ranks. [51] Guest himself did not want to go down in history as the man who wrecked their historic Liberal Party. Even if he did finally become the architect of the coalition agreement for the 1918 election, he wrote to Lloyd George in August, advising him to:

> *pause before committing [himself] to any alliance with the*
> *Conservatives, except for the purpose of the War.*[52]

Irrespective of the discussions with the Conservatives, relations remained poor between the various Liberal groupings. Lloyd George had even set up his own headquarters and set to work accumulating his own party funds. That said, a precarious unity had been maintained in parliament and there was still a small grain of hope that the two strains could be reunited for an election. In fact, in June 1918, a breakfast was organised between Asquith, Grey and Lloyd George in an attempt to reconcile the Liberal Party. However, Lloyd George refused to subordinate himself and his followers to the regular party machinery and Asquith preferred to maintain his position outside of and as an alternative to the government, even though he was offered the Woolsack. The Asquithian Liberals found themselves even more ostracised from this point onwards.

As a consequence of these failed talks, Lloyd George let Guest negotiate with the Conservatives. In July 1918, negotiations for an electoral agreement between the Coalition Liberals and the Conservatives got underway and Lloyd George appointed a committee of prominent Liberal supporters to manage the process under Addison's chairmanship. Throughout the summer and autumn, negotiations were by no means easy. The Conservatives sent a memorandum in September setting out their strategy for the upcoming elections which clearly assumed that the Asquithian Liberals were the enemy. [53] It only went to highlight that their whole attitude towards the Coalition Liberals and Liberal principles were ambiguous at best.

Why were the Conservatives tempted by a coalition? Firstly, the Conservatives were becoming increasingly nervous about the rising impact of Labour organisation throughout the period. Their concerns further increased when they looked over to Soviet Russia and the new Communist regime. The leaders realised that a strong leader would be needed to avert the Socialist danger, but no one in the party was really strong enough to face up to this challenge. Their anxieties were summed up by Walter Long in a letter to The Earl of Derby, British Ambassador in Paris, on 5th July:

> There is a very great change taking place in the country: the Socialists are increasing considerably in certain districts and are becoming very pugnacious and this has thoroughly frightened the middle class and led a great many of those who were our most bitter political opponents to reconsider their position, to approach leaders of our party, and to express the hope that all moderate men who believe in the Empire and in fair play will unite to resist the attacks of the Socialists. I am convinced that this is the only policy that can lead to success. I entirely share your views about L.G. but I think we must face the fact that, unless some catastrophe happens, in all human probability we shall go to the country as a government with him as our leader. I can see nobody else who is likely to command the support of the country.[54]

Even though the Conservatives were numerically stronger than both the Liberals and Labour, it was certainly in their interest to unite with Lloyd George. However, they cared little about Liberal values and this was a union made purely out of political interest, but still, in their eyes, it was a necessary one. Consequently, both the Coalition Liberals and the Conservatives were considering coalition at the same time.

The negotiations between Guest and the Conservatives went on for several months with difficult discussions on the issue of imperial preference (in essence, Tariff Reform). They also disagreed on the type of arrangement. Lloyd George's chief supporters wanted to emphasise welfare provision whilst Long wanted the deal limited to a 'war only' programme. This minimalist co-operation was dropped after Long fell ill and Bonar Law, who personally favoured a greater co-operation, took over the negotiations.

In October 1918, Lloyd George and Bonar Law hammered out a policy agreement and manifesto which provided reasonable compromises over Ireland, free trade and other contentious matters, but which contained a clear Liberal emphasis, especially in its ringing endorsement of a sweeping programme of social reform and construction. The basis of it was the letter of endorsement, which became known as the 'coupon', and would be sent to all the candidates of the parties who were deemed to be supporters of the government. In effect, the coalition's organisers dressed up the election as a vote of confidence in the government's conduct of the war, which fortunately for the coalition was beginning to go rather well.

The timing of the election presented Lloyd George with a problem. Originally, he had planned to organise a 'khaki' election by the end of 1918, assuming that the war would continue for another couple of years. Parliament had been sitting for the past eight years, and was increasingly losing touch with the outside world and unrepresentative of the population at large. The recently enacted Representation of the People Act meant that the new electoral register had been enormously enlarged by two and a half times, largely due to the inclusion of women for the first time. It was generally agreed that the khaki election would help return a government that could finally go on to win the war. Lloyd George still seemed like the most likely candidate to achieve victory and the election would give the extra dynamism and legitimacy required for him to finish the job.

By November, the sudden collapse of the German military and victory came as quite a surprise and now the Prime Minister and the Conservatives had to plan for the unusual situation of campaigning for a peacetime coalition. Twenty-four hours after the termination of hostilities, Lloyd George announced his intention of going to the polls immediately as leader of the coalition. The parties soon found that the old methods of political campaigning had become irrelevant and obsolete during the war. Not only had they not campaigned for a long time, but most MPs also found the electoral map completely redrawn with a lot more voters and the constituency boundaries significantly changed.

Within days it became clear that coalition would be incomplete when Labour announced its immediate withdrawal from the government after the Armistice.

Nevertheless, the coalition agreement that was set up meant that the party basis was wide enough to lend it a truly national aspect. Some Labour MPs even chose to stay with the coalition: for example, Stephen Walsh, who had an impregnable seat in the Ince division of Lancashire, ignored the decision and over the course of the week persuaded the Lancashire and Cheshire Miners' Federation to endorse his candidature and let him go on supporting the coalition.[55]

As Prime Minister of no party, Lloyd George had the particular advantage of being able to shift his emphasis to whatever issues were arousing the attention of the electors without worrying if his party supported it. Of course, the most important issue for the electorate was the peace terms that Britain would bring forward at the upcoming peace conference. The coalition, and in particular Lloyd George, emphasised the need for reconstruction and the desire to avoid destroying Germany financially. However, when it became clear that reparations and indemnities were far more important to the public, the coalition was flexible enough to backtrack.

Consequently, the coalition was widely popular with the country at large. Already in early 1918, it seemed that there was a growth in hostile feelings towards the traditional party politics. Harold Spender wrote in the *Contemporary Review* in February 1918, 'Coalition... is becoming a vested interest.'[56] Churchill certainly capitalised on this feeling of national unity and reconstruction in his election speech in November 1918:

> *Why should peace have nothing but the squabbles and the selfishness and the pettiness of daily life? Why if men and women, all classes, all parties, are able to work together for 5 years like a mighty machine to produce destruction, can they not work together for another five years to produce abundance?...*[57]

The majority of the coalition candidates were Conservatives, with just over 150 coupons given to Coalition Liberals. A small number was also allocated to the National Democratic Party, a pro-government 'patriotic Labour' splinter group.

Lloyd George set out his position at the start of the campaign in a speech he made on the 12th November in Downing Street to a group of Liberal MPs. In the speech he insisted that the principal issue of the election would be the nature of the peace and he urged that in the:

> *present instance no sense of revenge or greed should override the doctrines of righteousness'* and he called for the creation of a League of Nations.[58]

He also outlined a programme for raising standards of health and housing and bringing 'light and beauty' into the lives of those at present denied them. He offered reforms like minimum wages and shorter working hours, the development of public transportation and improvements in the purchase of land. Essentially, his speech reaffirmed his belief in liberal doctrines like free trade and home rule for Ireland. Although later this was described as 'a magnificent Liberal speech',[59] he did not stick to a Liberal agenda throughout the campaign; in fact, within four days of this speech, he was behaving with outright hostility to the main body of Liberals. For example, in his speech on 16th November, he did not make a single reference to his concern for the Liberal cause. This was classic Lloyd George: his opening speech enabled him to take some Liberals with him by providing a Liberal gloss on the points already agreed with the Conservatives, made his change of allegiance less blatant, and was also a good bargaining tool with the Conservatives who were aware that he still enjoyed support amongst the Liberals.

For their part, the Liberal Party was in an awful state of confusion. Deceived by what they saw as Lloyd George's betrayal they were unsure as to how to campaign against him and were indecisive throughout the election campaign. Asquith in particular remained extremely ambiguous towards both the coalition parties and the Labour Party throughout the campaign, refusing to take a strong stand against either. On 18th November, Asquith declared in a speech that he would give:

> hearty support and fullest co-operation to any government, by whatever name it is called, which grapples with the problem of reconstruction on progressive and democratic lines.

and summed up by advising Liberals to:

> throw their whole weight on the side of their patriotic and democratic programme, keeping their eyes open and their hands free. [60]

It was hardly a rallying cry to vote Liberal. The press severely attacked him, and the *Westminster Gazette* published:

> Mr. Asquith, let it be admitted, has been no match for the modern politicians who capture opinion and make and unmake Cabinets with the aid of their press auxiliaries, and in recent months he seems to some of his followers to have carried modesty and self-effacement to excess.[61]

Asquith had the same attitude towards Labour, refusing to completely oppose them but not willing to co-operate more closely with them either.

The coalition won the election with a decisive majority and Lloyd George's authority and national appeal were not in doubt. Out of the 159 couponed Liberals, 136 were elected, together with 333 of 364 couponed Conservatives. In all, 541 coupons were issued to candidates and 478 of them were elected. The Liberals collapsed with just 29 MPs elected. In the end Asquith himself lost his seat despite the fact that Lloyd George had specifically not issued a coupon against him. The results reflected the mood of a nation less interested in normal election issues than relief and the exaltation of victory. Politician after politician declared that the issues of pre-war were out of date and that the problems of peace and reconstruction demanded a national rather than a party solution. For Lloyd George it was a triumph, no one had ever attained such overwhelming authority. In fact, he seemed to have climbed to a rare pinnacle of personal domination, as two Labour MPs later told Stamfordham, he was the 'strongest man since Pitt'.[62] For his old party colleague it was a different story. Asquith had begun the war as the unchallenged leader of a decisive parliamentary majority. He ended it, four years later out of parliament altogether and with a party in tatters.[63]

Although the coalition was overwhelmingly successful in the 1918 elections, many questions were left unanswered, questions which could potentially destabilise the government. In particular, the coalition parties remained distinct, with two separate Whips' offices. The future relationship between them seemed relatively unclear. At the end of the day, Lloyd George had understood the necessity of having a party base and knew he could not win the election without the help of the Conservatives. After all, the context of the situation suited the Conservatives perfectly well and they could probably have won a fair number of seats without the coupon. But Lloyd George and the Conservatives proved to work well together. Lloyd George found in the Conservatives a party and the Conservatives found in Lloyd George the leadership Bonar Law failed to give them. Lloyd George was now at his height of popularity, but the honeymoon was not to last.

From Coupon To Corruption

The newly elected government started with enormous goodwill. As the *Morning Post* wrote:

> *there is a widespread universal desire to maintain and to extend in peace that sense of comradeship which has been won in war...* [64]

Most people endorsed the concept of a broad-based National Government that could see the country through its transition from war to peace. Party politics suddenly felt out of place in this post-war atmosphere and expectations ran high as millions saw in the coalition a new hope for a better age.

From the start, the government set out to be genuinely cross-party. The Cabinet was made up of eleven Conservatives, eight Liberals and one Labour. There was a similar mixture at the junior ministerial level. Even many of the MPs were a completely new breed; interestingly out of all the Conservative MPs, only fifteen per cent were from landed backgrounds and over one third were businessmen. The country had high hopes for this new government and it seemed that the Conservatives and Liberals had come together for the good of the people, and not simply out of political calculations.

However this unity was tested throughout the next four years as each of the parties struggled within the coalition.

In February 1920, the Labour element in government was largely removed by the almost simultaneous resignation of two Labour ministers. After this event, any claim that the coalition represented Labour was unrealistic. In fact there had been tensions before as the growth of the Labour Party had begun to concern the coalition members. For several months in a series of by-elections in 1919, Labour showed its ability to attract support in a wide diversity of constituencies and in virtually every contest Labour candidates significantly improved their gains, going on to win a three-cornered by-election at Spen Valley in December 1919. [65] The rise of Labour as a political force enabled the coalition leaders to unfairly make the link to the Bolshevik threat to the country and encouraged people to believe that the coalition was essential to halt Bolshevism.

In June 1921, the Coalition Liberal representation in the government was also seriously eroded. After a savage public brawl with Lloyd George,

Addison, who was probably the coalition's most loyal supporter, was forced out of government after a dispute over his salary. His departure symbolised the end of the government's effective commitment to social reform and to the new house-building and slum clearance that he had been leading. Another Liberal casualty was Edwin Montagu, who left the Cabinet in March 1922 after protesting about the government's pro-Greek policy in the Near East and Lloyd George's anti-Turk manoeuvres inflaming Muslim protest in India. Despite this important loss, Liberals did remain in government with Lloyd George, including Churchill, Alfred Mond and H.A.L. Fisher, but Addison and Montagu were certainly two important pillars of government and their resignations were a serious blow.

Coalition Liberals, including some senior Ministers, were becoming increasingly restless with coalition politics and were tempted to opt for reunion with the Asquithians. However, they held back fearing that if a complete merger was made, this would alienate some of the Liberals who supported Lloyd George. Similarly, they were reluctant to fight Asquithian Liberals in by-elections, which made Lloyd George's job particularly difficult. In fact, it got to the point where Lloyd George had absolutely no party machinery with which to work as the entire Liberal Party machinery was in Asquith's hands. This became a serious problem in by-elections, as there was virtually no local machine to uphold the coalition cause.

The Coalition Liberals were also uneasy on policy issues, in particular free trade. The 1919 budget, presented by Austen Chamberlain as Chancellor, caused great anxiety as it encouraged imperial preference. Although Chamberlain had a tough job redressing Britain's disastrous finances and debts, the Coalition Liberals felt that their precious free trade heritage was slowly but surely being undermined.

Ireland continued to be an important issue of contention between the Conservatives and the Coalition Liberals who immediately rejected the controversial policy of retaliation and reprisals and called for more conciliatory and less coercive policies.

Nevertheless, despite Liberal Ministers' unease at the course of government policy, it remained less of a problem than the gulf which divided them from their Asquithian brethren.

Conservatives For Coalition

Despite the loss of Labour and Liberal members, the coalition just about retained its bipartisan aspect, with its predominantly Conservative Ministers still surviving under Lloyd George. In 1921, Bonar Law fell ill and was forced into temporary retirement. He was succeeded by Austen Chamberlain, a staunch coalitionist who publicly renewed his commitment to closer alliance with his coalition partners.

However, as the coalition wore on, it became increasingly clear that the Conservatives were only in it to keep Lloyd George as Prime Minister rather than to implement any Liberal social and welfare reforms.

Firstly, there was growing alarm at Lloyd George's free-spending programme. Addison, as Minister of Health and responsible for housing, was a particular target for their wrath. When he implemented expensive subsidies to private builders to try to stimulate housing he was criticised by the 'anti-waste zealots'. Fisher, at the Board of Education, and Mond, as First Commissioner of Works, were not far behind on the Conservative hit list. Increasingly the Conservative backbench felt as if they were being led by the Coalition Liberals rather than swallowing Lloyd George into their organisation and programme.

Secondly, as Ireland had troubled the Coalition Liberals, so it also aroused fears among the Conservatives. The eventual outcome of the Irish troubles was the Free State treaty of December 1921, negotiated with Sinn Fein, which accorded an extreme degree of independence to the twenty-six Catholic counties of southern Ireland, and left Ulster in the lurch and unprotected against IRA reprisals. A wave of IRA atrocities in early 1922, culminating in the murder of Field-Marshal Sir Henry Wilson outside his home in Easton Square, added to Conservative concerns.

Conservative alarm about the policies of the coalition also focused on Lloyd George and his foreign policy. His conduct at the Genoa Conference in April 1922 drew particular criticism. The Prime Minister proposed to grant *de jure* recognition to Soviet Russia and wanted to bring the Bolsheviks and the defeated Germans (whose reparations he wanted to scale down) into the European diplomatic and financial systems. All these proposals roused alarms for the Conservatives. In March 1922, Lloyd George was effectively vetoed by a majority of his own Cabinet over the formal recognition of the Soviet Union and he was forced to propose a humiliating compromise.

From the Conservatives' viewpoint, the Prime Minister was lurching too far in a Liberal direction and carrying them with him as the dominant partner. During the winter of 1921-1922 they felt Lloyd George had 'swung to the left' when he tried to place a new emphasis on policies to remedy unemployment and to revive trade. It is hard to understand why Lloyd George chose to go this far; perhaps he was trying to gain votes from the increasingly strong Labour Party by claiming that the government was the true champion of social and industrial policy.[66]

Despite this, the Conservative backbench discontent was contained, at least until the Genoa Conference in 1922. As Bonar Law later said to Balfour after the fall of the government, the Prime Minister's approach to domestic and foreign problems genuinely transcended party barriers:

> L.G.'s character and habit of mind made him approach any new problem in a spirit of complete detachment from traditional prejudices or principles. This made him absolutely impartial between the parties which, for the head of a coalition government, was a great advantage.[67]

The Conservatives were in fact content to stick to the coalition for three reasons. Firstly, they agreed that the coalition occupied a creative middle role between 'the revolutionary and the reactionary' and that the major problems of the time were new and unheard of previously, and therefore necessitated a rational approach. Secondly, politicians felt the need to sustain unity in the post-war world, especially at such an important time of reconstruction. Finally, there was an overriding fear of organised Labour, caused by the tide of trade union militancy from the national railway strike of September-October 1919 to the 'Black Friday' mining dispute and the defeat of the 'Triple Alliance' unions in 1921. As Kenneth Morgan writes:

> Lloyd George was indeed on firm ground in claiming that, whatever their other differences, Liberals and Conservatives were as one in defending private enterprise and the basis of a free society.[68]

The anti-Bolshevist card was, above all others, the one for Lloyd George to play with the Conservatives.

However, this tacit agreement between the two parties gradually eroded. Not everyone was convinced by the 'anti-Bolshevik'. Up until now, the rhetoric had been used and abused to weld the two sides together, but this soon became obsolete and irrelevant. Most Liberals still liked to think of themselves as progressives and disapproved of the class prejudice. The *Manchester Guardian*, previously a great fan of Lloyd George and the coalition, called the 'socialist menace':

> a political bogey by which we decline to be terrified.[69]

Even Conservatives rejected anti-Bolshevism as a strategy. On the contrary, in their view, it would make better long-term sense to appeal to the working man's patriotism. In the end, as prospects of a dramatic Labour breakthrough receded and chances of an outright Conservative victory correspondingly improved, anti-Bolshevism lost much of its relevance. Essentially, party feeling steadily revived after 1919 and there was little that the coalition leaders could say or do to stop the political system settling back down to normal circumstances and the humdrum of everyday life again.

In particular the Conservatives began to get restless resenting the fact that over seventy per cent of parliament was Conservative and yet they only had twelve out of the twenty-one Cabinet positions. They disliked having to stand down at by-elections in favour of Coalition Liberals especially as the latter did not even have a functioning local party organisation with which to fight Labour. Lloyd George had been able to mesmerise the Conservatives at first, and they recognised he was a truly charismatic and powerful leader, but they soon became disenchanted and realised that the Coalition Liberals had become more of a burden to them than an advantage.

"Fusion Or Confusion"

Despite the problems with the various parties the general absence of partisan feeling within the government was impressive. This was partly due to Lloyd George's maintenance of a very strong executive. After the election his intention seemed to be to continue the political methods of the war years and the Cabinet remained firmly under his direct control. Ministers were often reprimanded when they fell out of line. When Lloyd George was in Paris, Churchill submitted some proposals to the Cabinet without running it past him, this resulted in a firm rebuke:

I am surprised that you should think it right to submit such a scheme to my colleagues before talking it over or at least before submitting it in the first instance to me...[70]

At times it seemed as if the Prime Minister simply used the Cabinet as a sounding board to try out ideas without giving them any great power. He also interfered in the running of various departments. He turned himself into a kind of collateral Minister of Labour when he played a major role in tackling the various industrial disputes between 1919 and 1921, employing, as Kenneth Morgan writes:

the whole formidable range of weapons in his political armoury – delay or coercion, summit diplomacy, or personal charm.[71]

He also spent many hours on foreign affairs, engrossed in shaping the post-war world and conducting over twenty major conferences with foreign heads of government.

During this post-war coalition, Lloyd George did not lose the authority or the enthusiasm and determination that won him the war. He remained the dominant personality and the coalition was formed around him. However, the management of the coalition was a very difficult task for the Prime Minister. At the end of the day, no merger of parties occurred and both remained completely separate and independent. The two sets of supporters sat as separate parties, under separate leaders, and were separately whipped.

His main problem however was a lack of a personal political base and party support. When he tried to remedy this by raising his own funds, this further increased resentment and criticisms. The Prime Minister acquired large sums of money by means of soliciting gifts, that is to say, he widely sold peerages and knighthoods. These sales were the origins of the notorious 'Lloyd George Fund'. The Conservatives, slightly hypocritically, objected to this method on both practical and moral objections. Many old-style Conservatives felt that Lloyd George's peers and 'dreadful knights' derived from a lower social order and were selected more on a cash basis than was customary (but let's not forget that the Conservatives happily sold peerages too for their own funding purposes). Lord Salisbury even called Lloyd George's methods, 'the adulteration of the peerage.'[72]

In an attempt to create a political base Lloyd George's supporters decided to try to form a coalition party, which would have effectively solved a lot of problems. From 1919 onwards, Lloyd George began to emphasise the notion of 'fusion', suggesting a nationwide merger of the coalition parties. He effectively wanted to persuade his Liberal government colleagues that old party labels were meaningless and that only a fusion of anti-socialist parties could cope adequately with the problems of the time. Initially there was enthusiasm from the new 'brand' of MPs, young officers returning from the atrocities of the war who were keen to get rid of party politics. However, the idea never developed and by March 1920, the plan for fusion had completely collapsed and nothing like it was proposed again. Both the Coalition Liberals and Conservatives rejected it as they saw in the idea too many negative reasons to join rather than a real ideological desire to unite the two parties. Bonar Law eventually proposed a better co-ordination between the two parties as the alternative. On 24th March 1920, *Punch's* cartoon summed up these sentiments: Lloyd George, depicted as the captain of a ship that was undergoing a refit, is asked by the mate whether she should be given a new name: ' "Fusion" or "Confusion" – It's all One To Me So Long As I'm Skipper', he replies.[73]

Descent From Olympus

Although he started out very strongly, as peacetime politics gradually returned, the Prime Minister was forced to give up his God-like status. The non-party men, invaluable during the war, were disappearing. After the Versailles Treaty, his Cabinet Secretariat became rather unnecessary and resembled more a piece of formal administrative machinery for recording and implementing decisions than any kind of prime-ministerial department. More significantly still, the 'Garden Suburb' was being reduced in status. The Prime Minister was slowly but surely obliged to accommodate himself to the varying pressures within the coalition. By March 1922, Lloyd George's authority over his own Cabinet ministers was increasingly strained. Percy Grigg, Principal Private Secretary to the Chancellor, believed that three quarters of them were now disloyal to him. Indeed, Lloyd George suffered a severe rebuff when his colleagues, led by Churchill himself, voted him down on the issue of the recognition of Soviet Russia at the Genoa Conference. He could no longer employ the same weapons as before, and his grip on the coalition was loosening.

Lloyd George had also failed to take parliament seriously enough and the MPs let him know this. In 1920, a sort of revolt against the Prime Minister's absences abroad occurred through a demonstration in support of General Dyer. More importantly, as Liberal leader of a largely Conservative majority, he lacked effective control through the Whips and this greatly hindered him. He did try to resolve this by spending more time in the Commons after 1920 but it was almost too late and his interjections and debates in the Commons almost always led to disastrous consequences. He had never been a great parliamentarian and although had been able to get away with it during the war, he struggled during peacetime.

His authoritative personality was far more suited to a war climate and increasingly his stubbornness to adapt to the new situation meant that he lost grip on the Cabinet and parliament and his personality was no longer enough to keep the system together.

Essentially, as the war receded, the interest in 'strong government' somewhat faded and Lloyd George's style of governing fell out of fashion. The coalition worked because the Executive dominated over the Legislature; in times of war this method had been accepted but now there were strong calls for a return to normality, which presupposed the dissolution of the coalition altogether. State control had worked effectively during the war because it was seen as necessary but it was neither a Liberal nor a Conservative principle and, although Lloyd George managed to 'de-control' the economy efficiently and quite successfully, the people were content to return to two-party politics.

The early signs of recession also undermined the coalition and meant that the government had to abandon its big reconstruction plans. This became particularly damaging for the coalition, as its main reason for existing was to implement these big peacetime social and economic reforms.

His fall was finally triggered by the Honours Scandal, which erupted in the summer of 1922, and the political and military crisis that brought Britain to the brink of war with Turkey in August 1922. The Chanak crisis over Turkey came in precisely the wrong area and at the wrong time. All at once, his weaknesses on every side were exposed.[74]

In the end this succession of disappointments, failures and humiliations led to the Conservative 'revolt' against the Prime Minister at the Carlton Club in October 1922: with 185 votes to 88, the Conservative MPs resolved to fight the upcoming election alone without Lloyd George and the Coalition Liberals. He and Chamberlain, his coalition partner, resigned and Bonar Law became Prime Minister. Parliament was dissolved and an election set. His crushing defeat at the December general election confirmed that his career as a political figure of major consequence had abruptly come to its end.

Although Lloyd George fell in disgrace, in particular for his corruption and wasteful methods of government, it would be wrong to completely characterise this coalition as a failure. As G. Searle writes, to conclude that the coalition as foredoomed to failure 'would be an abuse of wisdom of hindsight'.[75] Many of the policies initially proposed and implemented, especially in the sphere of foreign affairs, did command a consensus of national support. Skilful tacking from the Prime Minister did prevent movement to the left or to the right, and, despite being a small minority, the Coalition Liberals did get an opportunity to implement Liberal policies. The only other feasible alternative in 1918 would have probably been another coalition as none of the parties truly commanded enough national support, especially with the rise of the Labour Party during World War One. On the whole, Lloyd George's brand of coalition seemed the most convincing and plausible possibility.

A Tale Of Three Coalitions

The period between 1915 and 1922 was dominated by three very different coalition governments. Asquith's war coalition lacked authority and failed to keep pace with the demands of war. In contrast when Lloyd George took over, his coalition provided firm leadership, political unity and a much clearer military direction. Finally, after the coupon election his leadership skills became part of the problem as he drove a government into corruption and lead what many have described as the 'most unloved coalition of all'.[76]

Asquith had been drawn into coalition after it became clear that the war would not be won in a matter of months. The various military failings were seen as the fault of politicians and together with Bonar Law both men felt safer together than apart. It was an uneven relationship and one which did little to speed up the political response to events in Europe.

However it's all too easy to caricature this coalition as a failure. Compared to Lloyd George's regime it was certainly the weaker but many of the measures he adopted would have split the country if Asquith had adopted them earlier. His cautious approach to conscription and control of the economy showed indecision but a more single-minded leader may have struggled to win over the public and parties so early into the war.

In contrast, Lloyd George's premiership was quick to understand that the structures of decision making needed to change. A smaller war committee and better control of the military were strategic decisions that gave him great authority and were necessary tools for winning the war. He handled the Conservative party with more tact and gave Bonar Law a status that Asquith ignored.

Lloyd George's contribution to the war effort was outstanding but in the end it also helped bring disaster to the Liberal Party. The fall out between Asquith and the establishment of two Liberal parties was not just his fault and both leaders must share the blame. Asquith's quiet leadership avoided the party splitting as the country entered war, but his unwillingness to participate in government after his resignation contributed towards the split.

By the time of the coupon election and peacetime coalition many of the qualities that helped Lloyd George win the war quickly became reasons why he lost the peace. His overpowering leadership created more and more friction and his lack of a political party and base led him to unrealistic attempts to create a merged party. The Conservative partners were irritated at his social agenda and shared very few common values, whilst the Liberal Party remained out in the cold and his 'administration had seemed to ride roughshod over every principle that Liberals most valued'.[77] I think the lack of a clear political base led to the failings in Ireland where he managed to alienate all the political parties and it was his lack of party structure that led him to raise funds from the sale of honours. Taken together the coalition has been denounced by historians. Kenneth Morgan's summary is typical when he says the government will be remembered for its:

> *sabre-rattling in industrial relations, for presiding over mass*
> *unemployment on a scale unknown in British history, for the reprisals*
> *in Ireland and unsuccessful adventures in foreign affairs. It was*
> *credibly represented as debasing the tone and the currency of British*
> *public life. It was impregnated with the whiff of corruption, through*

the glittering millions of the Lloyd George fund, largely raised through the sale of honours, as its visible legacy.[78]

It was a sorry end for Lloyd George. His fall mostly reflected the fact that the national imperatives of wartime had given way to the sectional pressures of a new world in which party politics was back. By 1922, Lloyd George had finally stopped being the war hero and was 'whittled down to mere human'.[79]

Looking back on the seven year period there is no doubt that the middle coalition led by Lloyd George during the war was a successful one. Taken as a whole though the various coalitions did not cover themselves in glory. Not for the first time a coalition had left a leader without a party, a party in tatters and a country lacking firm leadership. It was a pattern that would return within a decade.

References

1. *Country Before Party: Coalition and the Idea of 'National Government' in Modern Britain 1885-1987*, G. R. Searle

2. Herbert Henry Asquith in *Political Lives*, Hugo Young

3. Kenneth O. Morgan 1902-1924 in *Coalitions in British Politics*, David Butler

4. *Manchester Guardian*, 1 May 1915

5. *British Politics and the Great War: Coalition and Conflict, 1915-1918*, John Turner

6. 'Asquith, Bonar Law and the First Coalition', Martin Pugh, *The Historical Journal*

7. *Ibid.*

8. *Ibid.*

9. *Asquith*, Roy Jenkins

10. *Memories and Reflections 1852-1927*, Herbert Asquith

11. Kenneth O. Morgan 1902-1924 in *Coalitions in British Politics*, David Butler

12. *Politicians at War, July 1914 to May 1915: A Prologue to the Triumph of Lloyd George*, Cameron Hazelhurst

13. *Ibid.*

14. *Observer*, 23 May 1915

15. *The Age of Balfour and Baldwin, 1902-1940*, John Ramsden

16. *Manchester Guardian*, 30 July 1915

17. *Country Before Party: Coalition and the Idea of 'National Government' in Modern Britain 1885-1987*, G. R. Searle

18. Asquith to Balfour, 18 September 1915, Asquith Papers

19. 'Asquith's Predicament, 1914-1918', Barry McGill, *The Journal of Modern History*, volume 39 (1967)

20. *Asquith*, Roy Jenkins

21. *Ibid.*

22. *Ibid.*

23. *Ibid.*

24. *Ibid.*

25. *British Politics and the Great War: Coalition and Conflict, 1915-1918*, John Turner

26. *Country Before Party: Coalition and the Idea of 'National Government' in Modern Britain 1885-1987*, G. R. Searle

27. Lloyd George to Gilbert Murray, 26 October 1927, Gilbert Murray Papers

28. 'Asquith's Predicament, 1914-1918', Barry McGill, *The Journal of Modern History*, volume 39 (1967)

29. *Observer*, 16 April 1916

30. *The Downfall of the Liberal Party, 1914–1935*, Trevor Wilson

31. *Asquith*, Roy Jenkins

32. *Daily Chronicle*, 30 November 1915

33. *Morning Post*, 30 November 1915

34. *Asquith*, Roy Jenkins

35. *The Times*, 4 December 1916

36. 'The Treasury: from Impotence to Power', War and the State: the Transformation of the British Government 1914-1919, Kathleen Burk

37. *British Politics and the Great War: Coalition and Conflict, 1915-1918*, John Turner

38. *Ibid.*

39. 'Lloyd George's Premiership: a Study in "Prime Ministerial Government"', Kenneth O. Morgan, *The Historical Journal* XIII

40. *British Politics and the Great War: Coalition and Conflict, 1915-1918*, John Turner, p.164

41. *Ibid.*, p.234

42. *The Downfall of the Liberal Party: 1914-1935*, Trevor Wilson, p.106

43. *Ibid.*, p.109

44. *The Times*, 10 May 1918

45. *Political Lives*, Hugo Young, p.28

46. *Country Before Party: Coalition and the Idea of 'National Government' in Modern Britain 1885-1987*, G. R. Searle, p.106

47. *British Politics and the Great War: Coalition and Conflict, 1915-1918*, John Turner, p.194-5

48. Extract from 8 June 1917, taken from *Four and a Half Years: A personal diary from June 1914 to January 1919*, volume II, Christopher Addison, p.459

49. *Country Before Party: Coalition and the Idea of 'National Government' in Modern Britain 1885-1987*, G. R. Searle

50. 'Lloyd George's Premiership: A Study in "Prime Ministerial Government" ', Kenneth O. Morgan, *The Historical Journal* XIII, p.130-150

51. *The Riddell Diaries, 1908-1923*, Lord Riddell, p.230

52. 'Lloyd George's Timing of the 1918 Election', Barry McGill, *The Journal of British Studies*, 14 (1974) p.115-116

53. 'Asquith's Predicament, 1914-1918', Barry McGill, *The Journal of Modern History*, volume 39 (1967) p.302

54. *British Politics and the Great War: Coalition and Conflict, 1915-1918*, John Turner, p.304

55. *Ibid.*, p.319

56. 'The War and the Parties', Harold Spender, *Contemporary Review*, 113 (1918) p.137-8

57. *Winston S. Churchill, Vol. IV: 1916-1922*, Martin Gilbert, p.171-2

58. *The Downfall of the Liberal Party: 1914-1935*, Trevor Wilson, p.136-139

59. *Manchester Guardian*, 13 November 1918

60. *The Downfall of the Liberal Party: 1914-1935*, Trevor Wilson, p.168

61. *Westminster Gazette*, 27 November 1918

62. Lord Stamfordham to Lloyd George, 19 March 1921, quoted in *Men and Power 1917-1918*, Lord Beaverbrook, p.338

63. Barry McGill, 'Asquith's Predicament, 1914-1918', Barry McGill, *The Journal of Modern History*, volume 39 (1967) p.303

64. *Morning Post*, 30 August 1917

65. *Consensus and Disunity: The Lloyd George Coalition Government 1918-1922*, Kenneth O. Morgan, p.46

66. Morgan, 1902-1924 in *Coalitions in British Politics*, David Butler, p.43

67. *Ibid.*, p.43

68. *Ibid.*, p.44

69. *Country Before Party: Coalition and the Idea of 'National Government' in Modern Britain 1885-1987*, G. R. Searle, p.141

70. 'Lloyd George's Premiership: A Study in "Prime Ministerial Government" ', Kenneth O. Morgan, *The Historical Journal* XIII, p.144

71. *Ibid.*, p.145

72. *Country Before Party: Coalition and the Idea of 'National Government' in Modern Britain 1885-1987*, G. R. Searle, p.139

73. *Punch*, 24 March 1920, Issue 223

74. 'Lloyd George's Premiership: A Study in "Prime Ministerial Government" ', Kenneth O. Morgan, *The Historical Journal* XIII, p.155

75. *Country Before Party: Coalition and the Idea of 'National Government' in Modern Britain 1885-1987*, G. R. Searle, p.146

76. *Consensus and Disunity: The Lloyd George Coalition Government 1918-1922*, Kenneth O. Morgan (Clarendon Press, 1979) p.vii

77. *Ibid.*

78. *Ibid.*, p.25

79. Kenneth O. Morgan 1902-1924 in *Coalitions in British Politics*, David Butler, p.50

4

A King's Coalition

A King's Coalition

It was an absurd and unhealthy situation, well calculated to muffle important issues and obscure the realities of the times.[1]

After the War the resumption of party politics was not straightforward. During the 1920s there were four general elections and all three parties saw their fortunes fluctuate. Labour formed its first ever government, then split; the Liberals split, then re-united; the Conservatives found themselves in the unusual position of having over 400 seats, but still not forming a government. It's hardly a surprise that the result of this turbulent decade was an economic crisis and a government of national unity.

At the heart of these events was a reluctant leader, Ramsay MacDonald. Like Lord Aberdeen decades before, he needed constant reassurance from the monarch and regularly threatened to resign. Although MacDonald had declared in 1924 that 'coalitions are detestable and dishonest' he was to go on to head a national coalition seven years later and in doing so paid a high personal price. In splitting the Labour Party and leading a Tory dominated government he became a hate figure in Labour circles. His name has acted as a warning to party leaders ever since on the perils of creating coalitions.

Three-Party Politics

The story starts at the collapse of the coalition that had continued after the end of the First World War. By 1922, Britain was ready to return to party politics, but the untangling of the coalition made politicians nervous. Conservative leaders were suspicious of Lloyd George and Churchill, not knowing if they might unite to create a centre party. A general election was held on 15th November 1922 and Bonar Law's Conservatives took full advantage of the divided opposition and won 344 seats. The Liberals were divided between Herbert Asquith's Liberals and David Lloyd George's National Liberals. This split allowed Labour to surpass the combined strength of both Liberal parties for the first time in both votes and seats.

Within a year, Stanley Baldwin had become leader of the Conservatives. Keen to impose his mark on the party he surprised everybody by calling an early election. He wanted a mandate to introduce protectionist policies to tackle unemployment, but also felt a snap election could further damage the divided Liberals. As Roy Jenkins explains Baldwin did not like three-party politics:

> He was uneasy with the fluid pattern of politics which existed in the post coalition situation. What Baldwin wanted was a reversion to the firm two party system of his youth, but with the Labour Party securely established as a great – not too great – party of state and the Liberal Party tucked up in the history books.[2]

Things did not go to plan and the Conservatives lost their majority but ended up as the largest party. Meanwhile MacDonald's Labour Party grew from strength to strength with 191 seats, and a now reunited Liberal Party was close behind on 158. It was one of those elections where nobody had won, but Baldwin had clearly lost.

The politicians faced a number of options:

> The curious balance of the parties in the House after the 1923 election led to a host of ingenious proposals about alliances and personalities for the new parliament.[3]

Some Conservatives wanted a coalition with the Liberals to stop Labour getting in and pushed horror stories about the danger posed by Labour. Winston Churchill, bruised by defeat himself, said that a Labour government would be 'a national misfortune'.[4] Other Conservatives feared the Liberals more and wanted them frozen out. There was even talk of a government of national trustees.

The concern amongst the established parties was more than matched by the Labour leadership. They were surprised at the number of seats gained and nervous at the task of forming a minority government. In the first few weeks of December 1923, MacDonald took soundings from key party members on the possibility of forming a minority administration. Opinion ranged from those who felt Labour would be damaged by failure, to those who felt that the opportunity to govern was worth the risks involved.

The Labour National Executive, the TUC General Council and the parliamentary Labour Party all held key meetings over this period. As the consultations dragged on MacDonald became convinced that taking office was the right course. Although he saw the risks of dealing with the growing economic crisis, he feared the political risk of allowing the Liberals a chance to get back into office and regain the ground they had lost to Labour in the last decade.

By 13th December all sides within the Labour movement were agreed that:

> *Should the necessity for forming a Labour government arise, the Parliamentary Party should at once accept full responsibility for the government of the country without compromising itself with any form of coalition.*[5]

Three days later, Asquith, the Liberal leader, declared he would not work with the Tories. The path for a Labour government was set.

Labour's First Attempt

This was the outcome Baldwin preferred and he was relaxed about giving up office. For Labour it was a big risk and leap into the unknown. The next few years were an enormous test and those voices that had urged caution were proved right. The administration lacked experience and MacDonald had very few men of talent to call on.

In a letter to veteran Labour MP, Arthur Henderson, he described the problem:

> *I have to admit that we are terribly short of men. There is no use blanking the fact. We shall have to put into office men who are not only untried, but whose capacity to face the permanent officials is very doubtful.*[6]

In echoes of the first years of Tony Blair's Labour administration, MacDonald was to complain that officials were dominating Ministers:

> *Details are over-whelming and Ministers have no time to work out policy with officials as servants, they are immersed in pressing business with officials as masters.*[7]

Henderson himself presented MacDonald with a problem. The two men did not have an easy relationship – MacDonald wanted him to take on the task of organising the Labour Party machine, whilst Henderson wanted to hold senior office. Henderson won the argument and became Home Secretary, but the distrust between the two men was to explode with time, creating turmoil in the party.

Whilst the administration was inexperienced, the Prime Minister himself faced self-doubt. A shy and self-conscious man, his private notes show little joy at becoming Prime Minister. Days after taking office he wrote 'queer unreal feeling about it, sometimes feel should like to run away home to Lossiemore to return to reality and free from these unreal dreams'.[8]

His character was also suspicious and controlling. There were stories that he insisted on opening all his own letters, and checking train times for staff. As his working day often ran from 7 a.m. to the early hours he soon realised that such picky habits would have to go, but like the rest of his Cabinet, he was on a fast learning curve. Faced with inexperience, suspicion, no parliamentary majority and an economic crisis the Labour government was, however, remarkably determined to survive. MacDonald summed up the Cabinet aims as 'security and confidence based on goodwill'. The "goodwill" reflected the need for the Tories and Liberals to refrain from endlessly defeating the government.

Throughout this period relations between the government and Liberals were key. Labour would not have been able to stay in office without Liberal support on key legislation. Liberal leader, Asquith knew he had a powerful voting block, but despite this MacDonald kept him at arm's length and no formal pact took place.

David Marquand explains why:

> The most obvious was that the Liberal and Labour parties were competing for the same consistency. Eighteen months before becoming Prime Minister, MacDonald had proclaimed defiantly that in Britain, 'we shall always tend to return to two great parties and that is the position today'. The two parties fighting for supremacy are Labour and the Tory Party.[9]

That may have been MacDonald's wish, but the Liberals, despite the damaging post-war split, had shown they still had considerable support and were not far behind Labour.

Blake believes the Liberals' failure to enter into a more formal agreement was a mistake:

> The Liberals were in a dilemma. We can now see that they made a fatal error in not securing some sort of agreed terms of co-operation with Labour. As it was they supported Labour from an entirely

independent position with no written treaty, not even an informal understanding.[10]

I think that despite shared political ground, this period was a part of a battle to show which of the opposition parties were stronger and the prospect of defeating each other was a greater motivation than working together. This was to prove the case when the Liberals decided to join forces with the Conservatives over the government's handling of a prosecution for sedition against the editor of the Daily Worker. When it was revealed that political pressure had been put on the Attorney General to withdraw the case, the opposition tabled what amounted to a censure vote. MacDonald lost and the nine-month Labour experiment was over. In the subsequent election on the 29th October, Baldwin saw a remarkable turnabout in support and won a large majority with 412 seats. Labour held on quite well with 151, but the Liberals, whose censure motion had triggered the election, fell badly to 40 seats and have never again made it into three figures. Their failure to negotiate a deal with MacDonald and subsequent triggering of an election have both been regarded as key events in the party's decline.

Baldwin's government faced desperate economic problems, not made any easier knowing that their previous attempts at economic and tariff reform had failed just a few years before. This time they took a more inclusive approach and appointed the free trader Winston Churchill as Chancellor and Neville Chamberlain, a reformer on social policy, as Minister of Health. The general strike of 1926 was a serious setback towards stabilising the economy and by 1927 progress on increasing trade and employment was limited. The party was losing by-elections and support was ebbing away.

Despite this, Baldwin remained confident that he could win the next election. His 200 seat majority looked comfortable and he judged the voters would accept that the difficult times were not of his own making. The election strategy was not ambitious; with a slogan of 'safety first', Baldwin was offering a 'no risk' party with a common-sense Prime Minister. As the 1929 election approached, Baldwin had every reason to assume that he had done enough and a divided opposition should secure him re-election. The election was a three-way battle and the first at which all three parties put up 500 candidates each.

The Conservatives went on to win the popular vote, but saw a massive drop in seats, losing 140 down to 260 MPs. Labour gained 126 extra seats and with 287 had the largest number of MPs. Holding the balance of power were 59 Liberal MPs. For Lloyd George there was an opportunity to be kingmaker, but neither Baldwin, nor MacDonald were interested in pacts. They seemed united in a desire to see off the Liberals and avoid giving the third party a lifeline. Lloyd George was disliked by both men and in these circumstances personality differences and tough political calculations combined to freeze the Liberals out of government yet again.

Heading Towards Crisis

MacDonald was back for a second term, still leading a minority administration, but this time with the authority of leading the largest party. It was an enormous vote of confidence and MacDonald, for the moment, was untouchable. It was not to last.

By the start of 1931, unemployment had hit over 2 million. For a first ever Labour government to see such an increase on its watch was unthinkable. They faced pressure on both fronts. From the left, tensions between unions and Ministers had grown and industrial action was on the increase. From the right, those that warned about economic disaster under Labour looked vindicated. MacDonald did his best to blame the crisis on capitalism, but as the situation got worse this was harder to sustain.

Labour's popularity was falling and by-election results showed a substantial drop in support. MacDonald now faced outright conflict with the unions as he desperately sought to tackle unemployment. In an attempt to take the politics out of the situation he accepted a Liberal suggestion to establish an Economy Committee and asked the opposition parties to nominate members. It was to prove a significant step as the Committee's recommendations were to trigger the beginning of the end for Labour. Roy Jenkins, in his excellent biography of Baldwin, described it as:

> A time bomb ticking away under the life of the government. The government had asked an outside and unfriendly body to make recommendations upon one of the most sensitive areas of politics.[11]

When the Committee finally reported to the Cabinet in May 1931 it sat for 12 hours to consider the findings and were divided on a recommendation to cut unemployment benefit. The situation became graver for MacDonald when Conservatives and Liberals united to support the proposed cut. It now became clear that the government would be defeated in a Commons vote. MacDonald sought and agreed a compromise with the opposition which suggested a smaller reduction in benefit, but still could not get his own party to agree. Undermined by the unions and his own Cabinet colleagues, MacDonald felt isolated. Within two years of a triumphant election result he now faced a party rebellion and a growing fear that he would bankrupt the country if a tough economic survival plan was not put in place.

What was to follow was a period of uncertainty and crisis similar to the days before Aberdeen formed his coalition government. As then, the monarch was to play a key role.

MacDonald was under enormous pressure and spent days torn between holding his party together, or pushing ahead with economic changes he knew were needed in the national interest. The summer saw increased problems with the failure of Germany to make reparation payments. This triggered a European exchange crisis hitting sterling, the most vulnerable currency, hardest. In the last three weeks of July the Bank of England lost £60 million in gold and foreign exchange.

The opposition looked on at this stage not prepared to attack, or assist. Baldwin, who enjoyed his long breaks, had no great appetite to return from his holiday home in France and from Aix wrote to his colleague Neville Chamberlain saying:

> I think in the long view it is all to the good that the government have to look after their own chickens as they come home to roost and get a lot of the dirt cleared up before we come in.[12]

Meanwhile the Liberals relations with Labour had improved. MacDonald had committed himself to a form of electoral reform and even had a private dinner with his old rival Lloyd George. There was some discussion of an emergency pact, but by August the economic crisis was growing and Lloyd George became ill, taking him out of action for two months.

Although there had been some tentative discussion about National Government, MacDonald does not appear to have taken it very seriously. For his part Baldwin was of the view that Labour would collapse and he could present the Conservatives as the true "national" party.

By late summer it was becoming clear to MacDonald that unless he acted fast he could no longer continue as a Prime Minister overseeing a divided

Cabinet and facing Commons defeats. He called a crisis Cabinet meeting late into the evening of August 23rd in one final attempt to resolve the conflict. This time MacDonald was able to get a majority of the Cabinet to agree to his financial proposals, but seven members including the key figure of Arthur Henderson announced they would resign. Such a mass resignation was now unavoidable. Any doubt MacDonald had about his own position became clear and by the following morning he'd decided he could not carry on and prepared to go to the Palace to resign. What followed was remarkable and probably the last time a monarch has played such a key role in forming a government.

Trips To The Palace

The King, George V, had been watching events unfold and was in contact with political and business leaders. The industrialist and ex-Prime Minister Sir Arthur Balfour had written him a memo arguing that:

> The time has come when even emergency measures may be necessary to avert a calamity which is not altogether incomparable with the Great War.[13]

The King had also kept in close contact with Baldwin. The Conservative leader had already served as Prime Minister and was prepared to serve again, if needed. He was well liked and trusted by his party and assumed that if MacDonald's government fell, the King would ask him to form an administration. The King, however, had different plans. In one of those strange twists of events, on the morning of 22nd August Baldwin had gone to see his friend Geoffrey Dawson, editor of the *Times*. As he discussed the political crisis he missed a call from the King asking him to go to Buckingham Palace before lunch. As a result, it was the Liberal leader Samuel who saw the King first.

At the meeting Samuel persuaded the King that a National Government with MacDonald as Prime Minister was a way forward. He agreed that:

> In view of the fact that necessary economics would prove most unpalatable to the working class, it would be to the general interest if they could be imposed by a Labour Cabinet.[14]

The Samuel meeting complete, the King then saw Baldwin later in the day. Baldwin was asked if he would serve in a National Government under MacDonald and had little alternative other than to agree. The King recorded that he was 'greatly pleased with Mr Baldwin's readiness to meet the crisis which had arisen and to sink party interest for the sake of the country', but what else could he have done, as Jenkins goes on to comment:

It is only necessary to reverse the meaning of the sentence to realise how difficult it would have been for Baldwin to have given a negative answer.[15]

The jigsaw nearing completion, the King then saw MacDonald later that night. MacDonald had come prepared to resign and told the King that his Cabinet was totally divided on the economic package. The King informed MacDonald that both Conservative and Liberal leaders would be prepared to serve under his premiership in a National Government. Within 30 minutes of the meeting MacDonald was forced to think again! His resignation was kept firmly in his pocket and an emergency meeting was set up between the three political leaders. The King's appeal had been critical. MacDonald's agreement was, however, conditional. This was not to be a coalition government, but an emergency national response pulling together key political leaders. The deal he agreed was to be temporary and after relevant emergency bills had been passed he wanted the King to agree to a fresh election.

The next day MacDonald informed the Cabinet of the turn of events, aware as he did, that he was going to face enormous anger from his own party.

He told the Cabinet that, 'in view of the gravity of the situation he had felt there was no other course open to him other than to assist in the formation of a National Government on a compromise basis for the purpose of meeting the present emergency'. According to those present he acknowledged that he would be 'denounced and ostracised'.[16]

Chamberlain's diary also records MacDonald's fears; 'he would help us get these proposals through although it means his death warrant'.[17] This was an enormous decision; no wonder he had changed his mind on several occasions, torn between national and party unity.

The easier route would have been to take Labour into opposition, rebuild, and allow the Conservatives and Liberals to form an economic crisis coalition. Whilst that would have been politically more acceptable to the Labour Party, it was not in MacDonald's character to walk away from the problem.

To have left government would have been giving in to the rebels and it seems to me very unlikely that the party would have been able to unite in opposition when they were so split in Cabinet. He must also have felt furious at the way the Cabinet had treated him. For their part many on the left no longer trusted MacDonald and the tag of betrayal began to stick.

The role of the King was also critical. MacDonald's diaries show how much importance he placed in George V. His support appealed to MacDonald's sense of civic duty and patriotism. It must have been incredible for Britain's first Labour Prime Minister to be told three times by the King that he must not resign. Ego and flattery will have played their part and it comes no higher than a situation where the monarch, Baldwin, Chamberlain and the Liberal leader were all urging him to take on the role. That is a persuasive alliance and, when you are irritated with your own party at the same time, you can see why MacDonald was attracted to the idea.

There was also a strong economic argument for MacDonald to stay on. He had become convinced that the only way to restore confidence in sterling was a National Government. There was a very real danger of an economic crash, the consequence of which would have hit those very voters Labour sought to protect. MacDonald would, rightly in my view, argue that his duty was to the principles of Labour, not the party. If Labour meant defending poorer people then he would justify splitting the party to save the economy. Henderson and others took a different view.

MacDonald was not the only leader taking risks in joining the National Government. Baldwin had twice served as Prime Minister and as leader of the Conservatives could easily have expected to step in and form a government.

At best he would have been Prime Minister of a minority Conservative government, at worst, he could have led the National Government. When the King formed the view that MacDonald should stay, Baldwin appears to have shown little resistance; in fact, he seemed rather keen. There is no record of dissent, so why was Baldwin so willing to take part?

Baldwin had shown signs in 1930 that he was sympathetic to helping the Labour government. In May of that year he told an audience in Sheffield:

I hold the view very strongly and, I know I have been criticised for it, that when a government has not got great experience in a minority government, it is essential if you can possibly support it that it should be able to speak with a strong voice to the countries of the world.[18]

It's true that he could not have defied the monarch, but I sense he was also aware that the problems faced by the country would be difficult for the Conservatives to solve without considerable damage to the party, as tough choices would be needed. He might want to let somebody else take the blame.

It was a gesture of political maturity which Baldwin hoped the country would welcome at some point. He clearly felt it would be a popular move and most politicians rather like the impression of working in the national interest. When he informed the Shadow Cabinet of his decision, again there was no opposition to it. Most of the abler Members assumed they would make it into the unity Cabinet and probably felt that the National Government would be a stepping stone to a full Conservative government within a few months. There was also a feeling that if they had formed a government at this point and implemented any hard economic measures it would look as if the "the party of the right" was hitting the poor, potentially damaging their future electoral prospects.

Supporting the National Government also had the twin advantage of splitting the Labour Party and removing the risk that the Liberals could have formed a Lib/Lab alliance. However, despite all of these political arguments in favour, David Marquand forms the conclusion that as all parties had decided to set aside political advantage maybe he was also acting out of a sense of duty.

Like MacDonald himself, in short, the Conservatives and Liberals acted as they did because they believed that it was their duty to do so.[19]

I think Baldwin probably felt that it was only a question of time before the temporary measure ended and he could become Prime Minister for a third time. He was indeed to gain that office again, but it was to be years not months before the "temporary" government fell.

Getting Down To Business

The King, satisfied with his work, left London with his good wishes. In a letter to MacDonald he said:

> *I wish you and your colleagues every success in the difficult task imposed upon you. I am happy to feel I have been able to return to my Highland home without changing my Prime Minister.*[20]

The business of government began and the first task was to create a united Cabinet with an agreed emergency programme of action. The Cabinet was reduced in size to just ten – four each for Labour and the Conservatives and two for the Liberals. Although very much in the minority, the Liberals were given the key posts of Home and Foreign Secretary. Labour kept the Chancellorship, with Snowden remaining in the post to continue with financial reforms that he had been unable to get approved under his own party.

When they met for the first time on the 20th August 1931, the mood was workmanlike, almost as if it was a War Cabinet. There was a minor ego skirmish over who should deputise for MacDonald and a rather odd batting list had to be created with Baldwin, Snowden and Samuel named in that order. Absent from any Cabinet line up was Henderson. He, and a majority of Labour MPs, would take no part in a National Government. In fact, MacDonald struggled to find junior ministers to represent the Labour Party. It must have been emotionally draining to find that colleagues were so opposed to what he was doing. In August when the full team of Ministers was sworn in, he wrote, 'strange eerie feeling glancing round – my worst fears re desertion of party realised. We are like marooned sailors on a desert island'.[21]

The task of forming a Cabinet completed, work immediately began on tackling the economic crisis. The level of deficit in the budget was £170 million – to balance the books Chancellor Snowden proposed a combination of a £76 million tax increase, cuts in salaries and unemployment benefit of 10 per cent. As if to reinforce the sense of national crisis, the King even agreed to a £50,000 cut in his income. These immediate measures helped to restore confidence, the sterling stabilised and France and America agreed to loan arrangements with the Bank of England. It was a start, but the underlying financial problems remained and foreign investors were still steadily withdrawing gold from Britain.

In parliament emergency measures were passed, but not without stormy protests from MacDonald's former colleagues. In the end just five Labour MPs voted for the emergency financial package.

MacDonald's bitterness was growing towards his old party. In his diary he noted:

> *Opposition getting out of hand and becoming like old East End vestry in its calibre, Labour has a scraggy tail.*[22]

As relations with the Labour opposition were getting worse, so too was the prospect of a quick economic recovery. Any hopes MacDonald may have had for a short period of National Government with the prospect of re-uniting Labour when the job was done were looking very unlikely as summer turned to autumn. The pressure on gold was mounting and if Britain was to avoid further collapse two options began to emerge; borrow more, or leave the gold standard. Attempts to reach further loan agreements with America failed and on the 21st September MPs voted to leave gold. It was a critical moment for the National Government, after all it had been brought about to bring financial order and this was a very public sign that it had failed and had been unable to avoid disaster.

MacDonald had to decide if now was the right time to abandon the coalition, or ask for more time. But time was not on his side: confidence in the government to resolve the crisis was likely to weaken and Conservative MPs began to sense the chance of power for themselves. In fact MacDonald had been giving thought to what happened next for some time. On 5th September he shared some early thoughts with Baldwin, trying to tease out how long the Conservatives would support the government. It's worth re-printing parts of the letter in some length as it is a very frank summary of the situation:

> *... how long can this government continue? My own impression is not very long, and, indeed, if we could get such a state of financial stability as would bear what undoubtedly would be the shock of an election, I would not stand in the way of a dissolution. The information I get is that your party will support us, but only for a comparatively brief time, as it is afraid that a prolongation of the existing position would weaken it when the election does come, and that as the days go on you will find more and more friction within your ranks. The Liberals are in*

the land of the Absolutely Unknown, and whatever happens now or whenever it does happen, is likely to see them in great jeopardy.

As regards to the present opposition: It has undoubtedly some rather detestable, but nevertheless electorally effective cries that must be dealt with very seriously. I have not left my party and have no intention of doing so, but if it were to have a majority or could even form a government after the next election, the country would again be faced with a financial crisis which would then in all probability break upon it and ruin it. I am sure you are considering all this, but I should like to put my views before you.

The present government will last so long as it deals only with the matters immediately before us. Can we draw any line between this time of crisis and a normal condition which is to follow? I do not see any such line. Undoubtedly it would be for the benefit of the country if we stayed on a little time after the immediate trouble is over, although, according to the information I have had up to this morning, that crisis is by no means over.[23]

As the weeks passed it seemed that the uncertainty would only be resolved by an election. The debate moved to what type of election it would be. All three parties could abandon the coalition and put their case independently, or the "temporary" unity government could attempt to get a mandate from the voters to complete its project. This was uncharted territory. A coalition formed after an election was one thing, but putting a "coalition party" to the country was untested.

Enthusiasm for a national election came from those outside politics. They saw party politics as a barrier to tackling the continuing problems and believed that if the three parties competed none would have the courage to put forward tough policies:

There lay an impatience with party politics and a belief that, at the very least, economic policy should be taken out of the party arena since it was far too important to be treated in a partisan way.[24]

Businessmen felt let down by the political process and formed a "league of industry" which planned to field candidates at the election and give politicians the elbow. The Bank of England even entered the debate announcing:

That a general election in which the three parties were acting independently should not be regarded as providing sufficient certainty for the establishment of a stable government ... an appeal to the electorate by a National Government on national policy devised to rectify the financial situation was more likely to be regarded with favour abroad.[25]

MacDonald, understanding the frustration, made the case for a non-aggressive election. He argued that if normal party fighting resumed it would not be in the national interests: 'A national appeal must be made by those who have formed the National Government.'[26] His only doubt was a nagging loyalty to Labour. He would have known that if Labour stood against the National Unity parties it would spell disaster for them. MacDonald seemed seriously troubled by this decision.

The King's aide, Wigram, hit the nail on the head in a note:

Without doubt he is a sentimentalist and an idealist. He does not like smashing up the Labour Party at the head of a Conservative administration. He does not know how to run with the hare and hunt with the hounds.[27]

As ever in politics events moved on, and as MacDonald prepared the ground for a national election, the Labour Party was to solve his private dilemma. For some time the Labour Party's National Executive had been considering what to do with MacDonald's membership of the party. By the end of September they had reached a decision to expel him and those fellow Labour MPs who were serving in government. It was to prove a fatal decision for Labour and any lingering loyalty, or doubts MacDonald had about calling the election were quickly removed.

The process of fighting a "coalition party" election was going to be complex. Manifesto and seat agreements between the Liberal and Conservative parties were a big enough challenge without the added complication of a Prime Minister who was now without a party and facing former colleagues standing against him. As well as party political problems, a major policy difference had to be resolved; the free trade versus protection debate was to dominate the pre-election discussions.

Negotiations took place between the parties and a formula was agreed that each party would issue its own manifesto with an overriding document from the Prime Minister setting out the need for co-operation whilst the economic crisis lasted. MacDonald's private papers reveal a fair amount of co-operation on the various manifesto statements with each party sending drafts to the other. There was never any real option of a joint manifesto as there was no prospect of the Conservative and Liberal parties agreeing a compromise between their different positions on free trade. MacDonald's instincts were to avoid the issue where possible, but his negotiating position was not strong. The Conservatives were the largest party in the coalition and MacDonald himself had no base to call on. If the Conservatives were to win the argument on protectionism it would push out the Liberals and lead to the charge that the National Government was a Trojan horse for the Conservatives. Neville Chamberlain was leading the election negotiations for the Conservatives and on the 25th September 1931 he sent MacDonald a draft election statement calling for, 'power to control imports whether by prohibition, tariffs or other measures'.[28]

It was a statement the Liberals could not live with and Chamberlain and the Conservatives were forced to accept a compromise phrase that talked of 'other measures to control imports, but did not rule out tariffs in particular'. MacDonald and the Liberals felt increasingly uneasy as the negotiations between the three parties continued. There was no escaping the dominance of the Conservatives. In a remarkably frank letter to Baldwin, MacDonald expressed his concerns at being swallowed up by the Conservatives:

Who is the 'we' seeking power? The united Cabinet or a majority? The new House will be Conservative ... because in present exigencies it must be so. Neither the Liberals nor us can put enough candidates in the field to give us the security of adequate numbers ... Must we then be able to show national unity only by becoming parties to an election which in fact means that if we say we are not ruling tariffs out, we are consenting to their being introduced whether we like it or not? That is the dilemma. It is caused not by the wording of a statement, but by the unknown action of those in favour of tariffs. Will they use a majority we have helped to give them irrespective of us? For us to have to resign before the New Year and leave a Conservative majority in power for five years would cover us with such ridicule that I cannot agree to run the risk ... Do the Conservatives expect us to accept a formula which if the appeal to the country is successful leaves them at

*liberty within a week to disagree with us, turn us out and proceed to
rule without us?*[29]

For their part, the Conservative activists had doubts about supporting a
coalition government. In various letters to Central Office and Baldwin direct,
the party rank and file set out objections based on the protection issue and
concerns about MacDonald's leadership. A memo from Central Office urged
Baldwin to seek the leadership of the coalition himself.

*We feel bound to urge with the greatest possible emphasis that the
leadership of the National Party during the contest should be vested in
Mr Baldwin and that Mr MacDonald should resign the leadership
before the election starts. We have ample evidence that the party
organisation and large numbers of Conservatives throughout the
country would not tolerate an appeal based on Conservative policy
with Mr MacDonald as leader.*[30]

A week after the compromise wording on tariffs had been drafted both sides
remained at loggerheads. Various drafts from the Conservatives and Liberals
were sent to the Prime Minister who seemed close to giving up his attempt
to get a final agreement. On 25th September MacDonald again wrote to
Baldwin in frank terms from Chequers:

*I think that I ought to let you know at once that I have met with great
difficulty regarding an early election. Some of your folks have been
talking a little too freely about their 'whole hog' tariff intentions and
have been saying too recklessly that they 'have the PM in our
pocket'.*[31]

Frustrated with the whole situation MacDonald turned to the King and
hinted he was ready to resign. He was told firmly to get on with the
negotiations, find a solution and that no resignation would be accepted.
Fuelled by some royal backbone, MacDonald decided on a put up, or shut
up, strategy. Over the first weekend in October at Chequers he set out three
options to colleagues; end the coalition, stay as a National Government
without an election, or fight an election as a united Cabinet.

It was decision time and faced with the break up of the National
Government at the last moment the Conservatives backed down and agreed
to compromise on free trade and fight a united campaign with MacDonald.

Within days parliament was dissolved and the National Government took its case to the country on the 27th October 1931.

It was to be a bitter campaign for MacDonald. The first Labour Prime Minister now leading an alliance of Tories and Liberals to defeat his old party. Even those that had understood the need for an emergency government felt fighting the election as a coalition was a step too far and they now literally turned against him as activists turned his portrait to the wall in Labour clubs up and down the country.

For his part MacDonald avoided directly attacking any former colleagues and stuck to his key theme of national unity to solve national problems. This was, he said, in his final election broadcast, 'a time of special distress which calls for the co-operation of all parties'.[32] On the whole the coalition candidates were able to avoid debating the split between free trade and protectionism even though both stuck to their separate positions in party manifestos. The election was a one sided affair with Conservatives and Liberals united against Henderson's Labour Party. The National Government wanted the country to blame Labour for the economic mess and put its faith in national unity at times of great economic unrest. A quick look at some of the press headlines at the time shows how the coalition used this argument against Labour:

The *Sunday Chronicle* of October 25th claimed, 'Vote for Britain Tuesday – Socialist policy is no use in the crisis' and in the *Daily Mirror* a day later: 'Vote for National Government and enable Mr MacDonald to stabilise the pound, balance our trade, ease the war debt burden – a vote for socialism is a vote for bankruptcy, despair and ruination.'[33]

Baldwin himself was encouraged to attack Labour to ensure that the coalition obtained a strong turnout. A letter from Conservative Central Office just twelve days before polling day warned of voter apathy:

> ... *people do not appreciate the necessity for a general election, and that many of them are in an apathetic mood and do not care much whether they vote or not. The more we can tell people in words of one syllable about the nature of the crisis, and the danger of a crash in the value of the pound if the Socialists get in, the better.*[34]

On the whole the three parties that stood under the coalition banners signed up to the shared objectives. Phrases like common cause, stable government and pulling together appeared. Strangely, one of the most patriotic came from the small group of national Labour supporters under a headline of national unity essential; their manifesto went on to say:

> Whilst our present conditions last, remedial action cannot be taken by political parties fighting partisan battles on platforms and in parliament.[35]

The Conservative activists were the least enthusiastic. According to Thorpe's study of the 1931 election some local parties just stamped 'national' on the front of existing Conservative leaflets![36]

Prime Minister Without A Party

In the end, the 27th October 1931 election was a landslide for the unity parties as they won 14.5 million votes compared to 6.5 million for Labour. The Conservatives had 471 seats, Coalition Liberals 33 and 13 for MacDonald's Labour supporters. In total the National Government had 551 supporters giving it a massive 500 majority. Labour was left with 46 MPs – five decades of progress wiped out by their former leader. It was not only a remarkable vote for MacDonald, but also Baldwin's Conservatives. It was the largest Conservative Party to ever sit in the House of Commons, and very hard to understand why Baldwin did not now become Prime Minister with MacDonald serving under him. The King recognised this position and shortly after the election, during a visit to Windsor Castle, the King sought out Mrs Baldwin:

> I want to tell you, Mrs Baldwin, that your husband has done what only one man in thousands would have done. He could have been Prime Minister, but he stood down to serve under another for what he thought was best for his country.[37]

Jenkins argues that Baldwin was torn on the issue:

> He was leader of by far the largest party, yet he felt committed by the Buckingham Palace arrangement to another Prime Minister.[38]

Although he may not have been Prime Minister, he was to have an enormous hold over MacDonald and within years would take that office for a third time.

The size of the Conservatives' majority was largely due to the withdrawal of 100 Liberal candidates. It's very unlikely they would have gained so many working class seats unless Labour had been so badly isolated. By taking part in the national coalition Baldwin had managed to create a very broad based national party – it was one nation Conservatism.

The problems of such a large majority dominated by one party were to hit home within hours of the election. MacDonald had to create a genuine cross-party Cabinet which also recognised the prominence of the Conservatives. It took a whole week to form, with Baldwin and MacDonald becoming more irritated with each other as list after list of Ministers was rejected.

On 3rd November MacDonald wrote to Baldwin from Downing Street to set out his dilemma:

> The trouble is not unwillingness to give you a very generous share, but that unfortunately the men cannot be produced, and I shall be very much blamed indeed by the country if I cannot show that there is a really national touch in the government with a meaning more comprehensive than that merely the three parties are represented on it.[39]

In the end the Conservatives took eleven of the Cabinet places, including Chancellor for Neville Chamberlain. Remarkably for such a small partner the Liberals – Simon and Samuel – took Foreign Office and Home Office. It was to be an uneasy arrangement. In his biography of Baldwin, David Marquand said:

> MacDonald could seldom afford to take a strong line since he had such a small personal following in parliament and in effect he became the prisoner of the Conservatives – his jailors were Baldwin and Chamberlain.[40]

For all sides the dynamics of working together created a tension. As Marquand observed in his essay on coalitions:

> The Liberals were even more anxious than MacDonald to show that they had not been captured by the Conservatives. That in turn made it necessary for the Conservatives to prove that Conservative principles were not being watered down and once principle reared its head, compromise became impossible.[41]

MacDonald was badly affected by the election result. Torn between the obvious satisfaction at his own personal triumph and the humiliation served on his former party. His fear of becoming cut off from Labour was now a reality and as he sat surrounded by Conservatives on his benches it must have been an alarming situation. His own letters at the time express a growing unease about his place in politics:

> What strange lands I have been pushed into. The first reaction is an increase in my anti-Tory instinct ... the oppression of my companionship crushes out every other feeling.[42]

Two weeks later his mood had worsened:

> Get no inspiration from the House of Commons; feeling completely out of harmony with it; point of view and interests of colleagues not mine. I am pulled up by the roots and even what I believe in, in these new conditions, seems dead.[43]

He yet again talked of resignation and his dislike of Tories in strong terms:

> I am worn out and feel more and more isolated. Better retire and get some vigour for work in the country to rally round Labour's policy of socialism. Close acquaintance with the Tories does not improve one's respect for nor interest in them.[44]

These are powerful and emotional words from a man who had just won an election on his personal record, now forced to admit the government he leads is made up of the Conservatives he cannot stand. It is as if he has done a deal with the devil and regretted it ever since and now longs to go back to the comfort zone of his roots with Labour.

His love of Labour remained strong and in private letters to former colleagues he sought to justify his action and then endlessly repeated his desire to help the Labour movement re-grow. His moods were not helped by the increasing bitterness shown towards him by former colleagues in response to these overtures.

Not all the Labour movement had deserted MacDonald. A few loyal allies had come together to fight the last election under a Labour unity government banner. They had fought 21 seats and 13 were elected. This small group was to provide MacDonald with a lifeline for his political isolation, but never developed into an alternative Labour Party that he could have grown.

Agreement To Differ

Meanwhile Chamberlain's influence on the government was growing. He was less consensual than Baldwin and asserted his Conservatism more than his elder colleague. He was never close to MacDonald and had once described him as a 'moral weakling'.[45] Chamberlain as Chancellor, and a passionate protectionist, had the tricky task of creating financial recovery without breaking up the government. He went to some lengths to try and persuade the free traders in government to change their minds and work through the export difficulties in sub-committees on which Liberals and Labour served. On January 15th 1932 he wrote to Lord Snowden, the former Labour Chancellor:

> *What you cannot know is the amount of pains I have taken to influence my colleagues, and a large part of the press, to restrain their impatience, and to prepare themselves to take a National rather than a party attitude.*[46]

The conclusion of the Chamberlain sub-committee was a recommendation that a general ten per cent tariff should be placed on imports, allowing for certain exceptions. Chamberlain's appeal to Snowden had fallen on deaf ears and when the recommendation went to Cabinet on the 21st January the Liberals and Snowden threatened resignation – not for the first time the coalition was in the balance. In what appears to be a rushed compromise it was agreed that on this issue alone the Cabinet could be split and the Liberals allowed to speak against it in parliament. It was a dangerous precedent to set; although allowing division to keep unity is pragmatic, it carries the danger that it becomes a habit. It's a warning future coalitions should note. The calculation MacDonald and Baldwin took was that the issue would be defused once the vote had taken place – they were wrong. The episode became known as the "agreement to differ", but as an arrangement it only lasted until the summer. Part of Chamberlain's measures had been to establish a trade tariff for the British Dominions. The details of this were to be agreed at a conference in Ottawa. The conference had gone some way to provide special tariff exceptions for the Dominion producers, but despite these the Ottawa proposals were a step too far for the Liberals and Snowden.

MacDonald had been desperate to avoid the resignation and had pleaded with Samuel to stay:

> Whatever use I may have rests on the fact that I represent a combination. If you go, I am no longer the head of a combination. I should be regarded as a limpet in office.[47]

The "agreement to differ" was stretched too far and they announced they would all quit the National Government. The battle between the Conservative protectionists and Liberal free trader was over. The Liberals bitterly complained that the Conservatives had gone against the spirit of National Government. Samuel set out this view at his last Cabinet:

> The country had put the various parties in office together in order to adopt an agreed policy, but on fiscal matters there has been no common policy. All the sacrifices had come from free traders.[48]

I think it is worth looking at the position of the Liberal Party at this point, as the decision to leave the Cabinet was to create yet another split within it. The Samuelite Liberals felt the strain of working with so many Conservatives and the free trade issue had been the final straw. Not all Liberals shared that view; Sir John Simon who along with Samuel had been in the Cabinet at the Foreign Office decided he would remain a "national Liberal". This group had come to regard the Liberals as too left leaning and they were prepared to cling to office rather than resign over free trade. Samuel regarded them as Tories: 'The Liberal nationals were in our opinion indistinguishable in policy and in action, then and then forward from Conservatives.'[49]

Most historians share this opinion and concluded that by the 1935 elections 'The Samuelites may be fairly classified with the Conservatives'.[50]

A closer look shows that they did attempt to create a party structure of their own. In fact the Liberal National Party was eventually wound up in 1968. It can't have been an easy choice – policy and principle on the issue of free trade versus power and influence. Leading Liberal, Geoffrey Shakespeare summed up the dilemma in a note to Simon:

> *Assuming we continue our support of the government, our lines of communication with the Liberal Party will be cut forever. Ottawa will be our Rubicon. There can be no re-crossing. Those who refuse to accept the Ottawa Agreement and wear sheets of repentance will be permitted to sit with Samuel and Mander in the seats of the mighty. Those Liberals who accept the Ottawa Agreement to preserve the National Unity will be cut off root and branch from the Liberal Party … If we still parade the name of Liberal it will really only be by false pretences because it must be clear to everyone that there is no future for us, but ultimate absorption in the Conservative Party.*[51]

Whatever the reasons the resignations meant the government faced yet another crisis in the summer of 1932. MacDonald now headed up a government with no Liberals or Labour followers in Cabinet – to describe it as a National Government was stretching the imagination.

A glance at the number of MPs shows that the former Labour Prime Minister was now really heading a Tory government. MacDonald saw the problem, he told the King:

> *The new government will also be, to all interests and purposes, a single party administration and I think your Majesty will find that a Prime Minister who does not belong to the party in power will become more and more an anomaly, and as policy develops his position will become more and more degrading.*[52]

The resignations were to mark the beginning of the end for the National Government, but Baldwin did not move against MacDonald. In a letter to him he said:

> *I see all the difficulties, but though the boat may rock when our allies jump off, it may well sail henceforth on a more even keel.*[53]

I think Baldwin acted with some considerable honour during this whole period. He was a willing and loyal deputy and his letters at the time even showed some fondness for MacDonald and concern for his health.

The same collection of private papers also shows that Baldwin's loyalty was not going unnoticed. I found a number of supporters who admired Baldwin for putting the country ahead of his own interest. Typical of the kind of comments he received was one signed by two admirers – Katherine and Isabel Forbes:

We feel that we must write and tell you how much we admire your public spirit and true patriotism in the present crisis, especially the way you were content to serve under Ramsay MacDonald when you might with justice have expected the premiership for yourself.[54]

In his study of the period Searle notes that women seemed to be particularly keen on Baldwin's leadership and liked his non-confrontational approach; given they represented 52 per cent of the electorate this was not unimportant.

Perhaps if he were younger and had not already held the office of Prime Minister, Baldwin may have moved at this junction to force an election and push MacDonald out. Jenkins' biography sums up Baldwin's position in relation to both MacDonald and Chamberlain:

The National Government in its first three years ....operated to an unusual extent on the second man in the government and the second man in turn depending to an equally unusual extent upon the second man in his own party.[55]

It seemed that the MacDonald and Baldwin era was drawing to a close as time moved towards a younger generation. In the end it was ill health and fatigue that brought the MacDonald government to a close.

By 1935, MacDonald's health was a cause of concern – his eyesight was failing and Baldwin noted:

It was tragic to see him in his closing days as Prime Minister, losing the thread of his speech and turning to ask a colleague why people were laughing – detested by his old friends and despised by the Conservatives.[56]

He had been suffering from ill health for some years with various eye complaints and a tendency to collapse at times of pressure. He was also prone to regular bouts of insomnia and regularly wrote of sleepless and worried nights. Of more concern though were the mood swings and depression. These seemed to impact on his work and were to lead to his eventual downfall. By January 1934, his own notes show the depth of his despair.

I am a little depressed about my own tired head. To speak now is a great effort and in the ground to be covered and the development of the agreement, I get more and more confused.[57]

By the autumn things had got worse:

Very tired and stupid – head a mere log, no memory, no energy, yawning all day.[58]

After seeing his doctor on the 16th May 1935, MacDonald went to the King to offer his resignation. Having talked MacDonald out of resigning on many previous occasions, this time he accepted it. There appears to have been some confusion over what would happen next. MacDonald thought that Chamberlain was most likely to take over; in fact, the King had requested Baldwin serve again. MacDonald's last Cabinet meeting took place on 5th June 1935. He made it clear to colleagues that his decision to quit had nothing to do with policy and thanked them all for the friendship and loyalty they had shown him. The Cabinet Minutes record Baldwin's warm response:

All had learned to admire his unfailing courtesy and kindness. The Prime Minister had never shown himself to be a party member of the Cabinet, but always a national member.[59]

Two days later during the afternoon of 7th June 1935, MacDonald went to formally surrender the Seals of Office at Buckingham Palace. Within twenty minutes Baldwin had become Prime Minister for the third time. Baldwin's new Cabinet remained just about one of national unity helped by the fact that Ramsey MacDonald's 34 year old son joined as Colonial Secretary. Within five months Baldwin had requested that parliament be devolved and an election date of the 14th November was set. Although he stood as a coalition leader, in reality the Conservatives were now free to rule alone and the coalition was all but over.

Decided To Be Undecided

Historians have not looked favourably on the period leading to and including the National Government. Roy Jenkins' opinion is fairly typical:

> My judgement that it was a disaster is quite independent of the hyperbole of contemporary 1930's political argument.[60]

He goes on to describe it as a:

> Gross over reaction to a relatively minor British financial crisis and the result was as undesirable for the tone and content of British politics as it was unrewarding for the participants.[61]

In his essay on coalition government, David Marquand believes they were genuinely acting in the national interest:

> They were party politicians, not saints. They did not want to damage their parties if they could help it and when they thought it was safe to do so, they pushed hard for their party's interest. But they were also patriotic men, who wished to do the right thing by their country. Their behaviour in August 1931 only makes sense on the assumption that they believe themselves to be putting party second and country first.[62]

It is true that the politics were muddled and the economic situation lurched from crisis to crisis with a national strike and high unemployment. The coalition government was brought in to solve the crisis and failed to deliver any quick solutions, but then so had both the Conservative and Labour governments in their attempts in the 1920s.

By 1929 when Labour failed again the country was running out of options. The Tories seemed reluctant to take on the challenge alone and by 1931 the logical conclusion was that all sides, with the King's strong support, should try to recapture the atmosphere of the wartime coalition which had ended a decade earlier.

The times demanded strong leadership matched with a firm programme of activity to tackle the economic problem. Neither Labour nor the Liberal party were in a position to deliver this. The Conservatives should have stepped up to the mark and it is the failure of Baldwin and Chamberlain to rise to the challenge that led to the coalition. In the end there was no alternative.

Not everybody agreed that a National Government was the best approach to deal with the nation's problems. It was seen by some as a 'coalition of old gangs and old gangsters with no policy and probably incapable of finding one'.[63] Churchill regarded it as a betrayal of national interest and Lloyd George became a strong critic.

This group argued that the old political systems and democracy had failed to provide the solutions.

It is certainly true that politicians are reluctant to take unpopular decisions and each of the various governments since the end of the First World War had paid more attention to winning votes than arguing for sacrifices to restore the economy. All three parties offered better times and standards of living when a period of belting down was more appropriate. By making these promises all three parties acted irresponsibly and should share the blame. The great waste of the national coalition is its failure to end this cycle. It was an opportunity to end the unwillingness of government to cut back drastically on public expenditure. If no single party dared embark on a serious programme of retrenchment and savings on the vast sums being wasted on social security benefits, the situation called for the formation of an all-party coalition which could spread the electoral risks. This opportunity was not taken and the coalition government threw away the goodwill.

Each of the parties was going through a period of rapid change and none really gained from the goalition.

The long term impact on the Liberals was not positive, in the short term though it was a remarkable achievement to have held both the Foreign and Home Office in Cabinet despite the comparative strengths the party had, enormously out numbered as it was by the Conservatives.

> If success in politics is measured mainly by the securing and holding of high office, the formation of the National Government in 1931 began a golden age for the Liberals. It brought about a situation in which despite the electoral decline and internal divisions of their party, it was possible for them to enjoy long careers and a security of tenure rare in British politics.[64]

The party was to emerge from this whole period much weaker and never to get near holding office again.

For the Labour Party the coalition was a rollercoaster. For a new party to form two governments in the twenties was a remarkable breakthrough, but to see its first Prime Minister then lead a National Government in opposition to the Labour movement was to haunt the party for decades.

Labour failed to solve the economic problems alone. They had pledged to solve unemployment and failed. They lacked direction and as Robert Skidelsky's review of the Depression says:

> They were overtaken not only by economic crisis, but by their own political and intellectual incapacity.[65]

Whilst it is true that unemployment doubled on their watch, the Conservatives' record was much better.

In his view of the national crisis, Phillip Williamson is more sympathetic to MacDonald:

> Any other government confronted by the economic recession from 1929 would have suffered enormous difficulties and in terms of its previous programmes and pledges would almost certainly have failed.[66]

After the coalition ended, Labour faced a decade of resentment and wilderness, only recovering after the Second World War.

You might think of all three parties, the Conservatives had most to celebrate from the decade, after all they had over 400 seats in the 1931 parliament. Roy Jenkins is highly critical of Baldwin's leadership, describing the events that led to the coalition as a 'monumental cock-up'.[67] The party had the opportunity to govern alone, but Baldwin:

> had burdened the Conservative Party with a penumbra of a semi-senile MacDonald and a vacuous Simon which made it much more flabby in the 1930s than the 1920s.[68]

Despite this the party did go on to rule alone for the rest of the 1930s and unlike its rivals emerged from the period united, not divided.

Like all coalitions relationships played an important part. This one included three leaders: Baldwin, MacDonald and George V. I think the sovereign played a key role, others disagree.

Williamson argues that the King was not the key to the coalition:

To conclude that the King was chiefly responsible for the outcome is to misconceive the true relationship between the crown and party politics – The King could not command.[69]

Technically this is true, but it fails to understand the ego of politicians – the private papers of both Baldwin and MacDonald reveal the importance they placed on the monarch. He was able to persuade MacDonald not to resign on at least a couple of occasions and his conversation with Baldwin secured the path for the national Cabinet. Baldwin would not have defied his monarch and MacDonald was flattered enough to reconsider his resignation. The King was critical to the process.

Much of this agreement was due to Baldwin and his relationship with MacDonald. The coalition could not have operated unless the chemistry had worked between these two leaders. Blake argues that they were temperamentally similar:

Baldwin was at heart as much of a romantic Celtic visionary as MacDonald.[70]

Despite their efforts to work together, in the end this was a failure of leadership that let the country down when between the Great Wars it needed strong direction.

I think the final word should go to Churchill: his commentary on the Baldwin-Chamberlain administrations sums up the failures of the coalition:

They are decided only to be undecided, resolved to be irresolute, adamant for drift, solid for fluidity, all powerful for impotence.[71]

References

1. *The Conservative Party from Peel to Thatcher*, Robert Blake

2. *Baldwin*, Roy Jenkins

3. *The Conservative Party from Peel to Thatcher*, Robert Blake

4. Winston Churchill

5. *Ramsay MacDonald*, David Marquand

6. Ramsay MacDonald letter to Arthur Henderson MP, from *Ramsay McDonald*, David Marquand

7. *Ramsay MacDonald*, David Marquand

8. *Ibid.*

9. *Ibid.*

10. *The Conservative Party from Peel to Thatcher*, Robert Blake

11. *Baldwin*, Roy Jenkins

12. *Ibid.*

13. Sir Arthur Balfour in *Country Before Party: Coalition and the Idea of 'National Government' in Modern Britain, 1885-1987*, G. R. Searle

14. *Baldwin: The Unexpected Prime Minister*, H Montgomery Hyde

15. *Baldwin*, Roy Jenkins

16. *Ramsay MacDonald*, David Marquand, p.637

17. *The Life of Neville Chamberlain*, Keith Feiling

18. *Baldwin: The Unexpected Prime Minister*, H Montgomery Hyde

19. David Marquand essay in *Coalitions in British Politics*, David Butler

20. *Ramsay MacDonald*, David Marquand

21. *Ibid.*

22. MacDonald Diary

23. Taken from a letter from MacDonald to Baldwin, Downing Street 5 September, Baldwin's Private Papers

24. *Country Before Party: Coalition and the Idea of 'National Government' in Modern Britain, 1885-1987*, G. R. Searle

25. *Ibid.*

26. *Ramsay MacDonald*, David Marquand

27. *Baldwin: The Unexpected Prime Minister*, H Montgomery Hyde

28. *Ramsay MacDonald*, David Marquand

29. *Ibid.*

30. Memo from Central Office, Baldwin's Private Papers

31. MacDonald to Baldwin, 25 September 1931 from Chequers, Baldwin's Private Papers

32. *Ibid.*

33. Arthur MacMahon's 'Review of the General Election of 1931', *American Political Science Review*, Vol. 26

34. Letter to Baldwin from Patrick Gower, Head of Publicity at Conservative Central Office, 15 October, 1931, Baldwin's Private Papers

35. *Country Before Party: Coalition and the Idea of 'National Government' in Modern Britain, 1885-1987*, G. R. Searle

36. *The British General Election of 1931*, Andrew Thorpe

37. *Stanley Baldwin*, G. M. Young

38. *Baldwin*, Roy Jenkins

39. Letter from MacDonald to Baldwin, 3 November 1931, Baldwin Private Papers

40. *Ramsay MacDonald*, David Marquand

41. David Marquand essay in *Coalitions in British Politics*, David Butler

42. *Ramsay MacDonald*, David Marquand

43. *Ibid.*

44. *Ibid.*

45. *The Life of Neville Chamberlain*, Keith Feiling

46. *Ramsay MacDonald*, David Marquand

47. *Ibid.*

48. *Coalitions in British Politics*, David Butler

49. *Personal and Literary Papers of Herbert, First Viscount Samuel*, Herbert Samuel, p.209

50. *The Downfall of the Liberal Party 1914-1935*, Trevor Wilson

51. The Runciman Papers, p.253, 23 September 1932

52. *Ramsay MacDonald*, David Marquand

53. *Baldwin Papers: A Conservative Statesman 1908-1947 ed.*, Philip Williamson & Edward Baldwin

54. Forbes letter to Baldwin, 31 August 1931, Baldwin's Private Papers

55. *Baldwin*, Roy Jenkins

56. *Baldwin: The Unexpected Prime Minister*, H Montgomery Hyde

57. *Ramsay MacDonald*, David Marquand

58. *Ibid.*

59. *Baldwin: The Unexpected Prime Minister*, H Montgomery Hyde

60. *Coalitions in British Politics*, David Butler

61. *The Empire at Bay: The Leo Amery Diaries, 1929-1945*, Leo Amery

62. *Country Before Party: Coalition and the Idea of 'National Government' in Modern Britain, 1885-1987*, G. R. Searle

63. Roy Jenkins, Lecture, 'Learning the Lessons of History'

64. *Ramsay MacDonald*, David Marquand

65. *Politicians and the Slump: The Labour Government of 1929-1931*, Robert Skidelsky

66. *Stanley Baldwin: Conservative Leadership and National Government Values*, Phillip Williamson & Stanley Baldwin

67. Roy Jenkins, Lecture, 'Learning the Lessons of History'

68. *Ramsay MacDonald*, David Marquand

69. *Stanley Baldwin: Conservative Leadership and National Government Values*, Phillip Williamson & Stanley Baldwin

70. *The Conservative Party from Peel to Thatcher*, Robert Blake

71. *Ibid.*

5

Winning War And Peace

Winning War And Peace

It is unlikely that there will be another cause uniting all politicians and nearly all Englishmen and, unless one is found, the achievement of Churchill's National Government will remain unique.[1]

The Churchill government is probably the only really successful coalition in modern British history. Although military victory was long coming, the government successfully led the country throughout the war and to a period of strong affluence and reform in the years after.

And yet, before the Second World War, none of this seemed possible. The 1930s saw the presence of bitter party conflicts and deep resentments. At the time, Churchill looked a very unlikely war leader. Often described as a man 'walking with destiny', he was not the obvious choice to bring the parties together and lead the country to victory. Despite having had the prestige of working with Lloyd George during the Great War, his achievements and personality provoked general distrust. Labour refused to work with him as they felt he had been heavy-handed with striking miners in the inter-war period, civil servants, like Lord Hankey, dismissed him as a 'wild elephant' and Chamberlain held bitter memories of working with him in the previous Conservative government. In fact by 1939, Churchill had made so many enemies that he was widely regarded in the party as an isolated demagogue, motivated above all by bitterness at his exclusion from office. At the outbreak of the war, no-one could have predicted that Churchill would lead a successful coalition and the country to an outstanding victory.

Into War Alone

At the start of the war the Conservatives had a parliamentary majority of well over two hundred. Chamberlain was in a relatively secure position as his critics were divided between Anthony Eden and Churchill. He had no reason to feel unduly threatened and decided that he and the Conservatives could govern alone at the start of the war.

However, right from the start his actions created concern. When Germany invaded Poland on 1st September, most expected Chamberlain to declare war immediately. And yet Britain did not do this until 3rd September. This delay created disquiet in the House: Arthur Greenwood, deputy leader of the Labour Party, privately told Chamberlain afterwards that without immediate action 'neither you nor I nor anyone else will be able to hold the House of Commons'.[2] Even Chamberlain's most loyal followers deserted him: on 2nd September, Sir John Simon carried a message to Chamberlain signed by eleven Cabinet ministers asking for war to be declared at once. But the damage, although repairable, had been done and sowed the seeds of doubt about the suitability of Chamberlain as a war leader.

The first year of war had interesting similarities with the First World War. In fact the country and its politicians were scarred by the conduct of politics during Lloyd George's coalition. Many of the figures in public life in 1939 had participated as ministers, administrators or experts during the Great War. All unanimously agreed that national unity was essential for Chamberlain in the Second World War. And yet, as G.R. Searle writes:

> history uncannily repeated itself and it again took almost three-quarters of a year before the country acquired a coalition government.[3]

Chamberlain decided to follow Lloyd George's 1916 example by creating a small War Cabinet, although his was actually slightly larger. The Cabinet was made up of nine members, none of whom were entirely released from departmental responsibilities. He even accepted Anthony Eden and his greatest rival, Churchill, into the government. Eden was given a minor department, the Dominions Office. Churchill's political stock had begun to recover as war became more likely and his strong line over re-armament and anti-appeasement now made him extremely popular nationwide. Chamberlain realised the importance of including him in the War Cabinet without giving him too much power. He offered Churchill the position of First Lord of the Admiralty with a seat in the War Cabinet, but sought to weaken him by bringing two other services into the Cabinet, the Secretaries of State for War and Air and a Minister for the Coordination of Defence. It was a clumsy and unwieldy arrangement but allowed Chamberlain to silence the most potentially dangerous source of party opposition whilst leaving effective power in his own hands.

Meanwhile relations with the other parties were not particularly good. Chamberlain dealt very badly with the Labour Party, only going through the motions of inviting them to join the government. In response Labour's

Parliamentary Party Executive unanimously resolved that members of the party would never join a ministry of which Chamberlain and Simon were two of the leading members. In effect they adopted 'patriotic opposition',[4] supporting the government in its war effort, but 'had no wish to exchange its place on the opposition benches for the responsibility of office'.[5] Labour found themselves trapped: on the one hand they were dangerously open to the charge of disloyalty, but when they did adopt patriotic measures, local party activists were dissatisfied.

The Prime Minister also offered Cabinet positions to the Liberals, who immediately turned them down, but by now their importance was much reduced with fewer than twenty MPs. At the end of 1939, there was little desire for a coalition, and the only real sign of co-operation came with an electoral truce, which was signed on 8th September by the three Chief Whips. This was to last for the duration of the war.

Chamberlain made himself increasingly unpopular with his poor management of the war economy. His government had recognised that the priority was to maximise war production on the Home Front as well as ensuring adequate manpower for the armed forces. However, by January 1940, Humbert Wolfe, from the Ministry of Labour, warned that in certain key munitions industries, the labour force would have to be increased by seventy per cent by the period July to September 1940. Production targets were set, but many argued that the government remained far too committed to a peacetime industrial policy. The government were also concerned about the threat of industrial unrest which might follow from higher inflation, so from early 1940 onwards, subsidies were introduced to keep down food prices and stabilise the cost of living.

The Labour opposition was highly critical of the government's economic policy: only a month after the outbreak of the war, William Beveridge launched a campaign to establish tighter state direction of the economy. On 3rd October, he wrote an article in *The Times* arguing that, sooner or later, the whole economy must be better planned. Labour critics also complained about the persistence of high unemployment, which still stood at one million in April 1940. As Jefferys notes:

> *a vigorous campaign was soon underway amongst those whose*
> *collective experience went back to the innovative days of the Lloyd*
> *George coalition during the Great War.*[6]

Dawson from *The Times* consistently pressed for a reformed War Cabinet and economic co-ordination along the lines proposed by Beveridge. After an important debate on the subject in February 1940, he noted, 'The P.M. was rather worried by *The Times* on the Economic Front'[7] and the *Manchester Guardian* wrote that, apart from the Treasury, there was no support for Chamberlain's line as parliament, the press, economists and industrialists all agreed with Labour.

Away from the Home Front there were problems abroad. The army looked under-resourced, hardly a unit of the British Expeditionary Force went to France properly equipped, while the Territorials were often short of supplies. Things were so bad that when the first secret session of war was held in parliament on 13th December 1939, a number of serving MPs sought leave from their regiments to air their complaints.

Other complaints were brought against the government. Many believed that Chamberlain's handling of personnel was poor and argued that the nation's best talents remained untapped. Disquiet grew in the Labour Party and by spring 1940, there were fifty-one resolutions on the agenda of the party conference calling for the termination of the by-election truce. Chamberlain's attitude to Labour did not help; he had no emotional rapport with them and felt intellectual disdain for Labour doctrines: as Attlee recalled, 'he always treated us like dirt'.[8] Things came to a head when the Labour NEC met to reaffirm that it would not join any new coalition led by Chamberlain. By now, even loyal Tories were conceding in private that the Prime Minister must somehow be moved to allow more sweeping changes to take place. There were talks of an open clash between loyal Chamberlainites and the next generation of Conservatives, nicknamed the 'glamour boys', and even of Lloyd George seeking to form a new alliance with Labour. The situation was beginning to have echoes of the last months of Asquith's failing government.

A Leader In Waiting

Although Chamberlain's critics were becoming more vocal over his methods of governing, they were unable to rally together and decide on a potential successor. The outside option was Lloyd George; he had expressed a strong air of defeatism about the war and even called for a negotiated peace. He was still seen as the nation's saviour, and his opinion influenced politicians and public opinion. However, he had no real power base or parliamentary support and he also lacked media support. The majority of newspaper proprietors decided that, in spite of their misplaced trust in appeasement, it was their patriotic duty to support the government.

Of more significance was the steady rise of Churchill. Between September 1939 and May 1940, he greatly enhanced his reputation and many people came to regard him as the national leader. It was not an easy position for him to hold: as Roy Jenkins has written:

> there was at once suspicion of him among most of his new ministerial colleagues and too much expectation of him among the press and public.[9]

By sending him to the Admiralty, Chamberlainites believed they had successfully confined his energy: as Boothby wrote to Lloyd George on 18th September:

> As a member of the government, who shall be nameless, put it to me last week, "We fixed him when we sent him to the Admiralty."[10]

For his part, Churchill meant to be a loyal colleague to Chamberlain, possibly because he thought that the time was not yet right for him to make a bid for the premiership, but, being Churchill, he could not help but give the impression he was promoting himself with every speech. He was the only colourful figure in the government and the only one who really stood out. When both he and Chamberlain gave speeches in the Commons that September it was Churchill who made the impact. As Harold Nicholson noted:

> one could feel the spirits of the House rising with every word. It was obvious afterwards that the PM's inadequacy and lack of inspiration had been demonstrated even to his warmest supporters. In those twenty minutes Churchill brought himself nearer the post of PM than he has ever been before.[11]

Churchill was also in the right place at the right time. Far from isolating him, his position at the Admiralty was ideal. At this stage of the war, there was no fighting on land and virtually no activity in the air so the actions of the Navy provided the only news and drama. Unlike many departments at this point, the Admiralty enjoyed good relations with the press, feeding them succulent items of news which the Ministry of Information was unable to obtain. Churchill especially had the trick of holding up the announcement of good news until he could announce it in a speech. He attached such importance to this that Vice-Admiral Hallett of the press section was posted to sea after releasing news items which the First Lord had wanted to announce himself.

As the Admiralty was the hub of the strategic war effort, Churchill soon immersed himself in the sphere of foreign affairs: by October 1939, he had been involved in his own secret discussions with Roosevelt, by-passing the British Embassy in Washington. But he looked beyond his own department and intervened in the running of every other. Now, probably without intention, Churchill behaved as though he were already Prime Minister. Despite meeting with Chamberlain almost once a day, in the first six weeks of war, Churchill directed no less than thirteen letters of substance to the Prime Minister, advising him on the conduct of war. As A.J.P. Taylor writes, 'this inexhaustible display of energy exasperated some of his colleagues and many civil servants even more so.'[12]

It was during this period that the public grew to admire Churchill's great wartime speeches. He made the first one on 1st October 1939, only a month after the outbreak of war; the very next day, the left wing popular press had seized the opportunity to create a 'Churchill boom'.[13] William Connor, the *Daily Mirror's* "Cassandra" wrote:

> *it is hardly premature to say that in popular imagination Churchill has already ousted Chamberlain as the dominant war figure.*[14]

It was not just the media that noted the impact; on the same day, Samuel Hoare, a loyal Chamberlainite and Lord Privy Seal, wrote to Lord Beaverbrook:

> *Certainly in the country he has a very big position...I should say that at the moment he is the one popular figure in the Cabinet.*[15]

The problem with these announcements was that they were always made on the authority of no-one but Churchill himself; in the eyes of the world, Britain had spoken but in the eyes of the British government, Churchill was trumpeting his personal views. For example, on 12th November, Churchill declared:

> *You may take it absolutely for certain that either all Britain and France stand for in the modern world will go down, or that Hitler, the Nazi*

regime, and the recurring German or Prussian menace to Europe will
be broken and destroyed.[16]

This speech had not been vetted by the Foreign Office beforehand and the undersecretary, R.A. Butler, had to tell the Italian Ambassador that:

Churchill's speech was in conflict with the government's views not only
in the present instant. As a matter of fact he always spoke only as Mr.
Churchill.[17]

At this point, the government was still considering serious peace proposals and Churchill's speeches were harming the negotiations. Chamberlain had tried to curb these speeches by demanding that Churchill submit all speeches to the Lord Privy Seal before the broadcasts, but naturally Churchill had refused.

All these factors meant that Churchill started catching Chamberlain up very quickly in the newly-developed opinion polls: a British Institute of Public Opinion (BIPO) poll of December 1939 showed that thirty per cent of people preferred Churchill to Chamberlain and now only fifty-two per cent wholeheartedly supported Chamberlain. Already by the end of 1939, many of the Prime Minister's loyal supporters were disappointed by his performance: as Lady Astor wrote:

I am sure that he meant it to be a fighting speech but its effect on me
was to make me wish that Winston were Prime Minister (this was only
momentary and I know it was wrong, but that was my reaction!)[18]

By April 1940, as Addison writes, 'Churchill had achieved something of the popular standing enjoyed by Lord Kitchener'[19] that is to say, he was regarded as a candidate for the premiership in outside circles, but the gap between his popular standing and his credibility in Whitehall was considerable.

Despite this obvious shift in balance between the two men, their relationship was very different to the hostile one that developed between Asquith and Lloyd George. The falling-out between those two leaders had resulted in the near death of the Liberal Party. It is to Churchill and Chamberlain's credit that their relationship was handled in a way which avoided the Conservatives suffering a similar fate. As Jenkins writes:

Throughout the whole of these early war months he was at pains to treat Chamberlain with respect and circumspection; which is generally a wise tactic for ministers in relation to the head of the government, particularly when substantial sections of the press and public are elevating the subordinate minister over his nominal chief...[20]

The first notable shift in power between Churchill and Chamberlain came during a reshuffle, caused when Lord Chatfield resigned from his rather empty role as Minister for the Coordination of Defence. Chamberlain appointed no successor, instead asking Churchill to preside over a Defence Committee, which consisted of the three ministers and the three chiefs of staff. However, this very quickly created problems as Churchill effectively behaved as Minister for Defence, constantly bullying the chiefs of staff and presenting the Committee with decisions which he had forced on the chiefs of staff beforehand. The other two service ministers eventually threatened to resign and appealed to Chamberlain to step in. Chamberlain agreed to chair the Committee himself but eventually gave in to Churchill's demands and, a week later, appointed him as his deputy, 'to concert and direct the general movement of our war action.'[21] Churchill had now won a key battle in controlling the war effort.

The End Of Chamberlain

It was a military event that was to trigger the end of Chamberlain's government. After the British declaration of war there had been little change to people's day-to-day life and the government quietly encouraged the belief that victory would be achieved through an economic blockade. The first serious British defeat in Norway made the country realise how tough winning the war would be. The evacuation of British troops from Norway started on 29th April and was publicly announced on 30th April. A two-day parliamentary debate on the subject was immediately scheduled for 7th and 8th May. Despite his critics, most believed that Chamberlain would survive this episode, as there was no really popular alternative. Lord Beaverbrook wrote:

I don't think Chamberlain will be turned out this time. But he remains in office with such an immense volume of disapproval in his own party that he had better retire.[22]

Chamberlain's speech was unconvincing and he was repeatedly interrupted by Labour members with cries of "Hitler missed the bus". At first he tried to blame Churchill by creating the impression that Churchill was personally responsible for the events in Norway. Harold Nicolson had noted before the start of the debate that 'the Whips are putting it about that it is all the fault of Winston who has made another forlorn failure...'[23]

The first damaging Conservative speech came from Admiral Sir Roger Keyes who appeared in the House in his full Admiral's uniform, complete with six rows of medals. He announced that he was speaking for the officers and the men of the fighting Navy against the incompetence and caution of the naval staff. Harold Nicolson described the impact of Keyes' intervention:

> *The House listens in breathless silence when he tells us how the Naval General Staff had assured him that a naval action at Trondheim was easy but unnecessary owing to the success of the military. There is a great gasp of astonishment. It is by far the most dramatic speech I have ever heard and when Keyes sits down there is thunderous applause.*[24]

When Leo Amery made his famous 'In the name of God, go' speech in the Commons, he explicitly demanded the replacement of the National Government by a new administration representing:

> *All the elements of real political power in this country, whether in this House or not.*[25]

His outburst was all the more telling as he was an old colleague and friend of Chamberlain and a disciple of his father Joseph Chamberlain. In Lloyd George's last ever address to the House, he called on Chamberlain to make an example of sacrifice:

> *Because there is nothing which can contribute more to victory in the war than that he should sacrifice the seals of office.*[26]

Churchill himself behaved in exemplary fashion during the debate and endeavoured to make the best possible case for the government: as Channon recalled, his speech was:

> *A magnificent piece of oratory... how much of the fire was real... we shall never know, but he amused and dazzled everyone with his virtuosity.*[27]

But even Churchill's loyalty was not enough to avoid an embarrassing vote. The government's majority fell from 220 to only 81, and although it had won the motion, the number of opposing votes and abstentions were significant enough to make Chamberlain finally understand that reform was necessary in order to retain his grip on both the Cabinet and parliament. Churchill advised him to fight on but it was now widely recognised that Chamberlain could only really last for another couple of weeks before having to resign from the premiership. Both Hugh Dalton and Clement Attlee, who would otherwise have preferred Halifax as premier, privately agreed that 'now it must be Churchill'.[28]

Chamberlain initially tried to hang on to power. First, he offered posts to Amery and other Conservative rebels but they stalled his plans by issuing a public statement that they would accept any Prime Minister who enjoyed the confidence of the country and could form a National Government that would include Labour and the Liberals. Under pressure, Chamberlain then approached Attlee and Greenwood from the Labour Party, inviting them to join his government. They took the idea to the annual conference in Bournemouth, but the answer they brought back was to deliver the fatal blow to Chamberlain. Labour declared that it would:

> Take its full and equal share as full partner in a new government under a new Prime Minister which would command the confidence of the nation.[29]

Chamberlain now understood that the end had come, and an hour later he went to Buckingham Palace and resigned. He recommended that Churchill should succeed him as Prime Minister. Technically, there was no upheaval, no interregnum as there had been in 1916 and again in 1931. This was a simple case where one Prime Minister resigned and after doing so named his successor. Labour's role in the destruction of Chamberlain's government was to prove crucial. Whereas Labour might have been admitted as a junior partner in a coalition government several months earlier, in the event, as Paul Addison says, they were not really given office at all; instead, 'they broke in and took it, on terms of equality'.[30]

Labour On Side

Churchill's arrival marked the real beginning of popular mobilisation for total war, the era of 'blood, toil, tears and sweat'. It was a tough and gruelling period to become Prime Minister and the rest of the country was a little apprehensive to see such "new" men governing the country. As Alan Bullock wrote:

> *The situation which faced the members of the new government left*
> *them no time to think about the future: they needed all their resolution*
> *to believe there was going to be a future at all.*[31]

With the fall of France, and the beginning of the Battle of Britain, the Prime Minister's priority was survival and stirring the nation to the tough battles ahead.

His first task however was to deal with the rather tricky predicament of having no party to command in the House, as Chamberlain remained leader of the Conservatives. To take control he decided to create a small War Cabinet, based on Lloyd George's 1916 model, and chose to establish a coalition balanced along party lines. The four members of the War Cabinet were himself, Chamberlain, Attlee and Greenwood, the leader and deputy leader of the Labour Party. The same balance was secured for the three Service Ministries as Churchill allocated one to each party. He solved the most difficult appointment by making himself Minister of Defence. He was also leader of the House, but in reality, Attlee often stood in for him.

The Labour Party was initially under-represented, especially in the lower ministerial ranks, holding only sixteen posts in contrast to the Conservatives' fifty-two, although in part this was because the Conservatives had more experience of government. Despite this imbalance it was a true National Government, with power genuinely shared between the two parties. Even if Churchill was not particularly fond of the Labour Party, he never lost sight of its importance. Labour politicians occupied several of the key positions on the Cabinet committees responsible for drafting social and economic policy. Their new-found importance was demonstrated by the appointment of Ernest Bevin, general secretary of the largest trade union, to the Ministry of Labour. As Keith Middlemas wrote, Bevin's appointment:

> *Was a clear recognition of trade union power to determine either way,*
> *supply, production, manpower and morale.*[32]

Finally, unlike during World War One, Churchill managed to convince the Conservative and Labour Chief Whips to occupy a joint office.

Labour were clearly quite happy with this initial arrangement and at the following annual conference, the leaders got formal approval for joining the government by 2,450,000 votes to 170,000. Although they started out at a serious disadvantage to the Conservatives, Attlee was to see Labour's position considerably improve during the war. In 1940, the party had eight ministerial and eight junior posts; by 1942, this number had increased to fourteen junior posts and finally, by 1945, the Labour Party held ten ministerial and seventeen junior posts.

The make-up of the Cabinet also showed how keen Churchill was to avoid unwanted divisions. By keeping Chamberlain on as Lord President of the Council, he treated him with consideration and courtesy. For the same reasons, Lord Halifax remained at the Foreign Office until 1940. As Lloyd George summed up, 'Churchill would not smash the Tory Party to save the country, as I smashed the Liberal Party.'[33] Churchill did not regard splitting the party as a badge of honour, and felt he could win the war and hold the Conservatives together. However his approach led to some criticism; in May 1940, *The Times* wrote that the new coalition was not 'a genuine National Government' in which the premier chose 'his colleagues on merit and not on the recommendation of any party manager'.[34]

Keeping Chamberlain on was essential for Churchill to have Conservative support. The Party unity was by no means wholehearted, and the Conservatives who had remained loyal to Chamberlain resented his overthrow. It would take a couple of days before backbenchers agreed to cheer Churchill in the Chamber rather than Chamberlain. Indeed, Churchill's most vocal supporters in these early weeks undoubtedly came from Labour – when the Conservatives persisted with their stony reception for Churchill, Labour would respond with loud cheering for the premier. These early days were difficult for the new Prime Minister and he clearly felt some pressure. In June he confided in a note to Stanley Baldwin, 'I cannot say that I have enjoyed being Prime Minister much so far'.[35]

Guilty Men

As Churchill gradually gained more support there was a growth in those who wanted to punish the politicians who had advocated appeasement. By early 1941, a resounding cry to get rid of Chamberlainites came from all the corners of the country, and it was only thanks to Churchill's expert handling of the situation that the Conservatives avoided this turning into a full-blown crisis. This was fuelled by a worsening of the military situation, which reached a serious low on 25th May 1940, when the army was forced to evacuate from Dunkirk. As General Mason-MacFarlane, Director of Military Information with the army, told an assembly of war correspondents:

> *I doubted if the British Army had ever found itself in a graver position than that in which the government of the past twenty years has now placed it.*[36]

With such stories, a clamour rose to make scapegoats of the appeasers, and the demand for resignations was voiced throughout the country. This campaign grew after the publication of the famous work, *Guilty Men*, written in four days by leading journalists (although it was anonymous at the time) and published in June 1940. It attacked and blamed Chamberlain and his associates for their appeasement policies towards Germany and for not preparing the country for total war. It was a popular piece of work, and a survey carried out by Mass-Observation claimed that sixty-two per cent wanted Chamberlain sacked from the government. The press quickly embarked upon what became known as "the attack of the appeasers": the *Daily Herald* led the way by placing the responsibility for the retreat of British forces on the shoulders of "the men of Munich" and called for Chamberlain and Kingsley Wood's resignations.[37]

The Daily Mirror called for the removal of survivors from the 'old loitering gang' who had brought about Dunkirk[38] and Aneurin Bevan in the *Tribune*, called for an inquiry into Dunkirk and the impeachment of those responsible.[39] Meanwhile MPs began to complain that the army had not been adequately prepared to fight in France.

Faced with this level of criticism, Chamberlain offered his resignation, but Churchill refused to accept, hoping he could maintain unity in the Cabinet, allowing the coalition to survive without creating a scapegoat. From the beginning of his premiership, Churchill had made it clear that he had no intention of trying to base himself within the anti-appeasement faction of the party. As Addison writes:

> Temperamentally he had no quarrel with Conservatism and although he gradually broke up and dispersed the old circle of appeasers, it was chiefly for the practical purposes of substituting his own rather than from any desire to settle old scores.[40]

On 6th June, at a War Cabinet meeting, Churchill lectured the Labour leaders and Archibald Sinclair, the Liberal Party leader, on the importance of calling off attacks on members of the previous government. The following day, he summoned the Chairman of the *Daily Mirror*, Cecil King. He told him that if the newspapers continued their attacks, the government would fall as they would have to resign along with Chamberlain since they were jointly responsible for the conduct of affairs since the outbreak of war. The Labour leaders immediately fell into line and both Greenwood and Attlee gave Chamberlain an assurance that they would try to muzzle the agitators in the Labour Party. One last attempt to dislodge the 'old gang' was launched and became known as the 'Under-Secretaries Plot'. Again, Churchill managed to defuse the situation by stating that:

> If anyone in the government wishes to criticise its workings or its composition they should resign and criticise from outside. He was going to make no changes of any kind and would sooner resign himself than be forced to do so... [41]

This immediately dashed the plot. Churchill had successfully prevented a witch-hunt and preserved political continuity; an end was finally put to the search for scapegoats when he made another of his magnificent speeches in the Commons on 18th June, explaining that an inquest into the past would be a:

> foolish and pernicious process. There are too many in it. Let each man search his conscience and search his speeches. I frequently search mine.[42]

The campaign to purge the government had failed, and instead Churchill was able to disperse the appeasers with foreign postings and dignified retirements. Although the hatchet was by no means buried, the Conservatives had at last reconciled themselves to the coalition, recognising that the national interest had become paramount.

Bit by bit, a real sense of National Government was growing and when in December 1940, the Independent Labour Party tabled a motion for a compromised peace, it was defeated by 341 votes to four. When the Communists took up the same cry, *The Daily Worker* was banned without provoking any unrest. There was an initial reshuffle in the Cabinet in October 1940, after Chamberlain was forced to retire, and only at this point, after much hesitation, was Churchill also elected leader of the Conservative Party. This gave him a firmer party base, and the removal of Chamberlain effectively took away his strongest opposition and obliged the Conservative backbenchers to give him more support. Churchill started to bring in non-partisan civil servants and businessmen, for example Sir John Anderson, a former civil servant, succeeded Chamberlain in the War Cabinet. Over the next few years, as the Prime Minister became more secure, his government began to acquire more obvious 'national' features.

The Challenge Of Sir Stafford

Although the coalition looked unified on the surface, there were grave problems below and 1942 marked the worst and most dangerous time for Churchill's leadership. When asked later to reflect on his most anxious period of the war, Churchill did not refer, as might be expected, to the danger of invasion in 1940, but without hesitation pointed to the summer of 1942. Britain had yet to win any significant victory against Nazi Germany and during the evacuation from Crete, some 13,000 Allied troops were killed as Germans launched their assault, and another 16,000 were evacuated, with the British Expeditionary Force now acquiring the new nickname 'Back Every Friday'.[43] Indeed, 1942 saw the greatest military failures; despite the arrival of Soviet Russia and the United States as allies, Singapore fell, two great battleships were sunk in the Far East, and in February, three German warships slipped through the English Channel en route from Brest to Germany evading the Royal Navy and the Royal Air Force. The Weekly Intelligence Reports described the period as 'the blackest week since Dunkirk'.[44] In June 1942, Tobruk finally fell, and Churchill knew when he accounted for the military failures to the Commons that it would require more than fine words, as Chips Channon wrote that there was no point in:

the Prime Minister coming back and making one of his magical
speeches. This time it would serve no purpose. The government must
be reformed and soon.[45]

As public opinion was increasingly disappointed with Churchill's war effort, the arrival of Sir Stafford Cripps, then British Ambassador in Russia, was to transform the situation. He was, according to Addison 'as though sent by providence to set the world right'.[46] As an Independent he put forward a personal programme of his own for winning the war and in doing so became extremely popular with the nation. Like Churchill, he started giving broadcasts and participated in the evening 'Postscript' series. In one such broadcast, he made a cleverly drawn comparison between the sacrifices and hardships being endured by the Russians, and the relative comfort of his audience by the fireside; a coded critique of the slackness of the British war effort. The effect of the broadcast was, as one might expect, sensational. From that day onwards, Cripps and the public felt that he would be the guiding leader on the Home Front, leaving Churchill to deal with strategy. He increasingly became thought of as the only credible leader to replace Churchill and fell for the illusion that he could supplant him and run the war more scientifically. Here was the first, and what would be the only, threat to the Prime Minister's leadership and Churchill knew he had to act fast to stop Cripps overwhelming him. Firstly, he restructured his government, offering Cripps the leadership of the House. It was in effect bait; the position offered limelight but no real power. Cripps took it and the more powerful post of Ministry of Production went to Oliver Lyttelton, a member of a famous Conservative family but himself a businessman with no political experience and as such not a potential rival.

The fall of Tobruk came as quite a shock and triggered speculation about Churchill's future. Nevertheless, he was still supported by seventy-eight per cent of the public and the politicians knew that no one would be able to usurp Churchill's authority without powerful Conservative endorsement. The malcontents in the Commons began to group under the leadership of Sir John Maldraw-Milner, Chairman of the Select Committee on National Expenditure, who put down a motion censuring the central conduct of the war. This could have been turned into a repeat of the 1940 debate which brought down Chamberlain, but the Prime Minister's opponents failed to capitalise on Churchill's mistakes and blew their case when they proposed that the King's brother, the Duke of Gloucester, be appointed as

Commander-in-Chief of Britain's armed forces. This provoked an outburst of sustained sarcastic cheering and as Channon described:

I at once saw Winston's face light up, he knew that he was saved.[47]

Churchill survived, winning with a margin of 476 to 25, but the episode left him aware that his position remained insecure unless handled very carefully.

When parliament reassembled in September, they still gave Churchill a rough ride. The Cripps threat was still present, and despite failing in a mission to calm Indian Nationalism, he was still very popular. Eventually, though, he overplayed his hand when he threatened resignation in a letter to Churchill on 3rd October 1942. The letter put on record that he was in fundamental disagreement over defence and would have resigned but for the pressure put on him not to do so at the critical moment before the battle in North Africa. Events however turned in Churchill's favour, with Montgomery's great victory of El Alamein after the Anglo-American landings in Africa. Churchill was quick to capitalise and insisted on Cripps' resignation. In the end he offered him the Ministry of Aircraft Production, which he took, but Cripps was no longer a member of the War Cabinet. This was the last time that Churchill's authority would be threatened.

A Brave New World

Alongside the military challenges the coalition had to tighten up economic controls and ensure the welfare of the population. What some regarded as a pragmatic war measure, others saw as the embryo of a superior social system. The *New Statesman* wrote:

We cannot actually achieve socialism during the war, but we can institute a whole series of government controls which after the war may be used for Socialist ends.[48]

In fact, the coalition had to introduce new welfare measures to relieve the pressures of a population having to endure the rigours of war. In June 1940, Attlee's Food Committee approved a scheme for free or subsidised milk to mothers and children less than five years of age. In July, the Board of Education decided that free school meals, which had hitherto been supplied only to undernourished children, should become generally available. The

Home Front, organised for war, was gradually becoming a model for the re-organisation of the peace.

This approach created some unrest among the Conservative backbenchers but their leaders, even the Chamberlainites, had to agree that change was coming. Lord Halifax wrote to Duff Cooper, Minister of Information in August 1940:

> *We were all conscious as the talk proceeded of the contrast between the reading of the Nation, and particularly the Treasury, to spend £9 million a day in war to protect a certain way of life and the unwillingness of the administrative authorities in peace to put up, shall we say, £10 million to assist in the reconditioning of Durham unless they could see the project earning a reasonable percentage.*[49]

For the time being, Churchill accepted the need for social reform and declared in December 1940:

> *When this war is won, as it surely will be, it must be one of our aims to establish a state of society where the advantages and privileges which have hitherto been enjoyed by only the few shall be far more widely shared by the many, and by the youth of the nation as a whole.*[50]

On the whole however he was more absorbed with winning the war and was happy to let Labour run with domestic reform whilst he dealt with the serious issue of strategy.

1943 was to become a momentous year for reconstruction. As survival for Britain became less of a need, and victory became almost a certainty, politicians' minds turned towards the reconstruction of the country after the end of the war. Until now, the problem had been conveniently buried, as Hugh Dalton writes, the war coalition was now 'allergic to post-war policy'.[51] Churchill had managed to avoid talking about reconstruction, strongly believing that there were other priorities that needed attending to, and greatly resented being constantly told about the need for post-war plans when 'we had nothing like won the war. People were always getting ahead of events'.[52] In January 1941, he had announced that Arthur Greenwood, Minister without Portfolio, had been moved from his job in charge of production to take on responsibility for post-war reconstruction. This appointment indicated that reconstruction was very low on the agenda, and in fact, the Reconstruction Committee met on only four occasions between 1941 and February 1942. But in 1943, the Prime Minister could no longer avoid the problem and reconstruction came to the forefront of British politics.

The Beveridge Report, produced at the request of the government to examine post-war issues, had been published in December 1942, and was to become momentous for British social policy, aspiring to introduce universal social security, and our modern-day NHS. It was a radical proposal compared to anything else that had been offered before and as Beveridge himself wrote:

> the policy outlined in the Report by-passes the socialist-capitalist controversy. It can be accepted by persons holding many different views on the controversy...[53]

In theory, Beveridge's task was simply to present advice to the government but in practice, he lobbied and campaigned in advance with the aim of getting the War Cabinet to accept his proposals.

The Cabinet was obliged to take the Beveridge Report seriously and found themselves having to focus more on domestic issues. However its contents created widespread concern. The War Cabinet, and in particular the Conservatives, were not impressed with the Report; they believed that people should prepare themselves for hard times and a post-war slump rather than expecting the State to provide new levels of support. Kingsley Wood, Chancellor of the Exchequer, declared that the plan involved 'an impracticable financial commitment'.[54] Labour leaders were also anxious for different reasons. They supported the plans, but believed that calls for immediate action could pose a serious threat to the coalition. It was finally decided that a motion welcoming it should be passed in the House, whilst emphasising that the Cabinet would undertake to review the Report, thereby refusing to make any firm commitments.

The debate did not run as smoothly as initially hoped. A group of forty-five MPs, the newly formed Tory Reform Committee, led by Quintin Hogg and Lord Hinchingbrooke, tabled an amendment demanding prompt legislation and the immediate creation of a Ministry of Social Security. Labour backbenchers supported them, calling for "Beveridge now" and rebellion from both sides grew. In the end the amendment was defeated by 338 to

121 votes, but it highlighted a serious rift between the coalition government and backbenchers.

The Beveridge Report also created serious fractures within the Conservative Party. Although the coalition had managed to survive this far with no serious sign of conflict, backbench Conservatives clearly resented the influence wielded by Labour in the government and Churchill's apparent indifference to the growing power of the left. Lord William Scott wrote to the Chief Whip in October 1942:

> throughout the country, the Conservative Party has become a cheap joke... you must agree with the fact that as an effective body of opinion either in the House or the country, the Conservative Party has ceased to exist.[55]

This disquiet worsened with the formal creation of the Tory Reform Committee in March 1943; they believed that, with the Beveridge Report, they had found a cause through which Conservatism could be revitalised. As Quintin Hogg himself argued, 'if you do not give the people social reform, they are going to give you social revolution.' In their opinion, the key to economic recovery was social progress. However, Conservatives outside the government looked upon much of the reconstruction programme as the work of the left. They accepted it reluctantly, from loyalty rather than conviction, and perhaps believed that it could be watered down when the Conservatives escaped from the coalition. There was a minor split in the party over the issue and in 1943, Sir Spencer Summers and others founded a highly secret conclave of some thirty MPs, the Progress Trust, with the primary aim of countering the influence of the Tory Reformers in the Party.

Within government the Reconstruction Priorities Committee had been created in early 1943 with the task of implementing the report's recommendations. Several public opinion surveys were conducted throughout the year and it became clear that the population's main concerns were housing and unemployment after the end of the war. The Cabinet set to work and the Prime Minister even made a broadcast in March 1943, devoted to describing a new impetus, the "four year plan", which outlined his vision of future economic and social recovery. His speech was, however, not matched with action, and for most of 1943, the War Cabinet produced no substantial piece of work that indicated a strong push for reform. On 2nd October 1944, *The Economist* wrote:

*Like the policemen in "Pirates of Penzance", Ministers say in chorus
"We Go, We Go" but like Gilbert's constables again, they do not go;
no visible headway is made...*[56]

Gradually, Churchill responded to the criticism and realised that plans
needed to be set up for the period of transition between war and peace and
along with Attlee he started discussing possible ideas. But deep down he
was still averse to change, and seriously believed that no commitments
would be made before the end of the war; a position which caused the first
serious strain between him and Attlee. Here lies the crux of the coalition's
survival – instead of allowing controversial measures to divide the coalition
it was held together by burying some of the deeper differences. The
Reconstruction phase produced a plethora of white papers but most of them
failed to tackle the underlying problems and almost none of them evolved
into bills before the end of the war.

In the end 'only two major measures, the Education Act and the new system
of family allowances, were successfully carried while the war was still in
progress'.[57] Rather than analysing each attempt at reform, I want to look at
one which showed how this style of compromise failed to tackle the problem
of unemployment, and one successful example, the Education Act.

In June 1941, Churchill appointed Rab Butler, a Chamberlainite, to the
Board of Education, a position regarded as a political backwater in wartime.
He thought Butler peculiar for wanting to take it on (as he'd also offered him
the choice of a Foreign Office position). But Butler saw things very
differently and believed it was one area where the system was clearly trailing
behind informed opinion. By the end of 1942, Butler's ideas had become a
white paper which was proceeding through the Lord President's Committee.
Butler had manoeuvred his proposals magnificently and reassured the two
Chancellors with whom he dealt that it would be a generation before the
Exchequer had to bear the full cost of the proposals. He had also persuaded
a doubtful Churchill that the plans were worth backing and the Prime
Minister had now come to the conclusion that 'educational reform was the
lesser evil than the Beveridge scheme'.[58] The Education Bill became a perfect
way to show the country that the government was taking immediate action
whilst avoiding the more radical demands discussed by Beveridge. Butler
spent most of his time resolving the major issue of religious education in
schools and convincing Conservatives to support him. He had to constantly
reassure the Conservative 1922 Committee that the position of the public

school would be safeguarded after the war, and had to give in to the party view on maintaining fees in a small number of direct-grant secondary schools.

The Education Bill became law in August 1944, and introduced secondary education for all children, the raising of the school-leaving age and the introduction of part-time continuation schools. The coalition united over the issue for various motives, the Conservatives had 'been brought to think the reforms less awful than they might'[59] and the Labour Party backed this long-awaited first item of coalition reconstruction policy despite the fact they thought it did not go far enough. Butler readily acknowledged that education had succeeded, as it was the least controversial reconstruction area; the Cabinet 'have been prompted to come the way of education because it has been very difficult to obtain agreement between the parties on any matters which involve property or the pocket.'[60]

Progress on employment policy was less successful. On 4th June 1944, Churchill asked Bevin to accompany him to Portsmouth to say farewell to some of the troops and Bevin recounts:

> *They were going off to face this terrific battle with great hearts and great courage. The one question they put to me when I went through their ranks was, 'Ernie, when we have done this job for you are we going back on the dole?'... Both the Prime Minister and I answered, 'No you are not.'* [61]

Employment policy was the single biggest area of concern for the population at large, as they remembered the terrible slump under Lloyd George after the First World War. The War Cabinet considered a draft white paper on the subject and Churchill declared it as bold, able and worthy of support.

When it was debated in parliament, a fair number of people supported it. The Conservative spokesman on industry declared:

> *My aim is that no man, except through his own fault, should ever have too many days without the prospect of a job.*[62]

Surprisingly, even industrialists, such as Sir Arnold Gridley, welcomed the content declaring that it was the best white paper produced by the party. However, the consensus on employment did not extend to the backbenches. Although both parties agreed that unemployment was a bad thing, they violently disagreed on how to resolve it. Labour believed that unemployment was inseparable from capitalism whilst the Conservatives believed that there was no cure for unemployment except a revival of trade.

The white paper tended to dodge these fundamental issues and was remarkably ambiguous on a number of subjects. It fell short of calling for full employment and called instead for a rather vague promise to create the conditions necessary for a 'high and stable level of employment'.[63] It also failed to make clear just how the government should raise money, warning that budget deficits should not be encouraged in the long term. The Conservative leadership preferred their traditional remedies to fight unemployment: stability of sterling, revival and expansion of export trade and the encouragement of private enterprise, whilst the Labour Party gave strong arguments for alternative methods of employment control.

In the end Conservative backbenchers were satisfied that the policies outlined were ambiguous enough to imply that employment policy would continue to operate within the framework of a private enterprise economy, and that there were no specific plans to control private investment. They also felt they had to embrace (however reluctantly) the government's reconstruction programme, as they were aware that it would be electorally damaging to oppose the principle of greater state responsibility for tackling unemployment.

Labour however felt let down, arguing with good reason that the resulting plan left several key issues unresolved. One of these was the relationship between public and private enterprise, which the Chancellor himself made little attempt to tackle during the life of the coalition. In the end though, Labour supported the plan, regarding the white paper as a starting point. It was however a fudge which failed to set a clear direction.

The poor quality of debate over unemployment measures was typical of the tension now emerging in the coalition. On the one hand, Labour concentrated its energies on pushing the Conservatives towards the implementation of agreed policies, while making clear its own preference for more fundamental social change. On the other hand, the Conservatives believed that coalition policy had reached the maximum level of reform possible for a post-war administration.

Despite this conflict there was remarkable progress on domestic reform with The National Health Service Paper of February 1943 followed by the Employment Policy proposals in May, the passing of the Butler Education

Act in August and in September the publication of the government's own proposals for social insurance, which largely embodied those of the Beveridge Report. However, most of these proposals stayed on paper and very little action was taken by the Cabinet and parliament. As Beveridge wrote to the editor of *The Times* on 18th July 1944:

> *It seems to me that any government under Winston will not do more for social progress than they are driven to by opposition and peace-making.*[64]

Clearly, Churchill and his party were not entirely convinced about the need for a brave new world, and their efforts at reconstruction were more about chasing public opinion. Even if small minorities within each party were moving towards what Addison calls a 'wartime consensus', they did not coalesce to create a truly inspiring blueprint for reform.

The Fall Of The Coalition

As early as March 1941, during his address to the Conservative Central Council, Churchill had made it clear he wanted the coalition to continue into peace. This is consistent with Churchill's past and general preference for non-partisan political systems. As G.R. Searle writes:

> *Churchill's wartime coalition in a way represented the culmination of a lifelong pursuit of a "National" government, unfettered by party traditions and restraints.*[65]

The same was initially true for the Labour Party, but their motives for wanting to continue the coalition were more practical as they, along with almost everybody else, believed that the Conservatives would win any upcoming election. All three parties also knew just how difficult it would be to run the country facing the problems which the peace would bring and because of this it was commonly assumed that the coalition would last beyond the end of the war.

Meanwhile, despite the government's attempts at reconstruction the public seemed unimpressed. In March 1944, Churchill complained in a broadcast that the coalition was receiving little applause for the bold progress it was making in social and economic affairs. The white paper on Employment Policy brought hardly a ripple of reaction and the health proposals were the subject of very little comment. It seems that people had formed extremely pessimistic expectations for the peacetime. A Home Intelligence Report commented on the social insurance white paper:

> *Many people, especially workers, while approving the plan, are*
> *sceptical as to its ever becoming law in anything like its present*
> *shape.*[66]

According to the report, one man in ten and one woman in five expected that he or she would have difficulty in finding a job.

This disillusionment was accompanied by a gradual but definite move to the left. By December 1942, about two people out of five had already changed their political outlook since the beginning of the war and the trend was essentially towards more left wing attitudes. The Labour Party started to benefit from this and voters increasingly preferred Attlee, despite his rather uninspiring air, to Churchill. As Jefferys writes:

> *By its ambiguous attitude to the Beveridge Report in particular, the*
> *government threw away its chance to shape and guide public*
> *expectations.*[67]

Opinion was also moving against the concept of coalition. In January 1944, when asked whether "after war shall we go back to the party system we had before the war?", forty-one per cent opted for a coalition government, as against forty-six per cent who wanted to return to a party system. In August 1945, when asked the same question, thirty-five per cent wanted an all-party government in the post-war world as against nine per cent who wanted a multi-party government and forty-two per cent who wanted a single-party government. These figures are hard to analyse, especially as opinion polls had only recently developed, but they do suggest that a sizeable portion of the population were not wedded to the concept of coalition in peacetime.

Between January and February 1943, there were six by-elections in England and Scotland, a period which many historians regard as a 'mini general election'. Although the electoral truce was still in action it was never very effective from the outset in preventing local contests between Conservative and Labour supporters, and from 1943 onwards there was an increasingly vigorous return to conventional forms of political activity in many parts of the country. The new contenders opposing coalition candidates were clearly Labour or Socialist, giving a definite sense that politics was returning to the normal pattern of Conservative versus Socialist. In the end the Conservatives did very badly in the by-elections as voters used them as a chance to vote against the party, but not the government or the war.

Between 1943 and 1945, the Conservatives' popularity worsened as they suffered more resounding by-election defeats by Common Wealth or Independent Socialist candidates. In April 1943, the by-election at Eddisbury was won by Warrant-Officer John Loverseed for Common Wealth, and Derbyshire West in 1944 by an Independent Labour candidate, Charles White. Both seats had been so safe in 1935 that neither had even been contested by Labour. In fact, in Derbyshire West the Tory majority of some 5,000 was turned into an independent Socialist majority of 4,500. The significance of these by-elections lay more in their demonstration of public feeling about reconstruction than in signalling any fundamental change in the party system. 'The electorate had become convinced that the Tory party, from its leadership down to its grass-roots, had no real commitment to what it valued most – a break from the past.'[68] Now, at the beginning of 1944, more than ever, traditional party politics were resurfacing.

And yet the significance of the results was not taken seriously by political pundits and the press. 'No Tory agent need yet be seriously alarmed'[69] proclaimed the *Guardian*, and Barrington-Ward at *The Times* wrote:

> So much for the foolish prophecy of that very nice ass Harold
> Macmillan who goes about saying that the Conservatives will be lucky
> to retain a hundred seats at the election.[70]

Most political correspondents refused to accept the depth of change taking place and remained convinced that Churchill would take the country by storm, as Lloyd George did in 1918, as 'the man who won the war'.

The political parties were in no-man's-land. They were not yet ready to end the coalition but there was no desire for the parties to 'fuse', as there had been under Lloyd George in 1920. There was never any question of party realignment, as Churchill's method of government had not changed or fragmented the political parties in the same way the First World War coalition had.

Gradually as war drew to a close politicians were recovering their old sense of party politics. At ministerial level, more serious rifts and controversial issues arose splitting the parties and creating serious tensions. In fact, by the end of 1944, the government had essentially exhausted the subjects on which they could agree and were left only with those on which they differed.

On 7th October 1944, the Labour Party announced that they would fight the next election as an independent party, and not as part of a coalition. The party was determined to avoid the fate that the Liberal Party had endured in 1918 with the 'coupon' election. Then in December 1944, there was a serious split in the coalition. The Greek communists had borne the main burden of the struggle against the Nazis in Greece, but after the Germans had left the country Churchill feared a rise in communism. During the ensuing civil war British troops found themselves fighting against the former Greek Resistance. British opinion was quite unprepared for this development. This immediately led to an uproar in the media and in parliament, and a motion of censure was introduced by Seymour Cocks of the Tribune group: although the motion was defeated by 281 votes to 32, only twenty-three Labour MPs supported the government with twenty-four voting against, and the rest abstaining.

Individuals within the coalition were finding it increasingly difficult to work together. Up until now, there had not been any major rivalry between the Labour and Conservative leaders: even though Attlee and Churchill were not close, they worked well together. However, in 1945, conflicts started appearing: for the first time, the Reconstruction Committee was unable to reach a compromise when Herbert Morrison and William Lloyd George, Minister for Fuel and Power, pressed for the re-organisation of the electricity industry into a public co-operation. As Addison writes:

> *Politicians were emerging at last into the light of the common day and when Germany surrendered on 7th May 1945, a return to full party politics was universally expected.*[71]

Now that the war was almost won and the parties knew they would not continue as a coalition, agreement was no longer necessary and negotiations came to a stop. A series of acrimonious Cabinet meetings had ended by effectively putting the lid on further new initiatives. Lord Beaverbrook told one correspondent:

> *Collaboration between the two parties is growing increasingly difficult. As victory draws nearer, the urge for a return to party warfare grows stronger and the stresses and strains of the coalition become harder to withstand.*[72]

Indeed, 'the time for pursuing common objectives had passed'.[73]

In October 1944, after the Labour Party announced their decision to fight the election, Churchill felt obliged to declare that it would be wrong to prolong the existing parliament as it had been sitting for over eight years. But he continued to believe that the government should remain united until the war in Japan was won. On 18th May 1945, just after the end of the war, Churchill drafted a letter with Attlee's assistance, proposing that either the coalition should continue until the end of the Japanese war or there should be an immediate election. Attlee, Bevin and Dalton were keen to continue the coalition for a couple of months but Morrison was against it and he convinced the NEC at the annual Labour conference to support his position and call for an immediate end to the coalition.

On 23rd May 1945, the coalition government came to an end after Attlee formerly rejected Churchill's offer of continued co-operation, made five days earlier. However, the Labour Party wanted to delay the general election for a couple of months in order to avoid a khaki election. With the coalition now in effect over, Churchill saw no purpose in postponing the poll until the autumn and immediately secured the King's agreement to dissolve parliament on 15th June with polling due to take place on 5th July.

The election was a landslide victory for the Labour Party as they returned 393 MPs, against only 213 for the Conservatives and their allies. The Conservative Party did not have a well-defined leadership under Churchill, and their ideas had not progressed enough to meet the voters' demands in 1945. A dramatic new world was emerging and the Conservatives were resistant to it. This was not helped by Churchill's habit of drifting into tirades against socialism, of which the radio speech when he compared socialism to the Gestapo, has become the most notorious. Press commentators on the whole agreed that Churchill had been unnecessarily provocative in attacking those who until recently had been loyal colleagues. The speech had caused great disillusionment, compounding the aggravation of an electorate already suffering from war-weariness. In the end the Conservatives lacked any real central theme or enthusiasm for social reform.

Some Conservatives had moved on and accepted reform as necessary; a few party members did attempt to make social issues more prominent in the campaign. For example, the Tory Reformer called for the introduction of Keynesian economic policies and Butler spoke of the opportunity in carrying out the 'greatest Social Reform Programme' in our country's history. But the majority, including former coalition ministers, came out as unashamed advocates of free enterprise capitalism, calling for the swift removal of economic controls and emphasising the link between reform and the revival of Britain's trading position. The campaigners for reform made little headway in a campaign dominated at national level by the Prime Minister. The electorate were left disappointed by the Conservatives' outdated policies.

Butler reflected that the party might have fared better if affirmation of post-war policies had not taken such a poor third place behind the exploitation of Churchill's position as war leader and negative attacks on the opposition. He noted:

> It was sad that the work done by the Post-War Problems Committee played so little part in the formulation of our Conservative campaign, and that the conduct of the election swept away much of the idealism which we wanted to instil and which emerged only in the 1945-1951 period in opposition.[74]

At the end of the day, the swing to the left, though strong, was by no means irreversible. If Churchill had used the period after 1942 to forge a popular post-war policy then wartime suspicions about the Conservative Party may have been at least partially overcome. Instead, he adhered only superficially to reconstruction, and in this sense he must bear a large share of personal responsibility for his crushing defeat at the polls in 1945.

Conservatives might complain that they had been too busy fighting the war to oil their party machinery, but it would be truer to say that they lost the election of 1945 by taking their victory under Churchill for granted. Churchill later claimed in his memoirs that the party organisation was much less well prepared for an election in 1945 than Labour, because the trade unions were the core of Labour's local organisation, and trade unionists had been obliged along with other members of reserved occupation to organise war production. The idea that Labour had a large number of agents on the Home Front is a myth; the Conservative Party organisation was in a very poor state by comparison with peacetime, but it does not follow that Labour had any great organisational advantage.

On the other hand, Labour caught the wartime mood of consensual reconstruction better than the Conservatives. Their campaign was both carefully orchestrated and purposefully conducted. The strategy was essentially quite a conservative one; had they gone to the country in 1939 with the 1945 programme, they would have been issuing a strongly radical challenge, but in 1945 they had only to consolidate and extend the consensus achieved under the coalition, and build upon the new foundations of popular opinion. The population were clearly in favour of a new welfare state: in response, Labour showed greater commitment to the Beveridge Report, whilst the Conservatives remained scarred and handicapped by being associated with inter-war depression.

The Prime Minister himself did not seem to take much interest in the final fate of the Conservative Party. In September 1944, Churchill had already confided that:

> *I have a strong feeling that my work is done. I have no message. I had a message. Now I only say "fight the damned Socialists". I do not believe in this brave new world.*[75]

Churchill had never been very interested by party politics, and he proved to be a poor leader for the Conservatives in their hour of need in 1945, but in Britain's hour of need he had been a saviour and is remembered as one of the most popular and successful politicians of all time.

Success Despite Defeat

The Churchill coalition was a remarkable success on many fronts. That the government could even consider a reform agenda as early as 1942, when victory was still far in the distance, is a remarkable feat by any standard. Although there were disagreements based on party lines, there were not the bitter arguments and resentments seen in other coalitions. Most importantly, Churchill avoided splitting his party, something both Lloyd George and Ramsay MacDonald failed to do when they led coalitions. And although he lost the 1945 election, it is to his credit that politics returned to normal so quickly after the war. As Searle writes:

> *the stability of the post-war years owed much to the common ground which had grown up between the main parties of government during the period of Churchill's premiership.*[76]

Over the greatest issue of all, the Second World War itself, the parties were united from the beginning and remained united until the end and differed over only details. His military leadership showed he had learned many of the lessons from the Great War. By establishing a War Cabinet and taking clear control, he avoided many of the weaknesses demonstrated by both Asquith and Chamberlain. The 1940 coalition would become the only genuine National Government in British history. Indeed, all three parties were involved, leaving only a minuscule Independent Labour Party of three and the solitary Communist to oppose the government, and were prepared to put country before party. Churchill was propelled to the unique position of commanding the almost unanimous allegiance of both parliament and country.

However, his rise to power was never inevitable. Up to the very last moment, Chamberlain could have stayed on, or, the more likely solution, Lord Halifax could have become Prime Minister. In the end though Churchill, with a little help from Labour, proved most adept at exploiting what was an unexpected political crisis.

Churchill himself had never been much of a party figure. For a number of years he had oscillated and varied between the Conservatives and the Liberals. As he wrote to Lloyd George (when trying to lure him into the Cabinet) in May 1940:

Like you I have no party of my own.[77]

He saw himself rather, as the 'father of his people' and as J. M. Lee noted:

The coalition was part of his personal dialogue with the nation.[78]

He did become leader of the Conservative Party in October 1940, but he never really led the party in a specific and well-defined direction; conducting the war strategy is what really interested him. What he lacked in great vision or imagination, the Prime Minister certainly made up for in his handling of administration, the swift assimilation of detail, the execution of policy and above all his stubbornness.

The Churchill coalition is in many ways a model for others to follow. It shows that strong leadership can be achieved without alienating coalition partners. Despite his mistrust of socialism he treated the Labour Party with respect, not the disdain Chamberlain demonstrated. His relations with Attlee were positive and showed none of the mistrust that Asquith held towards the

Conservatives and Bonar Laws in the First World War. And when he replaced Chamberlain, Churchill avoided the temptation of an anti-appeasement purge but showed tact in keeping Chamberlain on board. For all the impression of a tough wartime leader there was a tender and tactful political player who was able to craft and maintain a real national coalition.

The victory at war was not easily achieved and Britain paid a high cost, but had at least avoided defeat. The victory in peace could have been greater if Churchill had really believed in the need to implement reform. In the end though, the war was won and social reforms started, and it was a coalition combined with great leadership that had enabled these achievements to take place.

References

1. A.J.P. Taylor, '1932-1945' in *Coalitions in British Politics*, David Butler, p.94

2. *The Churchill Coalition and Wartime Politics 1940-1945*, Kevin Jefferys, p.16

3. *Country Before Party: Coalition and the Idea of 'National Government' in Modern Britain 1885-1987*, G. R. Searle, p.196

4. *The Churchill Coalition and Wartime Politics 1940-1945*, Kevin Jefferys, p.17

5. *Country Before Party: Coalition and the Idea of 'National Government' in Modern Britain 1885-1987*, G. R. Searle, p.197

6. *The Churchill Coalition and Wartime Politics 1940-1945*, Kevin Jefferys, p.19

7. *The Road to 1945: British Politics and the Second World War*, Paul Addison, p.66

8. *Ibid.*, p.61

9. *Churchill: A Biography*, Roy Jenkins, p.552

10. Boothby to Lloyd George, 18 Sep 1939, Lloyd George Papers G/2/13

11. *Churchill: A Biography*, Roy Jenkins, p.557

12. A.J.P. Taylor, '1932-1945' in *Coalitions in British Politics*, David Butler, p.80

13. *The Road to 1945: British Politics and the Second World War*, Paul Addison, p.79

14. *Daily Mirror*, 3 October 1939

15. *Churchill: A Biography*, Roy Jenkins, p.533

16. *The War Speeches of Churchill*, Charles Eade, p.119

17. *The Road to 1945: British Politics and the Second World War*, Paul Addison, p.82

18. *Ibid.*, p.66

19. *Ibid.*, p.80

20. *Churchill: A Biography*, Roy Jenkins, p.555

21. A.J.P. Taylor, '1932-1945' in *Coalitions in British Politics*, David Butler, p.81

22. *Ibid.*, p.83

23. *The Churchill Coalition and Wartime Politics 1940-1945*, Kevin Jefferys, p.21

24. *The Road to 1945: British Politics and the Second World War*, Paul Addison, p.95

25. Parliamentary Debate 5th Ser., vol.360, 1149-1150: 7 May 1940

26. A.J.P. Taylor, '1932-1945' in *Coalitions in British Politics*, David Butler, p.82-83

27. *'Chips': The Diaries of Sir Henry Channon*, R Rhode James (ed.), 8 May 1940, p.246

28. *The Fateful Years: Memoirs, 1931-1945*, Hugh Dalton, p.312

29. A.J.P. Taylor, '1932-1945' in *Coalitions in British Politics*, David Butler, p.84

30. *The Road to 1945: British Politics and the Second World War*, Paul Addison, p.62

31. *The Life and Times of Ernest Bevin, Vol. II Minister of Labour 1940-1945*, Alan Bullock, p.1

32. *Politics in Industrial Society: The Experience of the British system since 1911*, Keith Middlemas, p.271

33. *Country Before Party: Coalition and the Idea of 'National Government' in Modern Britain 1885-1987*, G. R. Searle, p.200

34. *The Times*, 10 May 1940

35. *The Churchill Coalition and Wartime Politics 1940-1945*, Kevin Jefferys, p.43

36. *The Road to 1945: British Politics and the Second World War*, Paul Addison, p.107

37. *Daily Herald*, 5 June 1940

38. *Daily Mirror*, 6 June 1940

39. *Tribune*, 7 June 1940

40. *The Road to 1945: British Politics and the Second World War*, Paul Addison, p.111

41. *Ibid.*, p.110

42. *Ibid.*

43. *The Churchill Coalition and Wartime Politics 1940-1945*, Kevin Jefferys, p.87

44. *The Road to 1945: British Politics and the Second World War*, Paul Addison, p.198

45. *'Chips': The Diaries of Sir Henry Channon*, R Rhode James (ed.), 9 January 1942, p.316

46. *The Road to 1945: British Politics and the Second World War*, Paul Addison, p.190

47. *'Chips': The Diaries of Sir Henry Channon*, R Rhode James (ed.), 1 July 1942, p.334

48. *New Statesman*, 1st June 1940

49. *The Road to 1945: British Politics and the Second World War*, Paul Addison, p.122

50. *Ibid.*, p.126

51. *The Fateful Years: Memoirs, 1931-1945*, Hugh Dalton, p.410

52. *The Churchill Coalition and Wartime Politics 1940-1945*, Kevin Jefferys, p.122

53. *Country Before Party: Coalition and the Idea of 'National Government' in Modern Britain 1885-1987*, G. R. Searle, p.217

54. *The Road to 1945: British Politics and the Second World War*, Paul Addison, p.220

55. *Ibid.*, p.231-2

56. *The Economist*, 2 October 1944

57. 'British Politics and Social Policy during the Second World War', Kevin Jefferys, *The Historical Journal*, 30 (1987) p.124

58. *The Road to 1945: British Politics and the Second World War*, Paul Addison, p.238

59. *The Churchill Coalition and Wartime Politics 1940-1945*, Kevin Jefferys, p.128

60. 'British Politics and Social Policy during the Second World War', Kevin Jefferys, *The Historical Journal*, 30 (1987) p.140

61. *The Road to 1945: British Politics and the Second World War*, Paul Addison, p.242

62. *Observer*, 12 March 1944

63. 'British Politics and Social Policy during the Second World War', Kevin Jefferys, *The Historical Journal*, 30 (1987) p.137

64. *The Times*, 18 July 1944

65. *Country Before Party: Coalition and the Idea of 'National Government' in Modern Britain 1885-1987*, G. R. Searle, p.205

66. *The Road to 1945: British Politics and the Second World War*, Paul Addison, p.247

67. *The Churchill Coalition and Wartime Politics 1940-1945*, Kevin Jefferys, p.140

68. *Ibid.*

69. *The Observer*, 12 March 1944

70. *The Road to 1945: British Politics and the Second World War*, Paul Addison, p.250

71. *Ibid.*, p.256

72. *The Churchill Coalition and Wartime Politics 1940-1945*, Kevin Jefferys, p.176

73. *Ibid.*, p.175

74. 'British Politics and Social Policy during the Second World War', Kevin Jefferys, *The Historical Journal*, 30 (1987) p.142

75. *The Churchill Coalition and Wartime Politics 1940-1945*, Kevin Jefferys, p.174

76. *Country Before Party: Coalition and the Idea of 'National Government' in Modern Britain 1885-1987*, Searle, p.219

77. *Ibid.*, p.199

78. *The Churchill Coalition 1940-1945*, J.M. Lee, p.15

6

The Uncle And Nephew Pact

The Uncle And Nephew Pact

I suppose inevitably supporting an unpopular government means the
unpopularity rubs off.[1]

Roy Jenkins

Post-war politics settled down to a regular pattern throughout the 1950s
and 1960s as the pendulum swung between majority Conservative and
Labour administrations. This continued up to the election of 1970 when
Edward Heath was elected as Conservative Prime Minister with a clear
majority, but four years later the situation had become more turbulent. In
one of the closest elections ever recorded, the Conservatives won the popular
vote with 37.9 per cent compared to Labour's 37.2 per cent, but due to
Britain's electoral system this resulted in Labour's Harold Wilson ending up
ahead by four seats. The Liberals, under the charismatic leadership of
Jeremy Thorpe, had one of their most successful elections in decades and
with 19 per cent of the vote had a potentially deal-breaking 14 MPs. All the
circumstances for a classic coalition were in place: with just 4 seats between
the two main parties and the Liberals holding the balance of power it looked
set for some kind of deal. Remarkably given the electoral arithmetic there
was to be no coalition. As ever personality played a part. Heath had been a
very reserved leader of the Conservative Party and was somewhat shocked
to find himself in a position of losing the election. Grumpy at the fact that
he won the majority of public votes, albeit by a whisker, he seemed reluctant
to accept defeat, but disliked the idea of entering into long protracted
negotiations with the smaller parties. Meanwhile, Thorpe, rather excited at
the prospect of power, was to find his hands tied by activists and MPs hostile
to any deal. The third player, Wilson, was very clear in his position and the
Shadow Cabinet issued the following statement shortly after the final results
were in:

> *Since the Conservatives have failed in their appeal for an increased*
> *majority, they lack the authority to give the lead the country is seeking.*
> *Therefore, the Labour party is prepared to form a government.*[2]

It was a straightforward and bold stance. Wilson and his team sat tight
making no attempts to form alliances, preferring to watch and see what
Heath did next. Tom McNally recalls what happened:

I was in Transport House at that time and I remember Harold was very relaxed on it, he said, 'everybody keep quiet and just leave them' – he called it the most expensive dirty weekend in British history – very Harold![3]

As sitting Prime Minister, with no overall majority in place, Heath believed it was his responsibility to create an administration. After the election he immediately went to see the Queen at Buckingham Palace, who herself had hurriedly returned from an official visit to Australia. Although there is no constitutional position set down, the monarch is thought to favour giving the incumbent Prime Minister the first option of forming a government when no party has a clear majority. Heath, somewhat reluctantly, decided to try and form a government turning first to the Liberals.

The parties had little in common, but at least on Europe, Heath felt the Liberals would not make totally unhappy bedfellows. At the time, the Liberals were also very supportive of maintaining a price and income policy, something which was a central issue to the Conservative government. Inflation was a key political concern and Heath felt the Liberals might be persuaded to at least form some arrangement on the basis of creating economic stability to reduce the impact of inflation.

Things did not start smoothly when Heath then spent most of Friday, the day of the election, trying to make contact with the Liberal leader. In classic Thorpe style he was conducting a procession around his constituency in Barnstable and could not be tracked down. When I spoke to Thorpe he recalls that Heath did eventually contact him by phone:

It was late, about 11.45, when Heath finally got through.[4]

Deal Or No Deal

It was Saturday when the two men eventually got together for what was a rather awkward meeting. Heath was clearly embarrassed at the need to horsetrade, whilst Thorpe rather enjoyed the limelight. There remains some dispute over the deal that was on offer. Heath appears to have offered a full coalition with a place in the Cabinet for Thorpe (probably the Home Office). In his biography Thorpe strongly denied that he was offered this:

I can state with utter conviction that no specific ministry was mentioned, or suggested.[5]

When I spoke to Thorpe in May 2007, he again denied any job was discussed. He was attracted to the idea of coalition and, having left Downing Street, proceeded to try and consult the party on the proposal. I am sure Thorpe would have enjoyed the luxury of holding office and would have seen little problem with joining the Cabinet and remaining leader at the same time. Others were not so convinced. David Steel as Whip at the time was alarmed at the pace Thorpe was setting and was annoyed that the first he heard of the talks was on the radio. Steel rushed to London to try and calm things down:

I thought he went to see Heath with indecent haste and was over keen to enter talks, but he rather enjoyed the theatre and the thought of being in power was obviously attractive.[6]

Thorpe disputes this, claiming he had been reluctant all along:

When the news broke that a meeting was to take place, many Liberals panicked and thought that I was about to sacrifice the very independence of the party which I had spent the last twenty-five years working to preserve. However, I felt that if the Prime Minister of the day requested a meeting one had an obligation to go.[7]

In our conversation he acknowledged that the party were concerned at the talks:

People were suspicious, some were even horrified as it was not usual to have talks with other parties, but I could not refuse to go and see the Prime Minister.[8]

Meanwhile Liberal Party activists up and down the country, shocked at the radio and news reports, were quickly organising themselves against any potential coalition with the Conservatives. There was a long-standing uneasiness about working with Conservatives that ran through the rank and file of the party. Even the more pragmatic members feared the party would be damaged by propping up a Conservative government that had lost its majority. Liberal Party HQ was flooded with calls over the weekend protesting at the talks and urging Thorpe to take no part. According to Paul Tyler, just elected as MP for Bodmin in 1974, it was not just activists that were concerned:

People kept coming up to me on my victory tour saying we did not vote for you to keep the Tories in.[9]

The real problem for Heath was that he had dramatically thrown away a Conservative majority. He had chosen to call an early election and get a new mandate from the electorate; instead he got a bloody nose. It would have been a brave decision for the Liberals to have sought to prop up a government in these circumstances, but if a strong commitment on electoral reform had been put forward it would have been a price that some activists may have felt worth taking. Late on Saturday evening Thorpe, now less enthusiastic having spoken to colleagues, told the Prime Minister he had lost the mandate to govern and that the only way he could gain support amongst the party for any deal would be a strong commitment and a meaningful Speaker's conference on proportional representation (PR).

They met again on Sunday and the Prime Minister offered a Speaker's conference on electoral reform, but there was no promise of a government whipped vote. Heath recognised this would be difficult and was not prepared to promise something that could not be delivered. Thorpe would have known that without this the chances of any change in the election system were non-existent.

By the end of the weekend it was pretty clear that Heath had failed to come to any agreement, but more embarrassingly he had the look of a man who had been defeated by the electorate and was still desperately clinging on to office. *The Spectator* described him as, 'the squatter in No. 10 Downing Street' and the image of Heath as a bad loser was set in stone for decades. As Heath began to realise that the game was up, Thorpe also realised that it would be impossible for him to gain support amongst his fellow Liberal MPs. They finally met on Monday morning and formally rejected Heath's offer. Paul Tyler was present:

> By the time of the meeting it had become clear there was no point in a deal as electoral reform was not on the agenda and the parliamentary arithmetic did not add up in any case. We met in a small room and rejected it in ten minutes, but had to keep the meeting going on to make it look like we'd taken the situation seriously.[10]

What happened next is best summarised by the published exchange of letters between the two leaders:

Heath to Thorpe:

> ... *When we met on Saturday afternoon, we agreed that ... the essential and urgent need was that an Administration should be formed which would have sufficient support in the new House of Commons to carry on the Queen's government.*
>
> *We noted that the leader of the Labour Party had issued a statement which made it clear that he would be prepared to form a minority government, but not to enter into any coalition, or understanding with other parties in the House ... I made clear my belief that it would be possible to construct a programme for the Queen's Speech on the opening of parliament which both the Conservative and the Liberal parties could honourably and in good conscience support ...*
>
> *I told you on Saturday that I thought that from the point of view of the stability and confidence of a new administration full Liberal participation in government was preferable to other possible arrangements ... We are now convinced that full Liberal participation in government, and thus in all the decisions of government, will be essential if we are to ensure a stable administration ... We do not think that, on its own, an arrangement for Liberal support would be sufficient ... You asked what were my views ... and I told you that I should have to consult my colleagues. I have now done so ... I am authorised to tell you that my colleagues and I in the present Cabinet would be prepared to support the setting up of a Speaker's Conference to consider the desirability and possibility of a change in our electoral arrangements ... We should be ready to co-operate in seeing that the conclusions and recommendations of the conference were put to parliament in the customary way.*[11]

Thorpe replied:

> *At our meetings on Saturday ... no commitment of any sort was entered into by me, save that I would report our discussions to my colleagues ...*
>
> *... on Sunday night, ... I made it clear that in my view, after preliminary soundings, there was no possibility of a Liberal-Conservative coalition proving acceptable, but that we might give consideration to offering support from the opposition benches to any*

minority government on an agreed, but limited programme. This you have now explicitly rejected.

After meeting my parliamentary colleagues in the Commons this morning this attitude was confirmed ... we believe that the only way in which the maximum degree of national co-operation can be achieved is for a government of national unity to be formed to include members of all parties ...

Accordingly, I do not believe that a Liberal presence in the Cabinet, designed to sustain your government, would prove acceptable.[12]

Instead of any coalition Thorpe and his party went on to argue that the time was right for some kind of national unity government. It was a rather bold request which was unlikely to have any success at all, but looked statesmanlike and avoided any impression that the Liberals had been rejected by the Conservatives. The national unity card is one which has always played well for the Liberals and was one of the reasons why their 1974 election vote had been so high in the first place. As the economy struggled there was a sense in which the public had been looking for their politicians to come together, and ironically if it had been possible to form a coalition it might have been quite popular with the voters. However, the calculations the Liberals made at this point was that propping up a dying Conservative government would not have been in the long-term interest of the party. Even if a foothold into government had been created, there was no doubt that the electoral tide was moving in Labour's direction and unless rapid progress had been made on proportional representation it would have been unlikely that the next election would have been fought on anything other than the first-past-the-post system.

The truth was these two men had never really built up any long-term relationship before the electorate flung them into this kind of discussion. Although Thorpe told me relations were very friendly, this was not an Ashdown/Blair relationship. Heath's heart was never really in it, he was devastated at losing the election and felt uneasy at having to belittle himself by seeking support from the Liberals. Thorpe was an awkward character to deal with and, although he may have been tempted with the glory of holding office himself, his ability to deliver it within the party would never have succeeded.

Ultimately, even if the two sides had been able to come together it seemed very unlikely that the coalition would have lasted more than a matter of months as it would still have been a few seats short of a majority if the Ulster Unionists decided to vote down the coalition. As Thorpe told me:

I always thought a deal was unlikely because of the arithmetic.[13]

The arithmetic, politics and personality just did not add up. David Steel summed the situation up:

My instincts were that it was a non-starter. The Prime Minister had sought a mandate and been rejected – to prop him up would have been a very odd thing to do and anyway the numbers between Liberals and Tories did not add up – the whole thing was bizarre.[14]

Wilson's patience paid off and he formed a minority government managing to govern throughout the late spring and summer months. His position was based on no alliance, other than the reluctance of the Conservatives to bring him down and face a new election. In fact, Conservatives and the Liberals had little appetite for playing party politics and both used language of national unity during the summer months.

In the Tory Party manifesto produced during September 1974, Heath virtually committed himself to a coalition:

We will consult and confer with the leaders of other parties and with the leaders of the great interest in the nation in order to secure for the government policies the consent and support of all men and women of goodwill.[15]

By the October 1974 election campaign itself he had gone further and declared:

The real hope of the British people is that a national coalition government including all parties should be formed.[16]

It was all rather desperate and suggested that Heath knew Wilson was heading for a victory. Wilson had waited for six months and felt it was time to turn to the country, and move his government from minority to majority rule. The appeal worked, but only just. The second election of 1974 was not much clearer, although Labour had 43 more seats than the Conservatives. His overall majority was just three – turbulent times were ahead.

New Leaders All Round

During the second Wilson government the Conservatives replaced Heath with Margaret Thatcher and the Liberals went through the nightmare of the Thorpe scandal. By 1976, Harold Wilson was very much the elder statesman with the opposition parties both having new leaders. Thatcher had shocked everybody by becoming the leader of the Conservative Party – she had put fire in their belly and began to restore confidence after their surprise defeat in 1974. Meanwhile the Liberals had turned to David Steel to begin the harder task of restoring credibility to a party which had been broken by scandal and tabloid headlines. However, Wilson was to produce the biggest shock of all by suddenly announcing his resignation in 1976. Jim Callaghan took over from him and spent the next few months seeing his Labour majority become smaller and smaller until by 1977 there was a serious chance of a vote of no confidence and Callaghan finding his premiership coming to an early and abrupt end.

As the Commons majority got smaller the prospect for some parliamentary arrangements got larger and minds started to focus on what might happen. The personalities of Callaghan and Steel were in marked contrast to Heath and Thorpe. The potential for coming to some kind of arrangement was made easier by the ease in which these two politicians worked together. Callaghan was a long-term Labour survivor who was seeing out his political career as Prime Minister, whilst Steel had instinctively been a consensus politician throughout his time in the Commons. As a relatively young leader of an insecure party he was keen to gain quick credibility for himself.

His Private Member's Bill on abortion had created a cross-party alliance, as had his involvement in the European referendum. Working on a major national campaign had also showed him how the big parties operated, and he liked what he saw:

> *This was an education in working with other parties, seeing how they get resources. If you wanted an executive jet, telephones or 50 electric typewriters, just make a call. It was a way of working which had escaped the Liberals.*[17]

He also knew that it was not credible for a party with so few MPs to claim that success could be achieved alone. Steel's approach to politics was instinctively inclusive. In his conference speech the year before he had said:

If the party was to go forward it would have to work with others on the way.[18]

Although, as one delegate told Steel a year later:

We understood from your speech last year that you were keen on marriage, but we didn't expect to find ourselves pushed to the altar quite so soon.[19]

The beginnings of the Lib/Lab pact began over the issue of devolution. During the 1976 session of parliament the government decided to introduce a Scotland and Wales Bill. Although the Liberals and Scottish Nationalists were supportive of this Bill, they were incensed when after fourteen days of debate the government decided to introduce a 'guillotine motion' thereby limiting the amount of debate that could take place. The Bill included issues that were close to the Liberals heart, such as proportional representation in the new devolved assemblies, that would now not get a chance to be debated within the proposed time limit. The government misjudged the mood of the House and the guillotine motion was lost by twenty-nine votes, defeated by a government rebellion, but more importantly Liberal and Nationalists votes. Steel admitted to me that he had not recognised the political consequences that would follow by voting down the guillotine. However, it acted as a wake-up call for the government and they began the process of cross-party talks to try and find a way forward on the issue of devolution. Thatcher's Conservatives refused to participate in the talks as they objected to the principle of devolution in itself. This left the Liberals with an opportunity to begin formal talks alone, something Steel regards as the embryonic stages of the Lib/Lab pact.

Inside and outside of parliament the Labour government was looking shaky. At the time opinion polls showed the Conservatives with a very large lead over Labour and after the devolution debacle there were other close votes in the Commons. The first mumblings of a no confidence vote began to be heard around the corridors of Westminster. There was every probability that the government could collapse and Steel had to quickly bring his colleagues together to decide what position they would take in any vote. Against this background, the larger than life Liberal MP for Rochdale, Cyril Smith, had already begun his own informal discussions about the possibility of some kind of physical arrangement between the two parties. In February, Smith rather clumsily wrote directly to Callaghan who responded saying he had felt it would be better for any discussions to take place at a more junior level. Smith was infuriated but a more constructive approach was to follow from the pen of Labour Whip, Cledwyn Hughes. He was friendly with leading Welsh Liberals and acted as a messenger for Steel. On the 17th March, Hughes wrote to Callaghan saying that Steel much preferred Callaghan's leadership to a Tory election win:

> As a new leader and a young man he felt it would be impertinent for him to approach you and he was glad, therefore, to have the opportunity of giving me these views.[20]

With this initial contact made events began to move faster. Party Whips made contact with Steel. Cabinet Member, Bill Rodgers, started discussions on policy and Michael Foot, leader of the House, began to play a critical role in pulling things together. He was an odd choice to become deal maker, but after his failed leadership bid he had built a strong relationship with Callaghan and as the seasoned political observer John Cole notes the two men could appeal to different wings of the party:

> In the perilous life of the minority Labour government the two men's backgrounds complimented each other perfectly, for they appeal to different strands of opinion, within their own party and beyond.[21]

Towards Agreement

The urgency for some form of agreement became more intense when Thatcher decided the time was right to strike and tabled a no confidence motion in the government for Wednesday, 23rd March. Consequently, the weekend before involved frantic meetings for both Callaghan and Steel as each prepared their own positions for the debate. Callaghan spent much of the weekend at Chequers in conversation with fellow Cabinet members as to the approach they should take. The critical decision he took was to seek out Steel before the Liberal Parliamentary Party could meet on Monday. This deal was always going to depend on the two leaders, but the initial contact, according to Callaghan's Biography by Kenneth Morgan, was not good:

> The first manoeuvres were unpromising. Steel's initial letter to Callaghan setting out the Liberals terms infuriated the Prime Minister, who flung it angrily on the floor.[22]

Tom McNally, Callaghan's close aide at the time was not present, but finds this surprising and suggests it was more likely Callaghan was being a bit over-dramatic than really angry. Callaghan, despite his 'Sunny Jim' public image, was often prone to:

> fierce (though sometimes calculated) outbursts of anger when he was under great pressure.[23]

On Monday 21st, after returning from his weekly haircut at Simpson's on the Strand, Callaghan met Steel alone for the first time at 6 p.m. in the Prime Minister's Commons office. It was an important point for the future of both parties and immediately the two men were able to work together in a comfortable and easy way. Although Callaghan and Steel were not close at the time there had been a vague family connection when years before Callaghan stayed with Steel's father-in-law in Sierra Leone, West Africa. It seems this had been a helpful ice-breaker in their relations. The two of them had also come across one another in parliamentary debates and shared taxis on a number of occasions.

According to Kenneth Morgan's biography the meeting was friendly:

> Callaghan, much the older man, was warm, almost paternal, towards the boyish Liberal leader.[24]

Thirty years on Steel readily agrees that the relations were warm and sees the paternal connection, but prefers to describe the relationship as more like 'uncle and nephew'.[25]

Tom McNally, close aide to Callaghan at the time, is convinced that without this easy relationship the pact would not have been born. He believes the age difference helped rather than hindered and the two men quickly learned to respect each other and understand their respective party problems:

> I suppose necessity makes strange bedfellows, but it also makes it a lot easier if there is a personal chemistry between the main candidates. I never heard Jim say anything about Steel that was not of the highest calibre. He liked Steel, he trusted him and appreciated his difficulties.[26]

In his own biography, Callaghan describes Steel warmly as:

> A determined man, but one whom I found scrupulous in his dealings and always considerate in his understandings of the government's problems.[27]

This first meeting lasted for approximately an hour at which Callaghan laid out very clearly that he believed a defeat on a no confidence vote on Wednesday would mean an immediate election which would be bad for both his government and the Liberals. Steel, however, was equally determined to put across the view that he did not fear an election and that for him the issue was not saving a government, but saving the country from a period of economic instability. He wanted an agreement which was based around controlling inflation, solving the devolution problem and other policy initiatives.

In the hours following the meeting the Liberal leader moved quickly to consult and secure agreement throughout the country on the principles behind any agreement. Wisely using trusted figures he consulted with local parties and sought to reassure a party, always cynical of its leaders, that they would have a say. The feedback was very clear. Although most MPs and local parties had no desire for a quick election they preferred to face the voters than end up with a watered down deal with Labour. Amongst the Liberal MPs former leader Jo Grimond and former leadership candidate David Penhaligon opposed the proposed pact.

Grimond argued that the Liberals would find themselves in no man's land – neither a full opposition party, nor part of government. Along with Penhaligon he also felt that if Steel was to go down this path the very least that he should get was a firm promise on PR for the next euro elections.[28]

Bluntly, colleagues told Steel they would back a deal, but it had better be good. If Labour wanted to stay in power then they were going to have to give a great deal in return. In reality though, the initial list of demands from the Liberals seemed to be realistic rather than over demanding. The Liberal list had six demands:

1. Regular meetings between the two parties based on a consultative committee which would discuss bills, policy statements and white papers.

2. An immediate meeting between Denis Healy and John Pardoe so the economic teams could see if agreement could be reached on an economic strategy to control price and income increases and reduce individual tax levels. This was seen as critical to any pact.

3. The government will introduce and support a bill for direct elections to the European Parliament based on a proportional system.

4. A new attempt to introduce devolution with a free vote on PR systems.

5. The government would abolish plans to introduce a local government direct labour bill and any plans for nationalisation must be put on hold.

6. Finally, the agreement should be made public.

The six areas were discussed at a second meeting between Steel and Callaghan. This time McNally, Callaghan's advisor, was present, along with Foot. The thorny issue of PR was the major sticking point. Labour were unhappy at a commitment on changing the voting system for European elections. Callaghan described it as an 'animal of a very different colour, for the party was against it and so was I'.[29] It is not surprising that Callaghan was nervous about agreeing anything on PR. McNally recalls a conversation with Callaghan that shows how anxious he was about alienating his own party:

> I always remember Jim saying to me – you keep your distance from this (negotiations) – you have a long career in this party – they never forgave MacDonald you know.[30]

Time was not on the side of the two parties. Thatcher was busy working on her no confidence speech with a vote due the next day. Throughout the Tuesday evening various drafts and meetings took place until the early hours when Steel appeared to have accepted a verbal promise on PR rather than binding agreements. Steel argued that:

> It seemed a pity that our failure to agree this one issue should vitiate the prospects of everything else and plunge us into an election.[31]

Steel had been prepared to accept Callaghan's private word that if there was a Commons vote on PR he would back it. It seems a remarkable act of faith and a missed opportunity at the same time. After all the Prime Minister was on the ropes facing defeat in less than 24 hours, surely the Liberal leader should have held out for more?

By the Wednesday morning of the no confidence vote, Callaghan still had to win the support of the Cabinet. Ministers were phoned early in the morning to be told that a special Cabinet meeting would take place at 12.00 noon.

As the world's media looked on, Callaghan informed colleagues of the late night Liberal deal. Tony Benn's diary records the momentous moment:

Jim opened Cabinet absolutely red-faced – I have never seen him so red. It was strange; he was scarlet. Michael [Foot] was white and drawn.[32]

After discussing it for an hour, a vote was taken. Four members of Cabinet voted against – Benn, Peter Shore, Stan Orme and Bruce Millan – but Callaghan had the backing of the key players.

The Cabinet's big hitters all supported the pact with varying degrees of enthusiasm. Healey said the deal was better than a pact with "Nats and Nutters".[33]

Benn came close to being sacked over his objections, but in the end the pact agreement did not result in a single Cabinet resignation.

Callaghan travelled the short distance from Downing Street to parliament knowing he now had an ace up his sleeve as Thatcher prepared to open the no confidence debate.

It was left to Callaghan to announce to the House that the agreement had been made. Amid rowdy scenes Callaghan made an economic case for the agreement, but faced endless interruption from the opposition and, typically, Dennis Skinner MP on his own side who sought reassurance that the Liberals would not be treated better than the Labour backbenchers. The level of noise increased as Steel spoke, arguing again that the country's interests were served by stability not a third election in three years. In an attempt to show that the Liberals were prepared to side with whoever was in government in the national interest, he said the 1974 talks with Heath had been based on a similar desire for stability.[34]

There was considerable disquiet amongst Labour MPs at the agreement with the Liberals. Although they supported Callaghan in the no confidence vote, 45 of them signed a Motion saying they would not agree to any binding agreement with the Liberals. Callaghan had to issue a statement making it clear that there was no coalition and no election commitments had been broken.

Thatcher was caught unawares and the vote of no confidence was lost by 24 votes. Throughout this whole period, to Steel's surprise, she had not consulted the Liberals over the no confidence vote. Now it was lost she would never forgive him for saving Callaghan. The Liberals paid a heavy price during her early premiership; she did not talk to Steel, or offer his party peerages. In the end, Callaghan had survived and the Lib/Lab pact was born.

Down To Business

The day-to-day working of the pact was never going to be smooth. The Conservatives were becoming more confident by the day and they happily exploited the weakness between the Liberals and the government. For their part the Conservatives were dismissive of the pact. They saw it quite differently from any deal Heath would have formed with Thorpe. Lord Hailsham said:

> If that had been concluded at the beginning of a parliament when it was the duty of politicians to accept the verdict of the poll and to make it work it would have been different. That was Ted Heath's purpose after the election of 1974, but that is not what the Lib/Lab pact is for. It does not accept the verdict of a recent poll. Its whole purpose and affect is to prevent a poll, to put off a general election as long as possible to prevent the people expressing any opinion whatsoever.[35]

Morale amongst the Cabinet was low as they saw little prospect of a revival and the Liberal Party saw its poll rating slump at a period when its parliamentary influence was the highest in decades. Against these political pressures the economy was turbulent and proved to be the first real test of the pact. As ever when parties work together, personalities were the key and the Liberal's Economic Spokesman, John Pardoe, and Chancellor, Denis Healey, never hit it off. Healey recalls in *The Time of My Life*:

> It was never easy working with the Liberals since Steel was unable to control his flock. I found it particularly difficult working with their economic spokesman John Pardoe, he was robust and intelligent enough, but sometimes he was simply Denis Healey with no redeeming features.[36]

Given the significance of the pact and the economy, it speaks volumes that John Pardoe only gets this one unflattering mention in Healey's 600 page autobiography.

Writing in *The Times* on 11th April 1977, Lord Winstanley explained the two men's relationship:

> *The other day John Pardoe said that there are several terrible things in the world today and one of them is the prospect of a Tory government under Margaret Thatcher. Mr Healey is said to have added that another is the prospect of regular meetings with John Pardoe!*[37]

David Steel was mystified that the two men did not work together better, and that Healey was not more grateful. He believes that Healey had more to gain from the stability which the pact brought to the economy. Healey's reputation as Chancellor depended on the Liberals and he should have engaged in the process more positively.

> *It's a strange thing because Healey out of all of the Cabinet should have been the most grateful because we helped with the battle on inflation. It was a major achievement and we were supporting them, but Healey got niggled by Pardoe's demands and did not like sharing his views with others.*[38]

The budget was due less than a week after the no confidence vote. Its contents had been agreed before the formation of the pact so the Liberals had a nasty surprise when one of its measures was to introduce a five and a half pence increase in fuel tax. For Liberals representing rural constituencies this was, and remains today, a sensitive issue. The Liberals could not vote for a budget with this measure in it and the government could not survive if it was to have its budget defeated. Eventually the government backed down and the fuel increase was removed at the committee stage of the Finance Bill, but it was an early warning of just how fragile the agreement was. It also demonstrated that if Callaghan needed to, he could step in and get his Ministers to back down without too much difficulty. McNally believed that on most issues fear of an election was enough to get a compromise:

I do not think it was particularly difficult because they could do the numbers and they also knew that a general election would have been a disaster, so in that respect, it was low politics.[39]

In this task Callaghan had a powerful ally in Michael Foot, who emerged during this period as a surprising force for the pact. As leader of the House he played a critical role in the day-to-day workings between the parties:

Michael Foot was the man who gave the Lib Lab pact its essential dynamism, who chaired the key inter-party committees, who saw Steel regularly in one to one meetings, and who was in Steel's words 'the front man throughout'.[40]

Foot's support for the pact was in part because, as leader of the House, he saw it as his job to maintain a majority, but he also had sympathy for the Liberal tradition drawn from his roots in Wales.

Having survived the budget, the pact now faced its first electoral test a few days later with a parliamentary by-election in the safe Labour seat of Birmingham Stechford (on 31st March). It was a disaster. The Conservatives gained the seat from Labour with a massive fifteen per cent increase in their vote. The Liberals ended up being pushed into fourth place behind the National Front.

It was a severe blow for both pact parties. A *Times* leader commenting on the result blamed Liberal links with Labour as a reason for soft Conservative voters deserting the party:

A proportion of Liberal votes usually thought to be rather over half, consists of voters who would normally vote Conservative if there was no Liberal candidate in their constituency. If they vote Liberal now they are voting for the maintenance of the Labour government in office. Voters who want to get the government out cannot be expected to vote for Liberal candidates who will keep the government in.[41]

For a party that depended on the votes of those dissatisfied with a government to help it win by-elections this was to be a key problem with the pact.

Liberal activists were aware of the early problems and pressure mounted for a full-scale debate on the wisdom of the pact when delegates arrived at the Scottish Liberal annual conference in mid June. As with so many of these so-called make or break events, the debate passed off without much drama and in the end the pact received overwhelming endorsement.

As the summer recess approached, Liberal MPs began to consider if the pact should continue into the new parliamentary session. Although progress had been made on devolution, other achievements looked pretty weak. If the party was to fight an election on its record then some firm victories would be needed, but to pull out early would look like the pact had failed and hand virtual victory to the Tories. Pardoe argued that the economic situation may get better in the next twelve months and having taken some of the pain it would be worth waiting to be associated with the gain when it came. The economic arguments were key and the party agreed to work on a new list of measures for Callaghan to consider. Some built on the original six proposals, but new ideas on first time home buyer rates, reform of the Official Secrets Act and employee profit sharing were added. According to McNally, one of the problems for the Liberals was a lack of clear policy, ideas and demands. Callaghan would often have to instruct his Ministers to find some new policy initiatives, then privately give them to their Liberal opposite number as if to try and balance things out.

After the usual round of meetings and discussions the new agreement was set in place on July 27th, giving time for the two leaders to have a break before facing the autumn party conferences. In the event these and the subsequent Queen's Speech passed off without too much drama and the pact began to have the feel of everyday life. There were early signs of a turnaround in the economy and one opinion poll even showed the Tory lead down under five points.

Elusive Electoral Reform

By the run up to the end of 1977 things looked less rosy. The issue of PR for election to the European Parliament was coming to a head with a debate due in Westminster. Steel sought a clear commitment to reform from the Prime Minister. Callaghan said he would vote for it, but only in a free vote and not with a government recommendation. It resulted in one of the frostier meetings between the two men and the issue was to become a running sore throughout the period of the pact.

For the Liberals, PR has always been at the heart of any discussion on coalition. Although there is a reluctance to admit it, for fear of self-interest, it remains the biggest prize for a third party to gain when it has leverage. The 1977 pact negotiations had not touched on changing the voting system for Westminster, but instead Steel had argued for voting reform in the European elections and any Scottish Parliament. It was a limited ambition, but was still to prove impossible against the forces opposed to change. When the vote came, the pro PR lobby was defeated by 87 votes.

The result was a major blow to the Liberals and on the surface looked like the end of the pact. Closer inspection of the votes shows that the majority of Labour MPs support PR, a point Callaghan went to great lengths to point out. In fact, it was pro-PR Conservatives who felt they had to vote against electoral reform, as it was an opportunity to damage the pact. Callaghan felt he had kept his part of the bargain by delivering 146 MPs in favour. The Liberals were very upset, but despite his anger Steel was not going to take any dramatic action. When he went to face his angry MPs he played a trick to test the mood. Walking into the room he said, 'OK guys let's call a general election'. It quickly sobered them all up, particularly when Jo Grimond told them that to trigger, then to fight a general election over proportional representation would be 'bonkers'.[42]

Grimond's intervention made a big difference. Not only was he a much admired former leader, but as one of those who had opposed the pact, his support for Steel at this stage showed colleagues that loyalty was the order of the day. However much they disliked it, there had been a vote and the Liberals had lost.

What emerged in the next few days was the strong determination of Steel and Callaghan to keep the pact going despite growing opposition in their parties. Steel threatened to resign at a meeting of MPs and repeated the threat in a letter to candidates. In the wider party the issue had now come to a head and in typical Liberal fashion activists forced the leadership to hold a Special Assembly. Confined to Westminster, deals and alliances can be formed, but they are often viewed with enormous suspicion in the party at large. This was a very public make or break affair for Steel and the government. In effect 2,000 Liberal Party delegates were to decide the fate of not just their leader but the government. The date was set for January 22nd 1978; there was no downplaying the importance of the Special Assembly. Steel spent much of his Christmas break and New Year initially trying to stop the assembly and then plotting to win the vote. As is often the case, leader's speeches don't win conference votes, but activist heroes do. In the 1970s, Cyril Smith was just the figure Steel needed to call for unity and his intervention helped win the day by a resounding margin of over 3 to 1 in favour of leaving the parliamentary party to decide when the pact should end. With hindsight Steel told me he was rather glad the assembly took place as it gave him more authority.

Delaying The Election

The early start of 1978 saw continued speculation over when Callaghan would call an election. This clearly put the pact under strain as all sides agreed it would be difficult to move from pact to election without some kind of cooling-off period. There appears to have been no suggestion that the two parties should seek to come to an electoral arrangement by forming deals over candidates in key seats. If anything, Steel was determined that his party should appear independent at the election and he publicly left open the prospect of working with the Conservatives if the next parliament was hung. Privately though Steel dreaded the thought and told Callaghan that a small Tory majority was his recurring nightmare.[43] Steel had also come to the view that it would not be helpful for the Liberals to be seen helping an increasingly unpopular Labour government hang on to power. Throughout spring Steel raised ending the pact with the Prime Minister on a number of occasions and in early May he suggested an early announcement that the pact would finish at the end of the parliamentary session in July. Callaghan argued that the financial markets would react badly and preferred to wait and make the announcement in July itself. There was some discussion about extending the arrangement into the autumn parliamentary term.

Seeing the PM in a vulnerable position Steel threw in a suggestion that they would be prepared to carry on into 1979 if there were votes on PR for Scotland and a referendum on PR for Westminster. It was a bold suggestion but at such a late stage in parliament unlikely to have any success as time was running out for the Callaghan government.

According to a letter from Liberal MP, Russell Johnston, Steel's problem was not just lack of time, but lack of ideas:

The problem was that while both you and Callaghan considered it to be the sensible thing to go onto May/June 1979, he didn't know what to offer you and we did know what to ask him for.[44]

Meanwhile Pardoe and Healey continued to argue, this time over a new range of economic measures, the most difficult of which was a proposal to increase National Insurance contributions by 2.5 per cent. Despite weeks of discussion to find a compromise the two parties could not agree, and when it came to a vote it was only the Liberal's decision to abstain that saved the government. It was a very uncomfortable situation and showed the pact had entered its dying days. In the end there was no big dramatic end, just a couple of paragraphs in a press release issued by Alan Beith, the Liberal Chief Whip, on 3rd August 1978, announcing the arrangement was over.

As MPs left for the summer break most expected they would not return until after an October general election. When Callaghan gave a message to the nation in early September, the waiting media expected him to start the campaign. Instead he announced there would be no election and in doing so made one of the worst political judgments for decades.

Steel believed that the timing of the election was critical and if Callaghan had gone to the country in October, history would have looked more favourably on the pact. Instead the disastrous events of the winter of 1978 not only damaged Callaghan's reputation, but also dragged the Liberals down with him.

The decision to delay the election had not been taken lightly. The Cabinet was split on the issue of when to face the country and Callaghan had brooded over it for ages, according to Bob Worcester.[45] He never trusted the polls that showed he could win in October, believing that unpopularity in key Labour regions such as the West Midlands would defeat him. Callaghan, a cautious man by instinct, chose to wait and see.

Labour was to face a winter of unrest on all fronts with industrial problems, economic decline and without the Liberals to support them, ultimately parliamentary defeat. Eventually Thatcher got the no confidence vote she wanted, and on 28th March 1979, the Prime Minister was defeated by one vote, 311 to 310, with the Liberals voting to bring down the government. For the first time in 50 years a government had left office due to a defeat in the Commons.

Thatcher went on to win the election with a comfortable majority. The Liberals went from 14 to 11 MPs. Little did anyone imagine that Labour would have to wait 18 years before they would hold office again. The 1980s were to be dominated by Thatcher and the Labour Party went on to split with the launch of the SDP.

Was It Worth It?

The Lib/Lab pact was never going to be a formal coalition. This was a speedy agreement that had limited objectives. For Callaghan it was needed to remain in power; for the Liberals it was a chance to delay the election in a post Thorpe era when poll ratings were low.

There is no doubt in my view that Steel was right to try and avoid an early election. The memory of Thorpe and loss of reputation was going to take time to heal. Steel himself was a young leader and he needed time to build a profile and credibility. The pact gave him a high profile and the party was seen in a position of influence, not ridicule. It gave the party time to rebuild in the local constituencies and Westminster.

Time, however, was not the only factor. Popularity matters and the Liberals found their growing influence did not result in growing support. Instead they were dragged down by Labour's unpopularity, and blamed for keeping them in power. Steel acknowledges that he underestimated the criticism he would face:

> We were lambasted for simply keeping in office a government which had outstayed its welcome.[46]

The lesson for future deals seems very clear: supporting a failing government is unlikely to reap many rewards from the voters.

The by-elections and polls during the lifetime of the pact confirm this. There were three electoral problems for the party. They lost support from Liberal voters annoyed that they were keeping an unpopular government in place. Secondly, the third party normally benefits from anti-government votes, but they were now part of that government, and finally soft Conservatives were turned off fearing Liberals were closet socialists.

It was a triple whammy and positioning the party in these circumstances was very difficult. Steel tried to claim the Liberals helped curtail the extremes of Labour, but it was a tough message to get across.

Despite unpopularity at the polls, the Liberals can take some credit for the economic stability which began to occur during the period of the pact. Callaghan had inherited an inflation rate of 21 per cent, but by January 1978 inflation was down to single figures and at 9.9 per cent was at its lowest since the price explosion of October 1973 under the Heath government. The interest rates on home loans had gone from double figures down to 8.5 per cent and there were signs in the opinion polls that a feel good factor was beginning to emerge. The Liberals could also point to some specific policy successes as they had been able to influence government proposals on industrial democracy, reduce petrol tax levies by 5.5p and had pushed Labour into doing more to support small businesses.

However, these were not eye-catching issues and at the end of the day it was very difficult for the Liberals to point to tangible policy achievements which would capture the public imagination. As for Liberal activists, the failure to deliver on proportional representation for the European elections, or progress devolution were big disappointments.

So could Steel have pushed for more and used his influence to a greater extent?

There is no doubt that the government was on the ropes and Steel had the power to defeat it. In these circumstances you would have thought that his negotiating hand was stronger, but there was a game of double bluff being played and Callaghan knew very well that the young Liberal leader did not want to pull the trigger for an election. It was also going to be very hard for Callaghan to deliver on proportional representation and as the parliamentary vote on the issue showed without a Whip over 100 Labour MPs were against the change. Even if Callaghan had struck a deal with Steel, it is questionable that he could have delivered. McNally explains why PR was tough for Callaghan:

> When you then move onto the question of PR the Cabinet were less keen on the low politics in terms of surviving an election – on this issue when it came to discussions about Callaghan trying to get the

various policies on European elections through there was much more hostility[47]

There would have been some in his own party that would have preferred to have seen the government fall than make huge constitutional changes such as proportional representation. But why did Steel not push harder for these issues in negotiations, or even raise them?

McNally thinks that perhaps Steel could have pushed further, but acknowledges the difficulty:

Yes, on the issue of PR, I might make the only criticism of Steel. Could he have been tougher in his negotiations? I think he probably could, but even then there would have been those in the Labour Party who would have been happy to have taken the ship down with them rather than agree to PR.[48]

Steel argues that such fundamental constitutional change could not have been made as part of this pact. This was not similar to the situation that was to emerge in Scotland in 1999, where there had been a coalition agreed and a set of policies negotiated immediately after an election. This was an emergency situation, there had been very little planning and it was a pact born out of crisis rather than one born out of a general election. In those circumstances Steel did not feel he had either a strong enough hand, or enough time to put in place a proper coalition which could have included a deal on proportional representation. Steel said:

This was quite unlike a proper coalition, it was not after an election, nor was there time to prepare; this was arranged over a weekend with a vote of 'no confidence' quickly coming down the track. You did not have the space that Jim Wallace and Donald Dewar had in Scotland so it was not possible to negotiate. If I was going into a coalition I would have pushed much harder, but the circumstances here were different.[49]

This is a general problem with coalitions according to Roy Jenkins:

I think it does show that the middle of a parliament is a terribly difficult time in which to make a satisfactory arrangement. If an arrangement is going to be done try to do it at the beginning or perhaps don't do it at all.[50]

Steel also acknowledges some mistakes and miscalculations during the period:

> One miscalculation made was on the vote for PR for Europe. I had assumed that a 100 or so of the pro-electoral reform Conservatives would support us in that vote and that we could win, but because it had been part of the pact even these Conservatives felt bound to vote against it.[51]

It is all too easy to criticise Steel for missed opportunities and to look back on the Liberal pact as a failed adventure which dragged the party down due to the unpopularity of Callaghan after the winter of discontent. But the winter of discontent was not Steel's fault – the pact had ended by then and the timing of an election cannot be blamed on Steel; he had no influence over that. If the election had taken place in October the outcome could have been different and the legacy of the pact more positive. Steel believed that by October 1978 the public image of the pact was good and it would have worked to the party's advantage if there had been an election.

If things had gone to plan and Callaghan had called an election at the right time when the economic indicators were shifting, history could have looked even more favourably on the pact. It could have resulted in another Callaghan government and the possibility that another deal could have been made. Under those terms, Steel might have been able to negotiate a tougher package for the party to include Westminster PR.

But it was not to be, and Steel's hopes were dashed:

> As it turned out by the time the election did come, Labour was very unpopular and although the pact had finished some months earlier the Liberals ended up getting the blame. Having been what is regarded as an electoral advantage, the pact now became a heavy minus. I was initially buoyed up and confident that the pact would work well in a campaign for us, but all of this was to be dashed when Callaghan delayed the election.[52]

Steel is right with his analysis. In October many of the political cards were within the government's hands, they had experienced a good 15 month period of positive news, the regular banana skins that had disturbed the government had not taken place, Healey had began to turn the economy round and in the two year period when the pact was in place the government had moved from a period when they were sixteen per cent behind the Conservatives to one which showed them almost neck and neck. In these circumstances the Lib/Lab relationship would have been regarded as a major success.

For Callaghan the pact was a remarkable achievement for a man who had come to office unexpectedly and faced enormous difficulties. The economic situation was poor and his parliamentary majority was almost non-existent, but he had been able to survive and give himself a battling chance of remaining in power by forming an unusual and remarkable political alliance. It was very much his pact and his agreement. It is unthinkable that either Wilson or Healey could have ever entered into this kind of arrangement. He had a natural dignity and authority about him and his straight talking earned the respect of many around him. He was not a factional politician himself and was able to work easily with, and respect, Steel. In setting up the pact he gave away no real policy benefits to the Liberals. He did not undermine any Labour principles, but in return was able to keep his party in power. It was a remarkable achievement and if he had got the timing of the election right he could potentially have benefited at the polls.

McNally believes it was a significant achievement not just for Labour, but also for the country:

> I feel very strongly that if Britain had faced a general election in 1976 it would have been another election in less than three years and there would have been a lot of talk about is Britain governable. The truth is that the Lib/Lab pact gave the Labour government a chance to carry through quite a successful rescue of the British economy and restored credibility for not only Labour, but Britain in the international markets.[53]

Thirty years on David Steel looks back at the period with no regrets at all:

> I have no real regrets, we got a lot out of it. My only slight regret was that the one thing I had no control over was the time of the election. Could we have screwed more out for Liberal advantage? It would have been very difficult. Could we have benefited from a conference for PR? We would have been laughed at if that was what we gained. I never felt out of my depth, but certainly, yes, I felt shaky sometimes and went without sleep at the weekend because of the enormity of the decision that was being made.[54]

But it was a brave decision, a tough decision and the right one to take for the Liberals at that time. Similarly, Callaghan had done the right thing for Labour through his actions.

It is also a tribute to the two men that they were able to arrange this pact with dignity and honesty in very difficult circumstances. It was very much their arrangement, a pact between men not parties. As Steel told me:

> It's fair to describe it as a Steel/Callaghan pact – the Labour Party was not happy about it and the Liberals, as usual, were difficult and had to be cajoled along – it was always a battle.[55]

The question remaining though is if it was the right thing for the country. It helped give a period of economic stability and as McNally argues showed Britain was governable by avoiding a third quick election.

Kenneth Morgan agrees:

> It was a good thing for the country without doubt and enabled the government to pass very good measures and things had picked up from the darkest hours.[56]

But it also allowed the government to enter into the winter of discontent and the misery that that inflicted on people. It held back the fresh start that Britain needed. There is no doubt that by the 1978-79 parliament, Britain was getting ready for change. Thatcher was to bring a much needed reform and redirection to the country and, like it or not, clear leadership. Did the pact just delay that? Yes, in part, but that fresh start did not really begin until her post-Falklands phase in 1983. Her 1979 election campaign and the period that followed were just as unsettling as the Callaghan period before.

The pact did its job, nothing more, nothing less. It allowed a government to govern, and an economy to stabilise. For the Liberals, however, it was another missed opportunity to change the voting system. That prize remained elusive and it would be twenty years before the chance came again.

References

1. Liberal History Society Pamphlet

2. *Coalitions in British Politics*, David Butler, p.102

3. Tom McNally Interview, 29 January 2007

4. Jeremy Thorpe Interview, 2 May 2007

5. *Ibid.*

6. David Steel Interview, 27 February 2007

7. *In My Own Time*, Jeremy Thorpe

8. Jeremy Thorpe Interview, 2 May 2007

9. Lord Tyler Interview, 24 April 2007

10. *Ibid.*

11. *In My Own Time*, Jeremy Thorpe

12. Jeremy Thorpe Interview, 2 May 2007

13. *Ibid.*

14. David Steel Interview, 27 February 2007

15. *Edward Heath: A Biography*, John Campbell

16. *Ibid.*

17. David Steel Interview, 27 February 2007

18. *A House Divided*, David Steel

19. Speech to Liberal Party Assembly, David Steel

20. *Callaghan: A Life*, Kenneth O. Morgan, p.566

21. *As It Seemed To Me: Political Memoirs*, John Cole, p.170

22. *Callaghan: A Life*, Kenneth O. Morgan

23. *Ibid.*

24. *Ibid.*

25. David Steel Interview, 27 February 2007

26. Tom McNally Interview, 29 January 2007

27. *Time and Chance*, James Callaghan

28. *Jo Grimond: Towards the Sound of Gunfire*, Michael McManus

29. *Time and Chance*, James Callaghan

30. Tom McNally Interview, 29 January 2007

31. *A House Divided*, David Steel

32. Tony Benn Diary

33. *Callaghan: A Life*, Kenneth O. Morgan p.568

34. Hansard, 25 March 1977

35. *The Times*, 5 April 1977

36. *The Time of My Life*, Denis Healey

37. *The Times*, 11 April 1977

38. David Steel Interview, 27 February 2007

39. Tom McNally Interview, 29 January 2007

40. *Michael Foot: A Life*, Kenneth O. Morgan

41. *The Times*, April 1977

42. David Steel Interview, 27 February 2007

43. *Against Goliath*, David Steel

44. David Steel Papers

45. Bob Worcester Interview, 27 February 2007

46. David Steel Interview, 27 February 2007

47. Tom McNally Interview, 29 January 2007

48. *Ibid.*

49. David Steel Interview, 27 February 2007

50. Roy Jenkins, Liberal History Society Pamphlet (#49)

51. David Steel Interview, 27 February 2007

52. *Ibid.*

53. Tom McNally Interview, 29 January 2007

54. David Steel Interview, 27 February 2007

55. *Ibid.*

56. Kenneth Morgan Interview, 26 March 2007

7

Traffic Lights
And Jamaican Flags

Traffic Lights And Jamaican Flags

If you end up with a coalition government next time, well then we can both sit and cry together.

Marcello Pera, former Italian Speaker

Britain is unusual in Europe as it is one of the few countries that has single party rule. As we have seen in previous chapters coalitions are rare and occur at times of crisis, whereas for the rest of Europe power sharing is the norm. On the whole this is explained by the mainland European systems of proportional representation that have created multi-party politics.

Each and every country has its own peculiarities, but I was interested to see if there were common themes and lessons that Britain could learn from.

There are many questions that arise from the European models:

- How do politicians from opposing parties move from an election campaign to sitting round the same Cabinet table?

- What is the process for negotiating an agreement and how does it deal with policy differences?

- How are splits avoided on a day-to-day basis?

- What happens when an unexpected event takes place outside of the agreement document?

These are all process issues, but I also wanted to see if coalitions deliver good or bad government.

I decided to pick out three countries – Germany, Austria and Italy – to take a more detailed look at their recent coalition experiences.

Not So Grand A Coalition

Germany is no stranger to coalition governments and for much of its history various 'traffic light' combinations have been formed with the big parties on the left (Social Democratic Party or SPD) and right (Christian Democratic Union or CDU) arranging deals with the minority groups. Even by German standards nothing could really have prepared them for what was to take place on 18th September 2005. With just a few handfuls of votes separating the SPD and CDU the result ended up being disputed for days, until after eight weeks of negotiations the two big rivals finally ended up forming a Grand Coalition.

I don't think for a minute a similar arrangement could happen between Labour and Conservative, but I was interested to see just how this deal was brokered.

In the months before the election, Chancellor Gerhard Schroeder's SPD Party had been suffering from unpopularity and although there was little enthusiasm for his right wing opponent, Angela Merkel, most predicted she would win. Although her lead reduced during the campaign itself, few commentators predicted just how close the election would end up:

> When the exit polls began circulating pundits were amazed that while the margin had been shrinking most polls forecast a victory for the combined opposition of the Christian and Free Democrats. Even days before the vote they said the CDU would top 40%.[1]

When I spoke to the SPD Chief Whip, Olaf Scholz, he said his party was just as surprised:

> Many in the party didn't really think it could get into a winning position during the campaign and so they just did not expect that the result would end up as close as it was. They were very surprised when it was that close. Many thought we would lose, so to get a draw felt like a victory for us. There was an enormous amount of enthusiasm and that is why we claimed victory so quickly.[2]

In fact the results showed that the CDU had narrowly outperformed the SPD by less than a full percentage point, but had failed to win enough votes to command a majority. The tight result led to both sides claiming victory with Merkel and Schroeder moving swiftly to seek the Chancellorship. Merkel rightly pointed out that the CDU had gained more seats and votes at the election whilst Schroeder claimed that people had combined to vote for more of the left wing parties and, therefore, he and his party were best placed to take charge.

Both sides immediately set about trying to find partners amongst the smaller parties. It seemed initially plausible that a three-party coalition might be formed between the SPD, Free Democratic Party (FDP) and the Greens, the so-called 'traffic light' coalition based on party colours. This fizzled out when the FDP refused to work with Schroeder.

The other option was a "Jamaican style"[3] coalition of CDU, SPD and Greens, but there were just too many policy differences to be able to come together. Realistically there was never much chance that these talks would work because of various policy differences which had emerged over the previous years.

With other options running out, the prospect of a Grand Coalition between the SPD and CDU looked more serious and exploratory talks began a week after the election. In theory there were a number of areas where the two parties could find some common ground, particularly in relation to elements of tax cuts proposed by the SPD. There were, however, very different views on how health reform could be taken forward and on labour laws there were strong differences on how to deal with Germany's powerful trade unions. Policy issues though were secondary to the issue of personalities. Both Merkel and Schroeder publicly declared they would not enter a coalition while the other was in charge. Until one of them gave up their claim to the Chancellorship, the talks were in gridlock. This was difficult for Schroeder as he had been so wildly predicted to lose he now saw himself as the 'comeback kid' who had recovered incredibly during the election campaign. For him the close result was a moral victory and he needed time to come down from the high of the campaign. Eventually, by the 10th October he publicly relinquished his claim to the Chancellor's post saying that he would not play a role in any coalition agreement. His decision meant the talks could get underway in earnest. In reality the SPD did not believe they had a great claim to the Chancellorship anyway, but by denouncing it they gained enormous leverage in negotiations with the CDU on both policy and positions in the coalition.

From this point on, the coalition talks took another seven weeks to be completed. Despite this uncertainty, the media and public seemed very relaxed about the long delay. The media found the negotiations great cinema, and put very little pressure on the politicians to speed the process up. Similarly the voters did not seem particularly unperturbed by what was taking place. Such a delay would be unthinkable in British politics.

Speaking to Ludovic Seagal from *The Economist* who had observed this period in some detail, he believed that the general view of the public was that they just wanted their politicians to work together to resolve things and would allow time for that to take place.[4]

When I asked German born Gisela Stuart MP why the public were so relaxed, she said it was part history, part cultural:

> It has now become part of Germany's culture. They believe that if they can avoid attacking each other they can gain, but I think in part it is drawn from the history of conflict and being surrounded by neighbours who you need to get on with.[5]

The first big breakthrough in the negotiations came with an agreement to make cuts in the public budget in an effort to bring Germany back in line with EU stability growth rules. Other measures quickly followed on increasing VAT and the creation of a new higher tax band for high earners. The most controversial issues on health care reform were sidestepped during the discussions with a pledge to revisit them later on in the coalition's life. The SPD claimed they had won most of the negotiations, but looking at the detail, it seems that many of the policy areas they asked the CDU to drop had actually been unpopular CDU policies. In reality Merkel was able to throw away some unpopular issues and, at the same time, allow the SPD to claim victory for it.

By the end of November 2005, just as Merkel was ready to announce that negotiations were completed there were a couple of final twists. In the final days two high profile resignations took place; Franz Muntesering, the SPD Chairman, quit believing his authority had been undermined when he failed to be nominated as his own party's General Secretary. On the right of politics Edmund Stoiber, the CSU leader of Bavaria, announced he would not join the coalition, still bitter that he had failed to beat Merkel as leader of the German right. The coalition survived the resignations, but it showed just how volatile the political consensus was.

In mid November the three parties each held their own special congress to approve the coalition pact. There was very little resistance from party activists on both sides. The SPD members were still surprised at being in a position to share power and the CDU were delighted to have secured the Chancellorship for their leader. There were enough public wins for both sides to be able to sell it to their party activists.

The jury is still out on the Grand Coalition. Business and media leaders argue it is turning into a 'do nothing' government that will have very little long-term stability. They had hoped for more dynamic policy developments, but now think they are getting watered down policies that are not fit to tackle Germany's most pressing problems. An opinion poll at the end of 2006, showed that 78 per cent of Germans shared this concern. In May 2007, regional elections in Bremen gave the coalition leaders further food for thought. A Grand Coalition in Bremen's regional parliament ended up losing seats to the non-coalition parties with a big increase in votes to the Green and smaller parties on the left. Although the result was regional, most leading newspapers in Germany felt the coalition partner in Berlin should take careful note.

> The results could be taken straight from the grand coalition chapter of a political science text book. Rule one: small parties profit in the medium term from the numerical and actual dominance of the two parties in a grand coalition. Rule two: the smaller governing party usually fares worse than the bigger one.[6]

Much of the coalition's popularity depends on the success of Merkel. Although she has been disappointing on domestic reforms, her standing rose when she became EU President. As Seagal said:

> You only ever see Merkel on a red carpet and that has certainly increased her profile, but she still faces tough challenges over the economy, health care and taxation.[7]

I found the politicians I spoke to remained very positive about the coalition and felt it would survive, although mainly because nobody would want to break rank and bring it down. Both parties have a vested interest in being seen to do a good job now they find themselves in joint government. Scholz of the SPD summed up his party's view and said:

> Both parties can gain if the coalition makes a good job. We are not so concerned about making clear the difference between the parties.[8]

Privately, the SPD thinks it is only a matter of time before they will be able to form a coalition themselves. Given that there are more parties on the left of politics in Germany, the SPD hopes that at the next election they will be able to form a left-leaning alliance which gets them back into power.

Does Consensus Deliver?

There are a number of lessons to learn from Germany. The length of the coalition agreement is, in my view, a problem. The agreement they negotiated was for two years, but at the end of that period the coalition partners are either going to need to re-set priorities, or face a very long period of election campaigning. With key state elections taking place within this period, the coalition is going to come under enormous pressure unless it has a clear programme in place.

The second clear message was the level of trust and co-operation between the two parties.

When I visited the impressive new parliament building, the SPD's Whips office was directly above the CDU's Whips office. I was told they are regularly rushing up and down the stairs to have informal chats. Built into this is a weekly formal meeting between the Whips offices, and the political leaders have a regular breakfast meeting to iron out any potential coalition problems, but above all else what everybody told me was that trust is a key element to a good working coalition.

The third observation concerns policy. The German and British systems are very different. In Britain our political parties tend to fight from different and strongly held positions and one argument wins through. In Germany the more consensual approach means that ideas develop in debate and through co-operation.

This according to Stuart is fine during times of economic strength, but consensus, she argues, does not work if you need radical solutions during a crisis.

> *If you need a radical or a tough solution that could create losers, it's hard to maintain consensus.*[9]

I tend to agree that the approach to policy in the Grand Coalition is weak. The Merkel-led government has kicked health reform into the long grass and apart from German pride in her Presidency of Europe, is seen as underperforming.

Coalitions, however, formed between a larger party and smaller partner that share some ideological ground, can be more effective.

Given the closeness of the election result and the hostilities there have been between Merkel and Schroeder it is an incredible tribute to the German political system that they have been able to come together and create this coalition. Whether it is delivering a set of policies to tackle the country's problems remains in doubt, but what is unquestionable is the patience and skill shown during the negotiations. If anyone is in any doubt about how hard that would be, just imagine a similar situation being created between Gordon Brown and David Cameron – unthinkable in this country, but workable in Germany.

Political Waltz

When you consider Austria's chequered history over the last couple of centuries, often occupied against its wishes and certainly at the heart of many of Europe's conflicts, it's not surprising that politics today is all about reassurance. There is a desire for Austria to have a strong and peaceful role and a sense that the political leaders want to unite and bring together the country more than ever before. Austria has four key parties:

1. The Austrian People's Party

2. The Social Democratic Party

3. A Freedom Party

4. A Green Party

This multi-party system combined with a PR electoral system has created a long sustained period of coalition governments since the war. Many of these have been quite peculiar combinations with left, right and far right combining at various points. I found after talking to various people in Austria that the public were very supportive of the coalition approach preferring co-operation to conflict. It is hard to understand how a nation can be so positive towards coalitions, but when I met with the former Speaker of the House, Andreas Khol, he told me that Austrians tend:

To know the compromise before they see the conflict.[10]

On the whole this approach has kept politics fairly stable and avoided any major conflicts over the years. The systems which Austria has developed to deal with this have become well structured and coalitions are so common that there is a well-laid formula to deal with their creation.

Typically the process will take the following path. During the election campaign itself opponents tend to avoid strong personal attacks on each other and don't speculate over the shape of a future coalition.

Parties are nervous about pre-judging a situation before it has taken place. Memories go back to the 1970s when the People's Party indicated it would work with the Freedom Party after an election, but doing this cost them votes and boxed them in unnecessarily during the post-election discussions. Remarkably it seems the media does not push the parties on this point and tends to avoid trying to trick parties into setting out what their post-election strategies might be. After the election takes place there is no immediate clamour to settle the uncertainty as the previous government continues in a caretaker capacity. The caretaker approach allows space for negotiations and also permits the business of government to continue unaffected.

Based on the election result the various political leaders begin discussions and possible partners start to emerge. The prospective partners then set up a process of committees to examine policy areas. Typically in Austria there are around 10-12 committees involving over 200 people participating in the negotiations between the parties. The process is relatively open and party members, not just MPs, are involved. The committees will consider the various election manifestos and policy positions and try to condense them down to find some common ground. The whole process can take weeks and often becomes a matter for public discussion. Vienna, after all, is a small city and most of the opinion formers know each other. A quiet conversation in a restaurant is unlikely to remain private; politicians in Austria probably went to school with the waiter – it is that kind of city! Such simple protracted discussions would be unthinkable in the British Parliamentary system with leaks and pressure being put on the politicians. When the committees have concluded their work they produce a government plan between the coalition partners. This can be quite a comprehensive document: in early 2007 the Grand Coalition Plan ran to 180 pages. In effect this document becomes the equivalent of the Queen's Speech for the government, but is much more detailed and the product of hours of joint work. Depending on the quality of the negotiations that have taken place these documents can end up as a watered-down set of policies creating a fudge between the partners, or at best, a fusion of ideas resulting in creative new legislation. The document becomes the coalition's formal agreement and the parties involved will sign up to it.

The parties then move onto the more delicate issue of allocating ministerial posts. The parties divide the ministerial posts between themselves; it is then left to each party to decide which person they appoint. Rather than spreading posts amongst the government the coalition partners take on a department each. There is a danger that this leads to a grouping together of government departments run by different parties. To avoid this, co-ordination is important. If, for example, the SPD run the education department there is a real danger that they can diverge in an un-agreed direction from the People's Party without properly clearing the policy in advance with their coalition partner.

However, the Austrians have made some provision to deal with this weakness. There is a very robust weekly process to keep the coalition on track and deal with unexpected events.

The regular meetings involve coalition parties holding a Co-ordination Committee every Friday with representatives from the Whips office, the relevant Minister's office and the leader's office. They discuss the key issues and Ministerial plans for the week ahead. This meeting then reports every Tuesday to the Chancellor's breakfast meeting at which the Chancellor and his deputy (who comes from the coalition smaller party) then settle any disagreements. After this meeting has taken place, what insiders describe as the 'bazaar' follows, allowing final negotiations to take place before the government and Cabinet meets to ratify the week's business. The system works, but it is the element of trust which is so critical and as Khol told me:

> *Great friendships can build up between opponents and issues become a real sense of honour when it comes to keeping promises and commitments.*[11]

Late night drinks and suppers often seal these relationships and there seems to be very little problem with keeping personality disagreements out of the process. It is a remarkably friendly system which sometimes seems rather too cosy. I also felt the policy by committee approach led to bland policy initiatives, something Khol acknowledges:

> *Often some of the boldest ideas of the individual parties can end up in the long grass of the various committees set up to look at policy.*[12]

He believes this is worse when a Grand Coalition is established between the two biggest parties – it almost inevitably results in a fudge. A coalition which he describes as being 'big plus small' where a main party finds a smaller ally potentially sympathetic in terms of philosophy is much more likely to produce clear and ambitious policies.

I put this point to one of Vienna's leading academics, Professor Gerlich. He explained that whilst the Grand Coalition did struggle to develop bolder policies this was part of a growing tendency by the bigger parties to move closer together as they feared that the minor parties were becoming more extreme. It seems that forming a coalition with your known rival is preferable to an uncomfortable coalition with an extreme party that could require very difficult compromises.[13] By combining, the establishment can protect itself.

A counter view to this was put forward by a number of diplomats in Vienna. They believed that one of the dangers of the major parties coming together was that it would actually fuel support for extreme parties. They argued that when the far right and Haider had such success in Austria during the nineties it was because the Austrians were beginning to question the cosy coalition between the established political parties and were looking for a more exciting alternative. Haider's appeal, they claimed, was less about popular right-wing policies and more about a desire to shake up the party system.

Apologise First

The most recent election campaign of October 2006 did break slightly with tradition. All the opinion polls had shown the Austrian People's Party would get re-elected and so the SPD decided they had absolutely nothing to lose by throwing everything they could at the People's Party, including personal attacks. It was the most negative campaign Austria had seen for years. When the election results were in, to everyone's surprise, it was a virtual tie between the People's Party and the SPD. All of a sudden, the two parties found themselves round the table working together in very awkward circumstances given the tone of the campaign.

One of the pre-conditions for the talks was that the SPD had to make a public apology, but the damage had been done, bitterness had been created and, unlike previous coalition negotiations, this one dragged on for some time until early January of 2007. Despite the length of the negotiations, most of the political establishment still believed that some kind of agreement would be reached, but it required the President to step in and knock heads together as the talks were taking such a long time. Eventually he put a deadline in place for the conclusion of negotiations and a final agreement was made. Having a President to act as a referee in such circumstances seems very useful to me. Although it had a shaky political start, commentators expect this coalition to last three or four years, and that normal good relations will quickly resume.

As Professor Gerlich said:

> *The arguments will soon be forgotten. There is so much double talk between front stage and then backstage behaviour that soon after a drink of wine, good relations will resume.*[14]

It does seem that alcohol is often a feature of European political alliances. In Austria, after the lengthy negotiations have taken place it is the tradition that the Chancellor Elect offers his coalition partners a bottle of champagne to celebrate and the first to take a drink will be his deputy (leader of the coalition's junior partner). The drink seals what is an enormously important relationship for the coalition; the Chancellor and Vice Chancellor are at the heart of the process and their relationship is key to a successful coalition.

Whilst Austria has a pretty good system for beginning a coalition they seem unsure about how to end it. After the details of the coalition agreement become law the coalition can run out of ideas, face tricky events and then head into a rather long pre-election period as the parties begin to look ahead to the election campaign. This often gives the government a realistic life of between 18 months to two years in which to carry out any good work – a cycle that prevents strong policy development. As the day-to-day negotiated programme dries up there is a danger that the parties will look at any favourable lead opinion poll and be tempted to cut and run early.

In the current Grand Coalition it will be tempting for either the SPD or the People's Party to look at a poll which shows them ahead and suddenly try and abandon the coalition and trigger an election. This is a dangerous strategy as the Austrian electorate is unlikely to thank the party that causes an unnecessary trip to the ballot box, but it remains an ongoing tension in Austrian politics.

I found the Austrian system very pragmatic. It provides stability and the public on the whole seem comfortable with it, but the rise of the far right during the last decade was a warning shot that the cosy coalitions may need to be more dynamic in the future.

When In Rome

If you take 23 parties, keep changing the electoral system and add a little bit of corruption it's no surprise that Italy has had 53 governments in almost as many years. I cannot say that I would recommend the system to Britain, but it was certainly entertaining to find out more. I guess for a country that was originally made up of over 300 different states it is not surprising that so many regional political factions and splinter groups remain in place today. Everybody I spoke to knows the system is far from perfect and they all joke about its inadequacies, but in a strange kind of way it just seems to work for Italy.

When I spoke to the former Speaker of the Italian Parliament, Marcello Pera, he was very philosophical about the political system and the wheeler dealing that takes place. When I asked him what advice he could give British politicians he simply said:

> If you end up with a coalition government next time, well then we can both sit and cry together.[15]

Post-war Italian government can be split into two distinct phases; the pre- and post-1992 period.

Prior to 1992, the system of government lurched from crisis to crisis and governments would fall with alarming frequency. Just the slightest difference in policy could cause one of the minor coalition parties to bring the government down, or demand a change in Prime Minister in return for continued support. The situation was so volatile that if parties did particularly well in mid-term elections they would use that as an opportunity to renegotiate the coalition agreement, or find new partners.

When I spoke to Professor James Walston, an expert on Italian politics, he described the Italian politics of this whole period, 'as being one of constant shifting sands'.[16]

He likened political parties to cars at a red light; each party would edge forward bit by bit trying to gain a small advantage, but without any real progress.

The political party leaders' approach throughout the 1970 and 1980s was to look for an immediate advantage without any long-term gain and if that immediate advantage meant a change of government, well, so be it. Although this created an unstable period with many changes of government, these were not major events. A changed government would perhaps involve a new Cabinet or new Ministers, but in this quickly changing world most of the politicians actually remained the same and just waited for their turn to come round again.

Professor Walston described it as:

> a revolving door with the same people always just coming in and out of office on a regular basis.[17]

It was impossible for Italy to sustain such instability and in 1992 the system was reformed. There were several driving factors behind this:

- The corruption in Italian politics which had now been exposed made people realise that a new political order was needed.

- The country was facing a serious economic crisis and Italy's role in Europe and its ability to remain as part of the pre-runner to the euro were under threat.

- There was also concern that communism was rising in the country and extremism was using the political instability to grow.

The key political players decided to try and change the electoral system to see if it would create more political stability and transparency for the public. Until this point the electorate had very little involvement in the formation of a government; once voters had performed their ballot box duty, it would then be left to the politicians to interpret the results in a series of literally smoke-filled rooms and thus create a government of their own making. Despite constantly turning out at elections the public were starting to demand a more open process and to understand what their votes would deliver in terms of a government. From about this point on, the system in Italy changed so that coalition deals shifted from being created post-election to more upfront pre-election arrangements where parties shared a platform and the voters knew which party would enter into which coalition. This has created some stability and since the early 1990s two men and political groupings have dominated Italian politics. Berlusconi's centre-right party had the longest post-war government from 1992 to 1996; Prodi's centre-left coalition ruled from 1996 to 2001. Berlusconi then came back into power from 2001, until he lost the most recent and very close election to Prodi by just 0.1 per cent of the vote in 2006.

The two characters are very contrasting: Berlusconi is a colourful, larger than life, wealthy individual who travels around in a fleet of luxury cars and private jets; Prodi, whose nickname is 'la mortadella', named after a bland sausage, prefers public transport and is a less flamboyant leader. However, in their own different ways, what the two men have created is the nearest equivalent to a two-party political system, even though their governments have been based on complex coalitions.

The Prodi coalition of 2006 has been vulnerable from the start due to the narrowness of its victory and dependence on nine partners. This came to a head on the 22nd February 2007, when Prodi tendered his resignation following a parliamentary defeat on the issue of deployment of troops in Afghanistan and plans to expand US air bases in Italy. Like so many coalition collapses before it, within a week Prodi was able to renegotiate with his coalition partners and remained as Prime Minister, but it was another warning of just how fragile coalition government is in Italy. According to polls in the summer of 2007, only twenty-two per cent of Italians believe Prodi will remain in office for one or two years at the most. It is a worrying figure and shows just how little optimism the Italians have about the stability of their government.

I was keen to understand how the process worked in detail and, in particular, how coalitions can be formed in advance of an election giving the electorate a greater understanding of what might happen after their votes were cast. Certainly the upfront coalition seems to have given the Italian people much more confidence in their voting system. The two main coalition opponents had created logos and titles for their coalitions and produced manifestos that began to mirror a party political structure. However, deals and arrangements between the political parties still take place all the time, but are most intense in the days after an election when the relative power of each party is known.

The task of allocating ministerial jobs to match the votes of each party is so complex, the Italians have actually created a manual (the 'Chenchi Manual') to help assist with this. Chenchi was a former Senator who decided that instead of the regular horse trading between parties he would create a points system to signify which jobs were more important than others. For example, if an Education Minister's job was worth 10 points, and an Agriculture Minister's worth 5 points, these sums would be added up to see how many points each party should get to reflect the number of seats they held in the coalition. The system is even more complex as point allocations are given to non-government appointments. Nevertheless, the Chenchi Manual seems to have been a successful tool in allocating jobs between parties.

On the whole, the task is much simpler when a coalition is formed of one large party with several smaller ones. Obviously in these circumstances the larger party calls the shots and takes the top jobs, but problems arise when there is a tighter balance between the coalition parties. The current coalition had this problem as it is dominated by two main parties; the Centrist Margheritas and the left wing Democrats. This has made the job on policy negotiations much harder.

The problems don't stop once you have allocated the key jobs between the parties. The party leaders then have to tackle their own internal party problems. The coalition is by definition made up of a number of different parties, but the parties themselves can often be mini-coalitions.

If a coalition depends on just a small number of votes the individual MP's influence is much greater than a British backbench MP. One of the real problems for any coalition is not just the small parties, but a few maverick MPs within those parties that can flex their muscle at various times and create serious problems.

The small parties remain very powerful in Italy and there are endless examples of fringe groups holding the government to ransom, with little incentive to stop them. After all, if the Italian Pension Party secures 200,000 votes then its role is to battle pension rights and be pretty determined about it. Similarly many of the Catholic-based parties have a long tradition of bringing down coalitions. In 2006, the issue of gay marriage was causing problems for the Prodi administration and his Catholic partners, but in the past issues relating to divorce and abortion have also been major stumbling blocks.

There is very little that can be done to stop the tail wagging the dog in this way, but most of the coalitions that have happened in recent years have, at least, tried to tie in their partners to a document and a clear policy direction. Prodi sought to overcome this problem by tying his coalition partners into a long document before the election. Initially running to 1,000 pages, it set out most key election issues. After the election this became a 300 page document which is in effect the 'coalition bible' and Prodi regularly uses it to knock the heads together of troublesome partners, pointing out that they have signed up to it and should stick to it. Trying to lead a political party let alone a coalition must require enormous patience and for over a decade Prodi and Berlusconi have survived by spending hours negotiating agreements, making and keeping deals.

According to the former Speaker, Pera, this requires:

An ability to be very flexible, pragmatic and not too ideological.[18]

Looking to the future, opinions amongst the journalists and diplomats I spoke to are divided as to where Italian politics is heading. Some argue it is moving towards a more bipolar system of parties, creating two ruling blocks that will try and develop a political position and philosophy rather than a grouping of separate opinions. They point to the election of Prodi who actually stood to lead the coalition without being a member of any of the parties within it. He has sought to create a very strong brand for the coalition and put in place a structure for its partners to elect the next leader based on a system of primary elections within the coalition.

By April 2007, the two largest parties in the government had agreed to merge into a single force. The merger between the Democrats of the left and the Centrist Margheritas is further evidence of the move towards reducing the factions in Italian politics, but as ever in Italy nothing is simple and the new party has struggled to establish clear leadership and structures.

There is also evidence that once Berlusconi finally retires, the centre-right may carry out a similar kind of restructuring, but they seem to favour a more flexible federation of parties rather than a merging of the party system. In part this is due to the difficult question of the Northern League, who would be uncomfortable about merging their identity with other right wing parties.

Others I spoke to argued that this was just an unrealistic hope – the divisions between parties would be too great and that coalitions will remain – perhaps becoming more focused and branded, but still essentially a collection of differing opinions.

In my view the current system does not provide much stability, but it seems that the Italian voters are just as pragmatic as their leaders. Apart from the outcry at the corruption in the late 1980s, they have dutifully voted with high turnouts in a system which they know is far from perfect for Italy. Maybe this is because there is less dependency on governments in Italy with a set of strong social structures based on families, business and the community. You look after your own and, in effect, this makes Italy an easy country to govern, but there are signs that Italy is a stressed country in need of leadership more than ever before. The standard of living is not great, there is a housing shortage, a low birth rate and industrial problems. If a strong political movement were to come along which would give some leadership this could quickly become popular.

I think it is quite a dangerous time for Italy, with the recent Prodi collapse showing just how vulnerable their government is. Unless the Italian system experiences another shake-up similar to the one after the corruption scams of the 1980s, then maybe the Italian people's patience will finally run out.

Caretakers And Referees

I chose three countries to look at in Europe to see whether we could learn anything in relation to the way in which their coalition governments have operated. In fact there are many other examples. Over the last 20 years, Ireland, France, Austria, Finland, Norway, Denmark, Holland, Belgium, Luxembourg, Switzerland, and Portugal have all experienced some form of coalition. Beyond Europe, Israel, Canada, Australia and India have experienced their political parties coming together. It is fair to say that Britain is pretty unique in not having a coalition government.

There are a number of observations and lessons that can be learnt from Europe. The most notable is the relaxed way in which the public and media respond to power sharing.

In Germany, for example, despite an eight-week delay in forming the government, I found little evidence of public disquiet. This is in stark contrast to the British experience where the public expects to know who is going to be Prime Minister within hours of the polls closing. The British media would jump on every meeting giving politicians little space to negotiate.

The other big difference is the constitutional position in the rest of Europe. Each country has a set of written procedures to help assist with the coalition formation. They also have a monarch, President or Speaker to act as the honest broker. Britain is once again unique in not having the parliamentary equivalent of a referee to deal with a drawn result.

The European models also have a system in place to allow government to continue while negotiations take place. A caretaker government is established (normally the outgoing government) after the election to allow the business of government to continue while the new government is formed. America is perhaps the best known example of this, as the defeated or outgoing President remains in office for two months before the inauguration takes place.

In Germany, if urgent decisions are required during the caretaker period then the incumbent will discuss it with his most likely successor. This happened in October 1998, when outgoing Chancellor Kohl consulted Schroeder over the conflict in Bosnia.

When the coalition is formed there are several interesting factors. The duration of agreement is often unclear. I think this is unhelpful and falsely assumes that an agreement can last the life of a parliament. What tends to happen is that they run out of steam. Having achieved any aims, they don't have a system to set a new agenda, and just drift towards the next election. This is a recurring theme throughout some of the European coalitions. It seems to me, that the solution is to either have a long coalition agreement which will cover the period of a parliament, or to have a short one with a structure for renewing and refreshing it on a regular basis.

The Queen's Speech cycle we have in Britain helps us with this as there is a natural pace to parliament. The European model seems to set themselves two-year coalition agreements which fizzle out midway through a parliament and there is a real danger in Germany and Austria that this will happen again.

The content and detail of the agreement varies in length and quality. Ben Seyd in his study of European coalitions notes that:

> *The greater the uncertainty the contracting parties feel about the future, and the greater their mutual mistrust, the more likely they are to form a 'tight' agreement that binds each other through policy committees and procedural rules.*[19]

This coalition agreement forms the basis of day-to-day discipline within a coalition. In Italy, Prodi went to great lengths to get each party to sign a document and regularly refers back to the agreement to try and keep parties in order. This document alone is not enough to manage the arrangement. The European models often have coalition committees, in fact, Blondel and Muller-Rommel in their study of coalitions said:

> *This was better described as a Board of Management entrusted for a period by its Godfather (the parties forming the coalition) with the mission of conducting jointly the affairs of the state.*[20]

In the countries I visited these formal meetings only tell half the story. The key to a successful coalition is the relationship between a Prime Minister and his deputy and the powerhouse for this is driven by the various Whips offices. I was impressed with the easy relations and trust between the parties, in particular how differences were resolved over a glass of wine!

This is not uncommon in Britain. There was genuine trust between Callaghan/Steel and Ashdown/Blair and government Ministers will regularly brief their opposite numbers. There is, however, one big difference. In Britain the media created a tension that tested these relationships. The culture of leaks and off the record briefings is so established in Westminster that I can't see how fallouts would be avoided between coalition parties.

Another factor worth considering is how the junior partner is allocated jobs in the coalition. There are two different European models. Some, such as Austria, allocate a whole government department to one party. This has the advantage of clearly identifying a party to a policy area and allowing them to develop ideas.

The alternative is to spread ministerial posts around departments, often as deputy to the main party spokesman.

Whilst the first model helps the smaller party create a strong identity in one area, the second is my preference, as it puts the minority partner at the heart of every decision.

By far the biggest weakness across Europe is the way coalitions implement policy. There are two distinct problems:

1. Policy is agreed by committee and results in a compromise that is unimaginative and short-term.

2. When the differences involved are so far apart that the policies put forward tend to avoid the issues of the day and government runs on automatic without direction. The current Grand Coalition in Germany is testament to this.

There is one final observation that I rather enjoyed. The frequency of coalitions has created an array of jargon to describe the various alliances that can be formed. Based on the colours of the political parties you get "traffic light coalitions" with Liberals, Greens and parties of the left, or "Jamaican coalitions" involving the right, Greens and Liberals. I am not sure how this would translate in Britain; you tend to get a bit of a mess if you mix blue, yellow and red!

I was impressed with the politicians I met throughout Europe in their ability to create friendships, bonds and work pragmatically with other parties, but I was less impressed with their commitment and passion to political values and ideas. It all felt very cosy at times. Surely to get good policies and good government, you need strong opposition. To create ideas you need healthy debate and, at times, rigorous arguments. This is hard to achieve in countries where compromise and co-operation are the order of the day. However, the bottom line is that many of those European countries that have coalitions have been successful for their own people and they seem content to let it continue.

References

Germany

1. *The Economist*, 22 September 2005

2. Olaf Scholz Interview, 15 March 2007

3. Based on the party colours matching the Jamaican flag

4. Ludovic Seagal (*The Economist*) Interview, February 2007

5. Gisela Stuart MP Interview, 7 May 2007

6. *Frankfurter Allgemeine Zeitung*, 14 May 2007

7. Ludovic Seagal (*The Economist*) Interview, February 2007

8. Olaf Scholz Interview, 15 March 2007

9. Gisela Stuart MP Interview, 7 May 2007

Austria

10. Andreas Khol Interview, 23 January 2007

11. *Ibid.*

12. *Ibid.*

13. Professor Gerlich Interview, 23 January 2007

14. *Ibid.*

Italy

15. Marcello Pera (former Speaker in Italian Government), 8 February 2007

16. Professor Walston Interview, 8 February 2007

17. *Ibid.*

18.   Marcello Pera (former Speaker in Italian Government), 8 February
       2007

Conclusion

19.   *Coalition Government in Britain: Lessons from Overseas*, Ben Seyd

20.   *Governing Together: The Extent & Limits of Joint Decision Making
       in Western European Cabinets*, Jean Blondel & Ferdinand Müller-
       Rommel

8

The Coalition
That Never Was

The Coalition That Never Was

I have no doubts that he was genuine – he always said to me this is the most important thing I want to do – but it was never the next thing he wanted to do and he just lost the opportunity.[1]

Ashdown on Blair

The political instability of the 1970s ended when Margaret Thatcher came to power in the 1979 election. For the next decade big election majorities and a divided opposition combined to rule out any real prospect of pacts. Nevertheless, coalition discussions were still a feature of the political landscape as both Labour and the Liberal-SDP Alliance became more and more desperate to defeat the Conservatives. After three successive election defeats the opposition parties could see no way for the centre-left to get into power if they kept splitting the anti-Thatcher vote.

By the start of the 1990s, the Thatcher era began to draw to an end and the polls showed that the Tories were in serious crisis. There seemed a real opportunity for Neil Kinnock's Labour to win through this time, without the problem of a divided opposition as the Alliance bubble had burst and the newly created Liberal Democrats were down to single figures in the polls.

Faced with defeat, the Tories' ability to survive kicked in and Thatcher was replaced by John Major. All of a sudden the landscape had changed. The Conservatives had done the electorate's job for them and Kinnock was left looking in need of help if he was to become Prime Minister.

Trojan Horses

With the polls now showing the two main parties neck and neck, Liberal Democrat leader, Paddy Ashdown began a series of initiatives to plan for a hung parliament. He made it clear to Kinnock that he would be prepared to support a Labour government if it would deliver on proportional representation.

During the 1992 election campaign, the Tories sensed public unease about a hung parliament and hidden deals; they played the issue well and it caused problems for both Labour and the Lib Dems.

When Labour launched its manifesto, Kinnock and his deputy, Roy Hattersley, were hijacked about post-election deals. The issue was to drag on throughout the campaign, increasing in significance as the Liberal vote appeared to be rising. Major jumped on hung parliament discussions as a sign of his opponent's weakness, describing the Liberal Democrats as 'Kinnock's Trojan horse with yellow posters'.[2] He also denounced PR saying it had nothing to do with fair play, but was all about power play. It was a superb move by Major and resulted in Labour and the Liberal Democrats getting in a tangle on both hung parliaments and then the details of PR systems, rather than their key messages just days before the election. The Liberal Democrats were badly damaged as soft Conservative voters thinking of voting for them became nervous that in reality they were voting to help let Labour in. At the time I was standing for parliament in Watford and I remember seeing my posters literally come down in the last week as the voters sensed a deal between Ashdown and Kinnock. For Labour it looked like an admission of defeat. Newspapers talked about deals on seats in any new Cabinet and press conferences were dominated by very direct questions to Kinnock on coalitions. It was a disaster and the whole hung parliament issue played its part in Labour's failure to win in 1992.

Bob Worcester, founder of MORI, acknowledges the problem, although remains convinced that Kinnock's loud cheering at a rally in Sheffield was more to blame:

> There is no doubt in my mind that the election was lost at the Sheffield rally, but it is true to say that this image, combined with the prospect of deals over hung parliaments turned off many potential votes.[3]

In the end, against all the odds, Major won with a slim, but comfortable majority of 38 seats. Kinnock's dreams were shattered and he quickly and emotionally resigned to be replaced by John Smith. A fourth election victory for the Conservatives, unthinkable during the Thatcher downfall, had just turned into a reality. Liberal and Labour activists across the country had miserable early morning journeys home as count after count went against them. It was a memory they would never forget.

The 1992 election had a big impact on future discussions on hung parliaments. Firstly, it made politicians nervous of discussing it, and never again allowing an election to be dominated by the issue. Secondly, it showed the need for better preparation – Kinnock and Ashdown had had no real dialogue before on how to handle the subject and finally the bitter taste of defeat made those involved determined that the next election would not slip away from them. Everything must be done to avoid a fifth defeat.

That said, Ashdown was glad there had not been a hung parliament:

> *I was pleased there was not a hung parliament. It would have been a nightmare as the only option would have been to support a Kinnock government that was still dominated by the unions; it would have been very uncomfortable. If Major had lost and Kinnock won, I think Labour would have been destroyed.*[4]

Tony Changes Everything

In the first half of 1994, two events were to trigger a change in relations between the Liberals and Labour.

By the spring of 1994, Ashdown had come to the conclusion that the Liberals should end the position of maintaining equal distance between the other two parties – known in Ashdown circles as equidistance. This private decision was the first key step towards closer relations with Labour.

Ashdown wanted to reposition the party, moving it towards a Blair agenda, but before Tony Blair existed. He felt that the best prospect for the party was to move into territory that Kinnock and now Smith could not capture. His plan was to push ahead and try and create a progressive Liberal force that would leave Smith's old Labour looking behind the times.

Then on Thursday 12th May 1994, Westminster was numbed by the sudden death of John Smith. Its emotional impact was enormous, but by the end of the day the political impact was sinking in. Ashdown wrote to Blair that night urging him to stand:

> *you are mad if you don't and the Labour Party is mad if they don't elect you.*[5]

He did, they did and so began a relationship between Ashdown and Blair that had potential to realign politics for a generation. It was also the point at which Ashdown had to rethink his strategy:

> *The moment Smith died I knew that there was no way I could win against the Blair bandwagon and take that political ground for us and*

that the new name of the game was to create a partnership to win the ground. I could sense at the next election we could not afford to not be part of the forces bringing about change. The tidal wave was coming; we had to be part of it.[6]

By late 1994, Ashdown and Blair had started informal discussions on how they could avoid the mistakes of 1992 and ensure that progressive politics won the next election. Personal chemistry, so often the key in these situations, was good from the start. Along with Cherie Blair and Jane Ashdown, the four arranged to meet and eat on a regular basis at each other's houses. Fuelled by wine and late night discussion the two leaders' discussions went far beyond what either of their parties would have imagined or agreed to.

I have often wondered why Blair was so keen to take part. He was certainly out to change the image of the Labour Party, his stand on Clause 4 had shown that, but by showing that he would engage with a Liberal centre party it was another strong signal that the left's influence on his party was over.

As Clare Short told me, his discussions with Ashdown were part of this repositioning:

It was important for him to do things that moved him away from the old Labour position.[7]

Blair became attracted to the idea of bringing about a progressive left of centre realignment during the summer after his election as leader. Ashdown was obviously key to this, but the role Roy Jenkins was to play was important and in doing so completed a rather tidy political circle. Jenkins' role in splitting Labour in the early 1980s when he helped establish the SDP had made him a hate figure for many in Labour circles. If Blair could win him over it would be a healing of divisions and send the strongest message that Labour was once again a party ready for government.

Ashdown told me that Jenkins influenced them both, but in different ways:

Jenkins was a paterfamilias for me – he did not invest me with a philosophical cause, I had that anyway, but he was the resource I turned to for wise advice and he would support me if I needed heavy weight support.[8]

For Blair, Ashdown believes Jenkins was more important:

For Blair, Jenkins was very different. He was the key to open the door to a new kind of centre-left politics. Jenkins was Blair's connection with the philosophical Liberal base of 1910 and this was his man of history brought into his living room.[9]

For his part Jenkins saw Blair as the best chance of killing the Labour left and creating a progressive Labour Party now the Liberal-SDP Alliance had failed. In 2001, Jenkins wrote:

One of the discussions which gave me great hope, in politics generally and in Tony Blair personally, was that we were both thinking in the same terms about healing the split on the centre-left and making the 21st century, in contrast with the essentially Conservative 20th century, a 'progressive century'.[10]

By mid 1994, a series of regular meetings began between the two leaders and both Jenkins and Ashdown felt able to trust Blair, believing he was genuine in wanting to co-operate. Blair may have been sincere about the progressive agenda but it's hard to believe he did not have a more practical incentive for talking. If the election was narrow then good relations with the Liberals would help in any negotiations – even if Blair had a majority of 40 he may still have needed Liberal votes unless he was to be beholden to his party's left-wing MPs.

What is surprising during this period is the depth of discussion that took place. Rather than focusing on likely election outcomes and possible pacts, the two men engaged in a fantasy game of 'what ifs' that even went into the prospect of a full open partnership not dependent on a small Labour majority. It was the kind of arrangement that fell short of a merger, but would have tied the two parties together. The two men were running way ahead of not only their parties, but also both their inner circles. As the private groups surrounding the men urged caution it was Roy Jenkins, beholden to no one, who pushed them down the realignment route. He saw the prospect of a new progressive movement that could stop the Tories from gaining power for years.

Outside these three men there can't have been many that saw this as realistic, but hours were spent on memos and position papers on just this prospect.

By early summer 1995, the meetings were becoming more formal and involved a wider circle. Robin Cook for Labour and Bob McLennan for the Liberals were to be given the key task of working up more detailed proposals on constitutional issues, in particular the tricky issue of PR. Even at this stage the media had little notion of the depth of the discussions. That was soon to change.

Having moved from private discussion to inner circle teams it was now time for wider debate amongst the two sets of MPs. Ashdown brought his plans to the regular Wednesday Parliamentary Party meeting on 10th May 1994, and described it as the worst meeting he had ever experienced. Ashdown has a habit of making every decision the most important there has ever been, but he was clearly irritated by the negative response he received and in his diaries says:

> I told the party bluntly that if you want a leader who will argue the myth of equidistance at the next election, it can't be me. You'll have to get someone else to do it.[11]

Ashdown told me that he regularly got frustrated with colleagues, but that some of this was his own fault:

> If I was to be brutally honest, I would say the problems were of my own making and by the way so were Blair's. The difficulty with both of us and why we had difficulty carrying our parties was because neither of us are of our party – we are both outsiders. That meant we did not have the natural instincts to touch the party in its erogenous zones if we wanted to get something done.[12]

It was not the last time he would have to threaten to resign in his determination to build a new relationship with Blair.

The 'project', as it was known, was in full operation by the conference season of 1995. Cook and McLennan had started work. Ashdown and Blair met regularly and Jenkins was still meeting with both men. As discussions speeded up they also became more focused on the issue of PR. Jenkins pushed this hard, believing that only if Blair would accept it would real progress be made, regarding it as the nuts and bolts of any new realignment. He felt that Blair was moving intellectually towards the argument behind changing the election system – although Ashdown recalls that Blair said he had serious intellectual reservations about it. The mixed messages are not surprising. It's unlikely that Blair would agree to anything based on belief alone. His calculation would assess the dangers of splitting the Labour Party on the issue and the negative impact such a move would have from a media that was warming to him. Blair was already taking a risk in developing cosy relations with the Liberals. To announce support for PR would have thrown his party into an internal row and lost him the support of *The Sun* at a time when all systems were ready for a general election. There was also little support within his party; of those in Shadow Cabinet only Cook expressed any real enthusiasm for PR.

The project was in danger of getting stuck on the issue of PR as Blair's reluctance to commit himself continued throughout 1996. Sensing Blair was going cold, Jenkins sent the young Labour leader off to Tuscany with a range of history books to convince him of the need to create a radical centre force in politics.[13]

By the start of 1997, with the election now months away, Blair appeared to cool on talks and the prospect of co-operation. The polls told him it was unlikely he would need the Liberals and his mind was focused on more important things. Jenkins sensed this when they had dinner on 19th January at Blair's house in Islington. It was as if reality had finally struck Blair and with victory so close there was little point in risking anything.

Ashdown recalls how Jenkins described the problem:

> *Roy Jenkins described Blair as somebody whose job it was to carry a very fragile crystal bowl from point A to B across a very slippery floor and arrive without dropping it. The crystal bowl was victory and Blair knew he had it in his hands and did not want to drop it.*[14]

Landslide

By late March the Major government finally ran out of time and an election was called for 1st May 1997. Although the prospect of any post-election arrangement looked unlikely, it did not stop the two parties working together informally during the campaign. What the Lib Dems described internally as "the two against one plan", involved daily conversations between campaign HQs to discuss messages and ways to keep the attack focused on the Conservatives, not each other.

In the end the result was remarkable – Blair was swept to power with a majority of 179. Election records were broken all over the place and all thoughts of a hung parliament had disappeared. It was a personal triumph for Blair, but Ashdown too, had reason to celebrate. With 46 MPs, his own party had achieved the highest tally since 1929. In the early hours after the election the new Prime Minister sought Ashdown out. Tom McNally, a veteran of the Callaghan Lib/Lab pact, now a Liberal Democrat Peer, recalls this story:

> When I was in Downing Street on the morning after the 1997 election doing an interview for the BBC I got a message to see Paddy straight away. I asked why and he said, 'I had a call from Blair and he says the project is still on.' I have always thought it amazing that in the most fantastic 24 hours of his life Blair called Paddy and, of course, even then I thought, well how the hell can the project still be on?[15]

In their early conversations after polling day there was no talk of any places in the Cabinet for the Liberals, or any need to have a coalition. The size of victory had made even the most ardent project supporter rule that out.

However, rather than turn his back on the Liberals after the election, Blair was keen to find new ways to keep the project alive. It became typical of his first term that he preferred a big tent approach to politics, trying to involve rather than alienate people.

It is hard to understand why a new Prime Minister with a massive mandate was still prepared to put so much energy into talking to the third party. David Steel believes the two men had just got so used to talking that they carried on:

> The truth is that Paddy and Blair got on well and enjoyed the planning – despite the fact that it was unwanted, unneeded and a distraction.[16]

If he had been as passionate about electoral and constitutional reform you could understand it, but Blair was not especially interested in these issues. It seems to come down to personality – Blair hates to disappoint and Ashdown had, along with Jenkins, created a strong bond that was going to be hard to break.

Jenkins remained committed to bringing the two parties together and following post-election discussions with Blair reported back to Ashdown that it was still Blair's intention to have the Lib Dems in government within months of the election. Even Ashdown with his endless enthusiasm for the project felt this was an optimistic assessment, but was still determined to stick out for PR. David Laws, the Party's Senior Policy Advisor at the time, explained why Ashdown stuck with it:

> the size of the prize of PR was just too much for Ashdown to give up, and there was frankly no real alternative to get PR than via more talks.[17]

In a memo to Blair he set out how co-operating could work and appeared to soften the Westminster PR demand with a bid for PR in the 1999 European elections as an act of good faith instead.[18]

A few days after the memo the two men had their first meeting after the election and Ashdown set out his desire to continue with the project and described the party's overall position, which 'will be one of constructive opposition and partnership where possible'.[19]

They met again a week later on 15th May and in his diaries Ashdown claims that Blair said he was still keen on merger. Ashdown meanwhile pushed hard on a need to change the voting system before any merger, or realignment could take place. Both seemed to agree on one common objective; to keep the Tories out of power for ten years. As the meeting ended Blair raised the idea of a single Cabinet Committee being established between senior party figures, which would allow wide ranging discussion to take place. And so the Joint Cabinet Committee (JCC) was born.

Liberals At Downing Street

The JCC became part of the day-to-day language for the Liberal Democrats and it was to dominate much of Ashdown's final two years of leadership. Along with the Cook/Maclennan talks on constitutional reform it proved the closest that the two parties ever got to any form of pact.

The beginnings of the JCC were controversial. Ashdown took Blair's suggestions for JCC to his regular 'Jo group' (the nickname for his inner circle), but senior party figures such as Maclennan and Chris Rennard were both hostile to the idea. Maclennan felt that it was taking the party in too deep with Labour and Rennard was concerned about the possible loss of identity for the party.

Nevertheless, the JCC began on the strict understanding that its work was limited to constitutional issues and a vehicle for any bilateral discussions that might happen between Labour Ministers and their Lib Dem Shadows. The formal announcement about establishing the JCC took place on the 22nd July. Despite the months of preparations it took party colleagues by surprise and even those MPs close to Ashdown, such as Malcolm Bruce and Matthew Taylor, went up the wall. A similar response happened when Paddy took it to the Parliamentary Party meeting later in the day. It wasn't so much the issue of the JCC that annoyed colleagues, but the fact that the announcement was made before they had been told; MPs rightly felt bounced into it.

It was a full three months before the Committee first met, and unlike previous visits to Downing Street this was very public. There was a photocall outside number 10 as Alan Beith, Bob Maclennan, Richard Holmes and Menzies Campbell all arrived. The press was allowed in to take shots around the Cabinet table and, for the first time in decades, Liberals found themselves at the heart of the government. Meetings continued to take place throughout the remainder of the year without much press interest. Ashdown's parliamentary colleagues were, however, very interested, waiting for his reports each week to find out what exactly had been discussed at the JCC. In reality, as Ashdown's detailed diaries now show, most key discussions took place at either planned or impromptu meetings with just Blair and Ashdown. One such occasion took place at the end of the handing over of Hong Kong to China. The two leaders were able to have a considerably long discussion over the issue of PR for Westminster walking round the airplane on the tarmac at an airport stopover.

Most weeks Ashdown seemed to keep sending letters and memos to Blair. The following was typical:

> One of the advantages of not being in government is that you have time to think – I have come to the conclusion that we may be missing the great opportunity for which we have both worked these last years.[20]

I think this particular letter shows that Ashdown was starting to get frustrated and his mood was shifting. Meanwhile Blair was now in the throws of leading a nation and the amount of time and interest he had was dwindling.

Each week as he met his Parliamentary Party, Ashdown seemed to grow more restless with those colleagues who questioned his strategy. There was a real danger of losing control of his own party as he continued to plug on with the project and JCC. Senior aides to Ashdown all warned him that it could end his leadership. Perhaps he wanted that? Perhaps he was deeply disappointed that there had not been a hung parliament?

David Steel, at the time deputy leader in the Lords, observed the unrest amongst colleagues as he attended meetings:

> *I was always slightly unhappy about the lengths that Ashdown was going to. I could see the restlessness in the Parliamentary Party and Ashdown's authority ebbing away.*[21]

Even those who were keen on the project had their doubts. McNally was a trusted ally of Ashdown. He recalls the mood each time Ashdown reported back on his and Blair's conversations.

> *I used to sit in Paddy's office where he would come back to kind of debrief us and we could not believe it. Some would say no, some would say this can't be true, but on the other hand most of us just thought well let's see how far this would run.*[22]

It's hard to work out the motives of the two men. Blair seems to blow hot and cold. At his most enthusiastic he still wanted to work for a full merger. Ashdown seemed less interested in a merger but described a partnership agreement for ten years based on PR and creating an arrangement that would keep the Conservatives from power.

At its most simplistic it seemed to boil down to Blair offering PR in return for the Liberals merging with Labour. Ashdown would not agree to a merger as his party would be swallowed up by Labour, but he couldn't get Blair to commit to PR and joint working. It was gridlock.

Throughout the summer of 1997, Blair kept delaying on PR and in June revealed his true concerns in a frank conversation recalled in *The Ashdown Diaries*, which gets to the heart of his doubts:

> *TB: If I give you PR, here's what my people say the last general election result would have been: we would have had an overall Commons majority of only nine seats, and you would have had a total of 146. Under those circumstances, why shouldn't you break away*

and return to equidistance? We would be tripling your seats and creating the very conditions under which we could not rely on you should things get difficult.

PA: I don't understand why this whole issue is up for review again. I thought we had already sorted this out. Are you now saying that PR itself is in question? If you are, then we shouldn't go ahead, even with the Cabinet committee, until we have sorted it out. You ask what's in it for you. Well, exactly what's always been in it for you. The absolute certainty of having a second term, and of keeping the Tories out for ten years. I thought you and I had agreed that that's what we wanted to do.

TB: But can I be sure of that? It might provide you with the opportunity to part company with us after the next election, if that was held under PR. In short, I believe that the only answer now is merger. It's the only way I can be certain that you are locked in with us for the long term.

PA: I have said this to you before and I will say it again: I am not prepared to contemplate a merger. And even if I were, I could not get it past my party, so I won't even try.[23]

By early 1998, most meetings of the Liberal Parliamentary Party were dominated by talk of the project. There was an obsession amongst some MPs over the subject as they wanted to know how many times Blair and Ashdown met and the detail of all the meetings. Ashdown was constantly on the back foot as he gave his weekly leader's report at the Wednesday night meetings. You could see the look of despair come across his face if Jackie Ballard or David Rendel, two left-leaning MPs, put their hands up to speak on the subject. Most MPs fell into one of three camps on the issue. Those pro-Ashdown and part of the inner circle were keen that the talks continued although they were not sure where it would end. Those firmly opposed, wanting an independent party, were annoyed at the secrecy and deeply mistrustful of Ashdown. A third group – by far the largest – were more interested in getting focus leaflets delivered to ensure they got re-elected and as long as Ashdown was not costing votes by talking to Blair they would watch with marginal interest. I got rather frustrated at the endless time wasted on the issue, but was firmly in the Ashdown camp believing he was right to continue with the project. After all his leadership had delivered a large number of seats, mine included, and when I looked at those who argued for the JCC they were on the more sound wing of the party in my judgement. It's also important to remember that at the time Blair was unstoppable, riding high in the polls, certainly heading for a second term and not yet as worryingly illiberal as he was to become. So there was appeal in hanging onto the shirt tails of such a popular Prime Minister. However, I had no idea at the time just how grand Ashdown's true plans were.

The Full Monty

His diaries during this year show that the JCC was just the tip of the iceberg and the real agenda was not just electoral reform, but what Ashdown's team called the Full Monty; involving two Lib Dems in the Cabinet and moves towards a merger.

Steel was surprised at just how far Ashdown was prepared to go.

> I thought I was a bit out in front of the party, but he was miles out in front.[24]

The discussions on changing the voting system dragged on and on until it was agreed to establish an electoral reform commission to be headed up by Roy Jenkins. This was to be Jenkins' last big political job. After such a distinguished career it's sad that Jenkins was to be used by Blair in this non-job which ended in a set of proposals left to gather dust.

It was clear to those involved that the Commission's work would take some time to complete and even if it were to get Blair's endorsement and parliamentary time there was little prospect of a new voting system at the next election. Ashdown was aware that without PR he had to help protect his new clutch of MPs and win yet more. Part of the Blair discussions involved very private work on how the two parties could help in a cluster of seats where the Labour vote could make the difference to a Lib Dem victory.

The latter was never grand enough to be described as a pre-election electoral pact, but there was little doubt amongst the two sides that they would keep in close contact about seats and tactics. The "two against one" strategy had worked at the last election and there seemed little point in abandoning it for full out war between the parties. Lord Razzall, the party's election chief under Ashdown and Charles Kennedy, always argued that the Lib Dems could not deal with the fire that the Labour Millbank machine could turn on the party.

But there was a problem in this strategy, illustrated well in a seat like mine in Winchester; I had won by just two votes in the May 1997 election and went on to face a rerun in a November by-election. Of course with such a slim majority the 6,000 or so Labour votes would make a big difference if they backed me. I was, however, alarmed at any discussion of asking Labour about backing off, or tactical voting. My slim majority was full of soft Conservative voters who would be furious to think I was just part of some Lib/Lab agreement. For every Labour vote gained it was my judgement that you would lose a couple of Tories if such an arrangement took place. Other colleagues were increasingly concerned that the JCC work was becoming more public and about the impact this would have on soft Tory votes.

Despite this, it was Ashdown's view that it was worthwhile sticking with the JCC. It was, in his opinion, delivering things the party wanted on freedom of information and devolution in Scotland and Wales. While Blair remained popular, Ashdown believed joint working would not damage the party's support in the country.

It was not just Lib Dems MPs that were growing restless with the talks. Deputy Labour leader, John Prescott had no time for other parties let alone deals with Liberals. He and fellow Cabinet Ministers, Frank Dobson and Margaret Beckett could not understand what Blair was playing at and were determined that the talks would remain as talks and nothing else. Enemies of the project regularly briefed the media. This in *The Express* was typical:

> *MPs close to Mr Prescott say he has 90% of the parliamentary Labour party on his side in his battle to bring a halt to the growing Lib/Lab love-in and, therefore, effectively holds a veto over Mr Blair.*[25]

In the end it was the failure to deliver on PR and the government's response to the Jenkins' Commission that was probably the final nail in the coffin for the project and the end of Ashdown's energy to lead the party. As Ashdown told me:

I can tell you the moment this thing became impossible to do and it was the day Jack Straw went on to Newsnight and rubbished the Jenkins review.[26]

Beginning Of The End

Jenkins had concluded his Commission work on changing the electoral system in the autumn. It had taken Labour some time to respond, when they eventually did, it was a clumsy effort that publicly embarrassed Ashdown.

Jack Straw was interviewed on *Newsnight* and dismissed the Commission's findings in what Ashdown describes as a hatchet job. Ashdown went to bed contemplating resignation within the week.

The following day, 30th October 1998, Ashdown used some of his strongest language with Blair:

It's always us who put the propositions to you. Then you and I agree how to go forward. Then at the last moment, it's discovered you can't. Then we, never you, go off and find a different way to keep the project on track and the whole depressing cycle starts over again. Frankly I don't know how long we can keep doing this and anyway I am not sure it's worth doing at all if it falls flat on it's face again.[27]

Perhaps this forced a guilty Blair into action, as over the next few weeks progress was made. It was to be a false dawn, but gave Ashdown a chance to get a very public pledge for joint working from Blair within a few weeks. They agreed on a joint declaration that actually expanded the work of the JCC, but it did not contain a single pledge on the timing of electoral reform. The document was released on Wednesday 11th November to an astonished Westminster. Having been humiliated on the Jenkins review just two weeks ago, Ashdown was now pushing on further with his project. It was hard for many colleagues to understand what was going on, but yet again Ashdown won the backing of his Parliamentary Party – even though, in his own words, he had tested everyone to the limit.

Paul Tyler, then Liberal Chief Whip, argues that Ashdown found it hard to admit the project had failed:

It was not easy for Paddy to go to the MPs and say "I think I may have been hoodwinked", and as it was the only act in town, and not doing any harm, he kept it going.[28]

Labour MPs were just as amazed at the joint declaration. It had been kept very secret and Westminster was astonished at the initiative. Clare Short told me there had never been any discussion or reference to it at Cabinet. Speculation on why Blair had signed focused on two theories. The commonly held view was that it gave Ashdown a lifeline after the humiliation over Jenkins. Others saw it as Blair wanting to keep his options open until the next election. As one Labour official said at the time:

You don't buy contents insurance the day before you're burgled, you buy it years in advance.[29]

If it had been a lifeline it seems Ashdown had run out of energy to grasp it. His patience had been tested to the limit and to a stunned Parliamentary Party on 20th January 1999, he announced his decision to quit.

By spring of 1999, the project became the problem or opportunity for the new leader, Charles Kennedy.

When Kennedy replaced Ashdown he was keen to be his own man. Kennedy had good relations with Blair, but was not as busy a politician as Ashdown. The prospect of endless time and meetings for little gain did not seem a sensible way for Kennedy to spend his days.

He felt it made no sense to keep talking about the Labour Party all the time with journalists. In particular, he was determined to try and end the media's obsession with seeing everything he did on how it would impact on the party's relations with Labour. The problem was he couldn't just walk away from Blair and the JCC and needed to disengage in a way which wouldn't embarrass either side. It was also not Kennedy's style to create a big fanfare over leaving it. There was some unfinished work which needed to be resolved on a couple of issues which were close to his heart.

The JCC was still in existence and in theory at least Labour had to formally respond to the Jenkins review of PR. Its work was also expanded to look at how the two parties could work more closely together on Kennedy's great passion for Europe. These two issues kept the JCC alive for a couple of years into the Kennedy leadership. At the same time it was the general view that the "two against one" policy had worked successfully in 1997, and both sides were keen to confirm this electoral strategy again. It made no sense to fall out with Labour in the run up to the 2001 election.

Blair and Kennedy had known each other for many years and had a good relationship. They both came into parliament at the same time and as rising stars regularly shared TV studios during the usual political media merry-go-round. They had an easy relationship and when Kennedy was elected as leader, Blair was very quick to make sure that he put in an early call to congratulate him. But the Kennedy team was keen to make a symbolical break with the Ashdown era. There was to be no walking through the door at 10 Downing Street and all the meetings that took place between the two were kept very private. Many of the MPs were unaware about the number of occasions they actually met. In fact it was on quite a regular basis, either in person or over the phone. Kennedy would take Anna Werrin, a close ally from his office, Razzall and Dick Newby to the meetings and would then share the contents of these meetings with his diary group, which met in his office, often pulled together very informally at around 6 o'clock for what Kennedy preferred to describe as 'a gossip'.

As ever the talks on PR never resulted in any particular proposal. Blair still hinted at reform for Westminster elections and there was some talk of PR for local elections. Nevertheless, much as Ashdown felt he needed to continue with talks just in case, the Kennedy team thought there would be no harm in keeping the door open. On the issue of Europe, Kennedy was extremely frustrated at Blair's refusal to grapple with the issue of joining the Euro. Kennedy had taken part in joint campaign events organised by Britain in Europe and continually pushed Blair on the issue. He hoped that the JCC might be able to do useful work in this area, but in reality much of the discussion over Europe involved the European institutions rather than the more significant issue of Britain's position on joining the new single currency. Again, the JCC promised much, but delivered very little. In a strange kind of way, Kennedy's laid-back approach to the JCC and his lack of enthusiasm for endless meetings created an atmosphere where Blair seemed to push harder and harder for co-operation with the Liberal Democrats. I sat in endless meetings over the subject and felt Kennedy showed a great deal of political maturity in not becoming mesmerised by the Prime Minister's trappings of Downing Street. This was a clear break from the Ashdown era and came to a head over the whole question of the devolved government in Wales.

Saying "No" To Tony

Although the Liberal Democrats had formed a well organized partnership with Labour in Scotland, in Wales things were not so clear cut. After Ron Davies had quit as the leader of the Welsh Assembly, the battle to replace him was between the Blair candidate, Alun Michael, and the more radical and eccentric candidate Rhodri Morgan. Michael was to win the Welsh leadership and went on to find himself the First Minister in Wales after Labour had won the majority of seats, but were three short of an overall majority. Unlike the Scottish situation where a Lib/Lab coalition had been formed, the Welsh Labour MPs decided to go it alone and try and run with a minority administration. The position was precarious and it was not long before the opposition parties in Cardiff had come together to try and put a vote of no confidence in Michael's leadership. This created a pivotal position for the small group of Liberal Democrats who could use their votes to either bring down, or prop up, Blair's man in Wales. Blair decided to intervene and made an appeal to Kennedy in February 2000, asking if the Lib Dem AMs would rally round Michael and support him in the no confidence vote. I remember discussing the whole issue with Kennedy, he was extremely reluctant to get involved in what he regarded as a devolved issue and dismissed Blair's first phone calls quite quickly. Blair then went further and tried to get Ashdown involved to see if he could bring Kennedy on board. In the same way that Ashdown had been quite heavily involved in the negotiations which had led to the Lib/Lab coalition in Scotland, he was keen to see if he could be helpful in supporting Blair's wishes for Wales. Ashdown believed the prize for supporting Michael could bring power sharing for the Lib Dems in Wales. Kennedy, surprisingly, did not seem irritated by the Ashdown intervention, but certainly wasn't persuaded by it. Upping the stakes, both Blair and Ashdown then sought out Jenkins to see if he could use his influence with Kennedy. Again Kennedy, despite his enormous affection for Jenkins, was unmoved and certainly at several meetings I attended kept repeating the line that this was a devolved issue. The whole episode allowed Kennedy to put a marker down letting Blair know that relations between the two men would be very different from the Ashdown era. It was typical Kennedy, rather than being proactive and getting involved in endless plots and manoeuvres he was prepared to sit back, observe events and stick very firmly to a position. Looking back he told me:

Although I was under pressure from all sides I was adamant that this was a devolved issue and not appropriate for the federal party leader to tell the Welsh party what they should do. At the end of the day it was their decision, not mine.[30]

In rejecting Blair's approach and supporting the decision of the Liberal Democrats in Wales he had marked a new era in Lib/Lab relations. In the event a coalition did in fact take place in Wales: Alun Michael resigned and Rhodri Morgan became leader and opened discussions with the Welsh Liberal Democrats, which led to a formal agreement.

Meanwhile the work of the JCC had failed to deliver anything tangible and the meetings became less and less frequent as thoughts moved towards the 2001 general election campaign. During the campaign there was co-operation on tactics, but again nothing that could be described as a pre-election arrangement. Labour won another landslide and the Liberal Democrat representation went up over the 50 seat mark for the first time in as many years.

After the election Charles was keen to bring the issue of the JCC to a head. He did this by letting it die away rather than any 'big bang' approach. He called together his newly elected MPs in the summer and told them that he wanted to end the process. This was very popular among most colleagues, particularly the newly elected ones, and by the time the party conference had begun, Kennedy had said that it was time to formally end the JCC. In line with both parties' desires to avoid much publicity, the phrase which was used around the Kennedy office was to 'park the JCC' rather than end it.

Reflecting on this Kennedy told me:

There was no point in calling off the JCC in dramatic style, it just died a natural death and in politics things move on and it had outgrown its purpose.[31]

So ended a process that had begun in the embers of the 1992 election when Liberal and Labour were in despair over their failure to defeat Thatcher and determined to find a new way to create progressive government. Ten years on with Labour now celebrating their second election victory, the need for the two parties to work together was no longer on the agenda. In fact the big political differences of the 2001 parliament were to be between Labour and the Liberal Democrats as the Blair government moved towards a more illiberal agenda and time and time again the Liberal Democrats found themselves opposing Labour on the issues of human rights and civil liberties.

In the end both sides understood what was going on, as Robin Cook recorded:

> They have decided not to pull out with a big fanfare, smashing the furniture as they go. Instead they simply won't activate the JCC and will say to Tony that it is up to the government to come up with something they would usefully discuss. This has the neat result of not putting on them the blame for the JCC being broken up and the onus on us to make it work.[32]

Ironically one of the closest levels of joint working between the political parties under Blair was to come under Kennedy's leadership. The London bomb attacks created a warlike atmosphere at Westminster as all three parties decided to pull together to respond to the terrorist threat. With London under attack in the 'war on terror', the Home Secretary, Charles Clarke, sought to respond with cross-party talks. During a six-month period Blair, the Conservative leader Michael Howard and Kennedy attempted to find consensus. The in-depth discussions took place between the Home Secretary, David Davies, his Tory shadow and myself, as Lib Dem home affairs spokesman. It was an insight into the process of negotiation and trust building. Clarke was very open from the start, inviting Davies and myself to the Home Office for regular briefings on the day of the attack and again two weeks later when the attempted second attacks failed. Some consensus was agreed, but it was Blair who broke the deal and sought to make politics out of the issue. Perhaps after seven years in office, all talk of consensus and big tents had disappeared – he was happier working alone. In the end Prime Ministers have to lead, act on instinct and consensus and co-operation are not happy bedfellows with conviction and confidence.

The Only Act In Town

Looking back on the Ashdown/Blair relationship, it came in two clear phases. Before the 1997 election most people I spoke to believed Ashdown was right to throw energy into the talks. Opinion is split on the post 1997 phase. David Steel told me he thought that by then:

It was unrealistic, it was one thing to discuss co-operation after the 1992 election and right to keep the lines of communication open, but once Blair had got that majority I thought the whole exercise was pointless.[33]

Others don't share the Steel view. David Laws, who was close to Ashdown, argues that post 1997 there was little to be lost in carrying on the talks as there was no alternative route to follow:

We lost nothing in the process and it could have led to all sorts of things.[34]

Although he acknowledges that delivering PR was unrealistic:

When Labour had such a large majority there were very powerful reasons for them not to deliver PR. Blair never fundamentally supported a change and after 1997 it would have required Blair to take a decision that would have spelt certain defeat for many of his MPs at the next election.[35]

Ashdown was certainly right to recognise that there was a major opportunity to reposition the Liberal Democrats after the fourth Tory election victory. With Labour in turmoil, led by a left-winger in Smith, the Liberals' strategy had to be to try and capture a progressive centre ground and move the Liberals ahead of where Labour were. The unforeseen death of Smith saw that opportunity disappear. Ashdown had to think quickly and reposition the party and again he took the right course recognising that Blair would be a pioneer of change. It was unlikely the Tories would be seen as the force of the future and the natural momentum of British politics was moving towards a Labour government. Blair was smart enough to see that he needed to create a new territory and a new label for his party and, however frustrating it may have been for Ashdown to see this territory disappearing away to Labour, he was right to try and get in on the act and link himself with Blair in some way.

It was also important for Blair and Ashdown to keep in regular contact during this period for two very pragmatic reasons irrespective of the shared ideology that they were developing. Firstly, if there had been a close election result in 1997 then having good solid preparation in advance would have been helpful. Secondly, the ability to fight an election campaign with both the Liberals and Labour focusing on one enemy, the Conservatives, was likely to enhance the chances of winning more seats.

Everything that Ashdown did up to this point made strategic sense for the party, but the difficulty is that Blair seemed to mesmerize Ashdown and when the two were together they went way beyond what would have been sensible, practical steps to take. Perhaps fuelled by Jenkins, neither man seemed to stop and reflect what could be practically achieved.

Looking back at the period, Ashdown readily acknowledges that he was somewhat of an:

> outsider to his party and did not understand that a party is something with deep roots, is a very strong club and could not be used as a vehicle by its leader to push forward a different agenda.[36]

Blair similarly suffered from the same problem. Nevertheless the approach to 1997 remained sensible, well planned and had the potential to deliver a number of policy initiatives for the Liberals which would have been unthinkable for the party to gain on its own. The consequence of both their actions clearly did not damage them electorally as there was no evidence that swing Conservative voters were put off from voting Liberal because they knew that Ashdown and Blair were in discussions. The landslide election for Labour was matched with an equally successful result for the Liberal Democrats.

It was after the 1997 election that opinions begin to differ on the Ashdown strategy. David Steel argues that the reality of the large majority meant very little could be gained and it is, on the face of it, amazing that within hours of the election result being declared, Blair still wanted to engage and talk to Ashdown. Surely at this point common sense should have kicked in. Ashdown should have accepted the election result and moved in a different direction, but here is the problem: What would that different direction have been? Why should Ashdown, because of the electoral arithmetic, walk away from Blair's overtures? The overwhelming support and popularity Blair had in the country was remarkable and there seemed no electoral danger in at least carrying on being associated with that success. As the Ashdown team had no Plan B they might as well continue with Plan A, develop it with Blair and see if something happened. If by having meetings, establishing the JCC and working closely together you could deliver, then it was a risk worth taking and at the time the risk was fairly limited.

Clare Short, however, argues that Ashdown missed his chance, was not focused enough on PR and got sidetracked on too many issues:

> If Ashdown had focused on the manifesto commitment on PR, rather than some of the big picture stuff he might have got somewhere.[37]

The only real downside to the period from May 1997 to Ashdown's resignation as leader was the amount of energy and time it took and the frustration it caused amongst his colleagues. Ashdown though believes it was the job of the leader of the third party to challenge his party and try and achieve the Liberals' aims. He can look back on the period and reflect that on issues relating to devolution in Scotland and Wales, freedom of information and PR for the European elections, the party was able to get its objectives achieved. Ashdown argues strongly that whilst his work with Blair was not damaging the party in electoral terms and was delivering Liberal policies, it was worth continuing.

However, behind all of these issues remained the one big frustration; failure to deliver on proper electoral reform at Westminster. Here it seems improbable that Blair was going to get some of his MPs, in essence, to vote to abolish themselves. With such a thumping majority and the polls predicting a similar one at the next election, it is very unlikely that he would have been able to have survived an enormous parliamentary rebellion from those MPs that would see a change in the electoral system as wiping out their political careers. This never realistically looked to be on the cards and it was a humiliation for Jenkins to have had his work so brutally dismissed by the Prime Minister and slightly naive of Ashdown to put such faith in the Jenkins Commission.

When I interviewed Clare Short she disagreed and felt Blair could have forced PR through the Commons:

> It was never going to lead to a coalition when you have such a large majority, but he could have given electoral reform. After all it was a manifesto commitment and the p arty would have put up with it.[38]

Ashdown believes that Blair's sincerity was not in question, but it was his commitment to be able to deliver against other priorities that was.

Looking back at the events, Ashdown quotes something which Blair said to him which he believes is a demonstration of Blair's view of politics:

I remember watching Roy Jenkins acceptance speech at Hillhead and I also remember watching the appalling speech of the Labour candidate and, I said to myself then, I am in the wrong party.[39]

Ashdown went on to say:

In almost all cases we agreed on policy except for constitutional reform; for me it was an iron in my soul, for him constitutional reform was a duty he owed to Smith and it is the irony of Blair that the most important things they had been able to do on changing government are on constitutional issues and the ones that Blair believes in least.[40]

Ashdown can look back on his period of leading the Liberal Democrats as one of great success for the party. He saw them achieve two very good election results, he passed on a healthy, successful party to his successor and rather than being wiped out by the Blair landslide, the Liberal Democrats were able to hang on to their shirt tails and gain considerable successes themselves. The planning and preparation was, as you would expect with Ashdown, of the highest military order, but ultimately the arithmetic did not favour a coalition. It would have been a great coalition, a great meeting of minds and the reunification of two parties whose histories had been intertwined for so long. In the end though it became the best coalition that never was.

References

1. Paddy Ashdown Interview, 6 March 2007

2. *Kinnock*, Martin Westlake

3. Bob Worcester Interview, 27 February 2007

4. Paddy Ashdown Interview, 6 March 2007

5. *The Ashdown Diaries Volume One*, Paddy Ashdown

6. Paddy Ashdown Interview, 6 March 2007

7. Clare Short Interview, 2 May 2007

8. Paddy Ashdown Interview, 6 March 2007

9. *Ibid.*

10. *The Progressive Century: The Future of the Centre-Left in Britain*, Neal Lawson & Neil Sherlock

11. *The Ashdown Diaries: 1988-1997, Vol I*, Paddy Ashdown

12. Paddy Ashdown Interview, 6 March 2007

13. *Blair*, Anthony Seldon

14. Paddy Ashdown Interview, 6 March 2007

15. Tom McNally Interview, 29 January 2007

16. David Steel Interview, 27 February 2007

17. David Laws Interview, 20 February, 2007

18. *The Ashdown Diaries: 1997-1999, Volume Two*, May 4th, Paddy Ashdown

19. *The Ashdown Diaries: 1997-1999, Volume Two*, Paddy Ashdown

20. *Ibid.*

21. David Steel Interview, 27 February 2007

22. Tom McNally Interview, 29 January 2007

23. *The Ashdown Diaries: 1997-1999, Volume Two*, Paddy Ashdown

24. David Steel Interview, 27 February 2007

25. *The Daily Express*, 13 January 1999

26. Paddy Ashdown Interview, 6 March 2007

27. *The Ashdown Diaries: 1997-1999, Volume Two*, Paddy Ashdown

28. Paul Tyler Interview, 24 April 2007

29. *The Guardian*, 12 November 1998

30. Charles Kennedy Interview, 9 May 2007

31. *Ibid.*

32. Robin Cook Diary, 23 July 2001

33. David Steel Interview, 27 February 2007

34. David Laws Interview, 20 February 2007

35. *Ibid.*

36. Paddy Ashdown Interview, 6 March 2007

37. Clare Short Interview, 24 April 2007

38. *Ibid.*

39. Paddy Ashdown Interview, 6 March 2007

40. *Ibid.*

9

Whisky And A Handshake

Whisky And A Handshake

There shall be a Scottish Parliament, although through long years those words were first a hope, then a belief, then a promise, now they are reality. Today there is a new voice in the land the voice of a democratic parliament, a voice to shape Scotland, a voice for the future.[1]

These words, spoken by Donald Dewar on 1st July 1999, marked the start of a new order in Scottish politics.

The establishment of Scotland's first parliament was to change the physical landscape north of the border: not only did it create Scotland's own government, but a new electoral system under proportional representation, and Britain's first real example of coalition government since the Second World War.

By the time the first election campaign started in 1999 it was clear that these elections would be very different. The parties were aware that one of the likely outcomes was that no party would have overall control and in my view this clearly coloured the style of the campaign.

Jim Wallace, leader of the Scottish Liberal Democrats at the time, acknowledges this:

There were occasions when the approach the party took was certainly less aggressive than it had been in a national campaign.[2]

For Labour, David Whitton, former Special Advisor to Donald Dewar, agreed that Labour took a similar approach:

During the election campaign our attention focused on the SNP and to a lesser degree the Tories, it's fair to say we went soft on the Liberals knowing they were likely coalition partners.[3]

There was a general acknowledgement that if you were campaigning against the people you could be sitting with around a Cabinet table within a few weeks, you laid off the personal attacks. Wallace argued that this was also the style of politics he wanted to put forward. He wanted a 'constructive election' matching the constructive opposition approach the Lib Dems were taking in Westminster. There was never any question of the party not keeping its identity and no hesitation about attacking where necessary, but during the passage of the Scottish Parliament legislation, relations had already been built up between the two parties and neither side wanted to damage that during the campaign itself.

The Scottish media had also realised this would be a very different type of election. They were as interested in the potential post-election power brokering as the actual campaign itself and constantly quizzed the parties on the subject.

Labour and the Liberal Democrats were both incredibly nervous about how to handle questions on a possible coalition. Neither wanted it to dominate the campaign and they quickly learned how to handle the 'what if?' questions from journalists. Wallace explained to me that he felt it was very important to have a clear answer to this question as it could not be totally dodged. He developed a formula to deal with this, stating that if no party achieved overall power then they would initially talk to the party with the largest number of seats.

The formula had the benefit of clarity and the added advantage that it left the decision in the hands of the electorate. Although it worked relatively well, Wallace acknowledges that the whole issue became a major distraction during the campaign and he regarded it as an 'albatross' around his neck. The other difficulty with the formula was that it limited the party's ability to negotiate after the election by announcing very clearly who they would approach in the first place. Despite the formula, the media and politicians played a game of cat and mouse. The press were determined to catch somebody out, whilst the parties wanted to enter the post-election period with as free a hand as possible. The parties almost succeeded until one of the last TV debates took place and the issue of tuition fees dominated the programme. The Liberal Democrats had stuck very clearly to their belief that tuition fees were wrong, but during the debate it became clear that this issue was a fundamental sticking point with Labour. With hindsight Wallace and his advisors were uneasy that such an issue had been able to dominate in this way, allowing them to publicly commit themselves to negotiating a bottom line over tuition fees.

The Negotiations Begin

Within hours of the results coming in, it was clear that Labour had failed to achieve an overall majority in Scotland. Labour had 56 seats, the SNP 35 and Liberals held the balance of power with 17.

Dewar took some time to understand what would be needed to form a coalition. After his result came in, he and his team headed back to Bude House. Waking at about 9.00 a.m. on the Friday morning he began thinking about the negotiations ahead. His first instinct was to resolve the situation by just offering the Liberal Democrats a couple of Cabinet places. By Sunday, he realised any deal would need to be built on policy not just positions. The first attempt was laughable, drafted on his own typewriter, it was a one page policy summary that was virtually a blank cheque to Labour. It seemed that working alone the First Minister elect was either trying to pull a fast one, or had little idea on how to set up a coalition.

Meanwhile the Liberal Democrats were much better prepared; at the turn of 1999 they had started to focus their attention on the likely make-up of any coalition. The Scottish Party was extremely occupied with the election itself, so Paddy Ashdown turned to David Laws for advice. Laws was Scottish MP Malcolm Bruce's researcher as well as the party's Senior Policy Advisor. Trusted by the Scots and Ashdown, he was a natural choice to work on preparing the first draft of any agreement. The previous year he had joined Bruce and Edward Davey MP on a fact-finding trip to New Zealand to look at public services. During the visit Laws picked up some helpful documents on New Zealand's own coalition experiences. These were to form the model of what was to become the partnership agreement in Scotland. As Ashdown and Wallace spent time on the campaign trail, Laws would tag along and get on with the background work. So by the time he flew to Edinburgh the Friday after polling day he was eager to get on with negotiations:

It was rather frustrating nothing much happened on Friday. I was surprised and thought more preparation would have been made; I guess they were all exhausted.[4]

Eventually a structure for discussion established itself and two rooms were set up within the dull sixties-style offices of the Lothian Regional Council building off the Royal Mile. On the top floor the long process began. In one room Laws and civil servants were drafting policy areas which would have heavy underlining where there was disagreement. These were then passed through to the negotiating teams headed up by Dewar and Wallace.

The next few days were fascinating, as the new parliament tried to find its feet, react to an unclear election result, keep public opinion satisfied and deal with a barrage of interest from the Prime Minister and other senior politicians in Westminster. It was important for Blair and Ashdown that these elections did not look confused and muddled. This was a flagship for devolution, but also, importantly for the Liberal Democrats, a showcase for how proportional representation could work. If these talks resulted in chaos it would have damaged both Scotland's first parliament and the principles of electoral reform.

Blair and Ashdown were determined to use what influence they had over the Scottish leaders to deliver some kind of coalition. The pressure at times became enormous and a glance at Ashdown's *Diaries* shows the amount of time he and Blair spent discussing the issue. From Dewar's and Wallace's perspectives this pressure became an irritation. Laws acknowledges that there was a lot of telephone traffic between Edinburgh and London. He was in the middle of it feeling a bit like a 'double double agent at times'.[5] He understood the Ashdown anxiety, but also wanted time to produce a good policy outcome.

> *Not all of the interference was unhelpful. On tuition fees Ashdown was able to make Blair understand just how important the issue was to the Liberal Democrats.*[6]

Wallace's telephone was ringing non-stop. He told me he hardly had a chance to get in the shower each morning before Ashdown was on the line.

Wallace and Dewar, however, were determined to take it at their pace and work issues through, but not at any cost. Wallace was still prepared to walk away from any agreement unless his demands could be met:

> *It was not, however, coalition at any price. Our willingness to have walked away if we could not have reached an acceptable agreement on tuition fees is evidence of that. But if agreement on a programme could be reached I was willing to be a partner in government.*[7]

As the talks went on the media were watching every step to see just exactly how they were proceeding. Camped outside the Lothian Headquarters they watched the comings and goings and waited in the local pub for a puff of white smoke to emerge. Given this was a very unusual position for both politicians and the press, the relationship seemed to work reasonably well. The media were not able to force the hand of the politicians to rush their discussions, and although there was some tension between the two political parties over leaking to the press, on the whole the talks were allowed to continue without much outside interference. The two teams were aware that they had a deadline to work to as the election of the Speaker for the parliament was due the following Wednesday and the First Minister was due to be elected on Thursday. At the time the sense was that the public would not want a protracted period of bargaining to take place. With hindsight all parties agree this was too tight a timescale. By 2003, the parties gave themselves a much longer period of eight days to complete the coalition discussions and by 2007, the discussions took even longer.

The key stumbling block was always going to be tuition fees. Blair, although determined that a coalition should be formed, was worried that an embarrassing back down on the issue would create him problems south of the border. Eventually both sides agreed to set up an inquiry to examine the problem. Although this had all the signs of a classic coalition fudge, it was in fact a very effective process. Blair's hopes of kicking the issue into the long grass failed to take into account the spirit of co-operation that was developing in Scotland. Labour also knew that the Liberal Democrats could break away from the coalition if they felt the inquiry got nowhere. In the end it created a serious solution and established an alternative higher education funding system. For the junior partner in the coalition it was a major policy victory and showed that holding your nerve could pay off.

Apart from tuition fees the other major sticking point was not on policy, but process. Laws was keen to have an annex to the agreement which would set out the protocols and arrangements on the day to day workings of the coalition. He felt so strongly about it that he had a major row with the Second Permanent Secretary, asking him to be removed from the negotiations.[8] The civil servants and Labour seemed happier to avoid formal arrangements. In the end Laws lost the argument, but in reality it did not matter, as Laws acknowledges:

> Donald and Jim trusted each other and on that basis it was felt the annex on formal process was not needed and I guess in such a small parliament it was less necessary.[9]

However, I think Laws was right to be anxious about the lack of detail on process. The arrangements were at times very informal, as Wallace and Dewar did indeed trust each other and their offices were close enough for regular quick gossips. The lack of formal structures on the day-to-day workings were overcome with handshakes and trust. But the lesson from Scotland is how events put that at risk. Dewar's unexpected death meant that handshake agreements died with him. He had made Wallace promises on PR for local government which were not set down in documents making it much harder to deliver after his death.

The two teams worked late into the night in the final few days of discussion, on the whole with good humour and occasional light-hearted moments. At one point the two teams were alarmed at a racket outside the offices only to discover the alley below was on the official city ghost tour and a guide was getting carried away with a ghostly howl.

For a deal based so much on two men, it was appropriate that the final agreement was reached at Bude House between Wallace and Dewar over a handshake and a glass of whisky.

Day To Day Work

The 'partnership agreement' was born and ended up as the underpinning for the coalition, making the day-to-day workings much more manageable. The final document was just over 4,000 words, a big improvement from Dewar's first single side of A4.

Wallace described the agreement as the glue that held relations together. After Dewar's death the agreement was key. As Wallace said in a lecture to Glasgow University in 2006:

> *Tellingly the existence of the original agreement and the express endorsement of it by Henry McLeish and Jack McConnell allowed Liberal Democrat MSPs to vote for each of them as First Minister.*[10]

It seems that the day-to-day working of the coalition in this first parliament was quite amicable. The partnership agreement had been the rock that had held colleagues together and often avoided splits between the parties at Cabinet.

Working relations in Cabinet were strong, Wallace said:

That when you sit round a Cabinet table although there is never any doubt that you are in a different party, you tend to work incredibly hard to overcome any differences.[11]

The key to success with this coalition had been the ability to put systems in place to deal with disagreements and avoid problems that could throw the agreement off track.

The structures are set out in some detail in Ben Seyd's study of the coalition and they are worth listing as a useful guide:

– A formal commitment to collective Cabinet responsibility and thus for both coalition partners to have sight of and an opportunity to comment on all policy decisions;

– The requirement for all information about impending policy decisions to be copied separately to the office of the First Minister and Deputy First Minister;

– Regular bilateral meetings between the First Minister and Deputy First Minister;

– A range of ministerial committees and working groups below Cabinet level (with Cabinet serving as a forum for signing off decisions rather than as a collective arena for co-ordination and management);

– Close working relations between the parties' special advisors;

– Dispute resolution via informal meetings of the First Minister and Deputy First Minister plus relevant policy Ministers.[12]

This final point is key, the First and Deputy Ministers in Holyrood offices are very close to each other and when problems arose, Wallace explains what went on:

Strive to find a solution is perhaps an understatement. It often involved intense negotiation. The team of special advisers on each side became very adept at talking to backbenchers and among themselves trying to identify possible options to break a logjam. But at the end of the day, if all else failed it landed on the desk of the First Minister and myself.[13]

One early issue that helped bring the sides closer together was the repeal of legislation concerning publicity on gay issues in schools, known as "Section

28". The tabloids' constant attacks on this actually helped make the Cabinet more united in its response. According to Whitton, Dewar went to some lengths to ensure unity by asking each Cabinet Minister in turn if they supported the policy: from that point on it became a real test of how the team would unite against criticism.[14]

Dewar's illness shortly into the life of the parliament became another test for the coalition. Labour were initially suspicious of how Wallace would perform as acting First Minister. When the first set of questions to him came up, the SNP leader, Alex Salmond, was looking to deliver some blows. Wallace performed well and the Labour advisors and MSPs were happy to cheer and clap along. It was another building block in the relations.

The coalition had a big impact on the Liberal Democrats, boosting their significance and creating a higher profile for individuals such as Jim Wallace and Nicol Stephen, but I was interested to find out if there is a danger that the smaller party gets lost in the system and becomes part of the establishment. Wallace said it was not a problem. One day he would act politically neutral as the Justice Minister, the next actively campaigning as a Liberal Democrat. One thing was for sure, the party members would never allow him to forget his roots:

> As the junior coalition partner I was very conscious of the need to maintain the party's distinctive identity. I think it took Labour some getting used to, but it was and remains important that on issues, which are not within the Executive's responsibility, there does not need to be an executive line. It still happens that the SNP will table debates on reserved issues over which the coalition parties are divided.[15]

Despite the reassurances of Wallace, it seems to me that a smaller party in a coalition can start to lose its identity, forgetting its ultimate purpose is to get into power alone, not as an appendage of others. In part, the 2007 election campaign illustrated this point: despite being in government for eight years the Liberal Democrats were effectively pushed out of the campaign. The whole of the run up to the election was dominated by a high profile battle between the SNP and Labour. Looking at the coverage, you would struggle to believe that the Liberal Democrats had been major players in Scotland's government.

Another key challenge for a coalition partner is to keep its party activists on board. I have written earlier about the battle David Steel had in 1977 with

Liberal activists over the pact with Labour. The Scottish Liberal Democrats had a much easier time in 1999.

At the time every single constituency party chair was consulted over the partnership agreement and a special conference was held which fully endorsed the decision. It is unlikely that the same level of consultation could be put in place on a UK wide scale, nevertheless the Westminster party is wisely looking to see what, if anything, can be learnt from the experience.

For party activists at a local level this whole arrangement can be very tough. Many of the activists unrealistically believed that because the Liberal Democrats were in power any of their policy ideas could suddenly become law. It also presented some difficulties for local campaigners in attacking Labour in local government elections when there was a direct race between the two parties. Meanwhile Labour activists had less to fear, as their party was never going to lose its identity given its larger status. Their main complaint was what they saw as a lack of discipline amongst Liberals within the coalition. The case of Donald Gorrie, a rather independent minded Liberal MSP, illustrates the problem. His vicious attacks on the expenditure of the new parliamentary building annoyed the Labour Party as Whitton said to me:

> We felt at times that the Liberals did not understand that
> responsibilities go with power.[16]

Whitton also acknowledges that the Labour Party had to learn how to work with others and was not very tolerant to the concept of power sharing:

> Labour members were not used to dealing with coalitions, many of
> them had come from large Labour dominated councils and were just
> not used to the idea of negotiating with other parties.[17]

A Second Coalition

Many of these problems had been ironed out by the next election in 2003. The coalition had been in place successfully for four years and the Liberal Democrats could boast achievements on keeping tuition fees out of Scotland and the introduction of free personal care for the elderly. Both sides entered the election with some confidence, but I wanted to understand how coalition partners could work together in parliament one week and the next week be fighting each other on the campaign trail. It certainly helped that there was a lack of significant battles between the two parties in key seats.

As Ben Seyd notes:

> One reason why in 2003 the coalition partners could campaign separately without risking difficult relations after the election was the limited electoral competition between them. In only five constituencies in Scotland did Labour and the Liberal Democrats occupy first and second place after the 1999 election; there were thus a few seats in which the main electoral competition in 2003 was between coalition partners. This reduces the potential for elections to undermine coalition unity.[18]

Both sides acknowledged that there could be a problem and some discussions took place about whether the coalition should have a cooling-off period before the election took place. There was never any discussion that the parties should join together and put forward a coalition platform to the electorate. During the campaign all parties ruled out saying who their preferred coalition partners would be in advance of the election. Interestingly though, polls carried out in Scotland showed that 45 per cent of the electorate would liked to have been told what the consequences were of voting for a certain party in relation to the potential government.[19]

Both coalition partners avoided attacking each other and focussed on what they had achieved. The danger with this approach is that you get a rather dull campaign without any real political debate. If parties are nervous about taking a strong position with post-election negotiations in mind, it is hard for the voters to sense what they will get in return. Douglas Fraser, political editor of the *Sunday Herald*, summed up the problem:

> Lib Dems acknowledge that they gave tuition fees too high a profile in the 1999 campaign as a coalition deal bottom line, and opted in 2003 to make a priority of everything and nothing. Those factors combined to give the public only a vague sense of the ways in which Lib Dems intended to 'make the difference' by 2007. Even council voting reform was denied the status of a coalition 'bottom line'.[20]

Against this backdrop it certainly helped that the war in Iraq was raging, as a political issue it created very clear dividing lines between the parties at a national level.

The 2003 election result again produced a situation where Labour could not govern without support and this time both parties were much better prepared for the negotiations that were to follow. More time was allowed for discussions to take place and a much longer and detailed document was put in place running to 14,000 words. Consultation was wider and greater attempts were made to involve backbench MSPs and in some cases the Liberal Democrats used local party activists to take part in the agreement discussions. On the Labour side the Chair of the Back Bench Group as well as the party's General Secretary were all involved. Both sides went much further than in 1999, and in doing so gave many more of the MSPs a sense of ownership which helped reduce potential conflicts in the future.

There was also an increase in the level of civil servant back-up, with each negotiating party given two officials to work solely with them. I believe making sure negotiating parties have strong advice and back-up is key to a successful agreement.

The 2003 election did raise a number of concerns for the coalition. Fewer than half of all Scots turned out to vote and the coalition parties' level of support was down from 1999. First Minister, Jack McConnell, was concerned enough to issue colleagues with a warning:

> We are in a really serious situation here. If Scotland is not well governed over the next four years then the devolution commitment Jim Wallace and I have had all our adult lives is threatened by a lack of public confidence.[21]

The growth of the SNP

For the next four years the coalition ran smoothly enough and Nicol Stephen, now leader of the Liberal Democrats, and Jack McConnell, the First Minister, although not as close as Dewar and Wallace, had a good working relationship.

By February 2007, when I visited Edinburgh, it was clear that the atmosphere was changing. There is no doubt from talking to close advisors on all sides that there was a build up in tension between the two parties in the run-up to the 2007 election. The increased threat from the SNP had created a nervy atmosphere as parties campaigned towards polling day.

The final result was a cliffhanger with the SNP becoming the largest party by just one seat, with 47 MSPs compared to Labour on 46. Yet again the Liberal Democrats, with 16, found themselves as king makers, even though now they were only the fourth largest party.

What followed was a long period of media speculation and horse trading, which did little to enhance the reputation of the parliament or coalition.

The Liberal Democrats quickly ruled out continuing their partnership with Labour. Even though there was just one seat in it, Nicol Stephen agreed that the party with the most seats had the authority to govern and he would respect that. Apart from the numbers there was a serious difference between the parties on funding local services. The Liberal Democrats' insistence on introducing a local income tax was likely to be tough for Labour to deliver. However, he was equally dismissive of working with Alex Salmond's Nationalists. The SNP plans for a referendum on independence within 100 days of the election was the stumbling block.

The Liberal position has been the cause of some press speculation. Some initially felt it was just a tough negotiating stance, others have suggested it is part of a wider plot with Labour to eventually defeat the SNP. They challenge Stephen's objection to the independence referendum pointing out that Salmond would have compromised on timing and format. This from Neal Ascherson is typical:

> It follows that given the feebleness of Nicol Stephen's arguments, there must be some other reason for his stubborn refusal to seek a deal.[22]

He goes on to speculate that pressure to reject the deal came from Gordon Brown and Ming Campbell as part of a wider deal on Lib/Lab relations in Westminster. I have to say I've found no evidence for this, but it is clear that if the Lib Dems had supported the SNP it would have created considerable ill will with their former coalition partners, certainly north of the border, and I suspect the ripples would have been felt in Westminster.

Meanwhile, Salmond began talks with the two Green MSPs. Although they could not help him provide a working majority, it was an attempt to broaden his base. They in turn suggested an arrangement described as confidence and supply. Robin Harper, Green co-leader, said:

We can vote against and campaign against policies that are being introduced with which we do not agree, at the same time guaranteeing not to go in a vote of confidence to bring the government down.[23]

In the end they struck a much looser agreement. The Greens voted for Salmond to become First Minister and in return the SNP agreed to back a Climate Change Bill and allow one of the two Green MSPs to chair a committee.

Despite all the uncertainty on 16th May 2007, Salmond became the first Nationalist to lead Scotland, heading up a minority government. In his acceptance speech he acknowledged the difficulties this would create:

The nature and composition of this third Scottish Parliament makes it imperative that this government will rely on the strength of argument in parliament and not the agreement of parliamentary strength. It will take patience, maturity and leadership on all sides of the Chamber ...[24]

The negotiations in 1999 and 2003 went relatively smoothly, without much criticism. The 2007 picture is murkier. There was considerable press criticism, some of which attacked the very idea of coalition government. This in the *Telegraph* was typical:

We are now into the shifting sands of coalition government, which is the worst background against which to take investment decisions if you are an existing or prospective employer. The reason is uncertainty. Now the future policies and such core issues as tax, planning and investment are subject to the vagaries of constant political horse trading the private sector has a whole new level of risk to contend with.[25]

Learning the lessons

So what lessons can we learn from the Scottish coalition experience?

On policy alone there have been successes. Some coalitions can result in a fudge or dumbing down. In Holyrood there is evidence of more radical thinking as the political heat is taken out of key issues. The creation of an alternative to tuition fees, a long term approach to health promotion and the environment have shown the parliament is prepared to tackle tough issues.

The Lib/Lab coalition took more long-term views about policy and without political point scoring; policies seem to have developed a way in which they may be harder in the very confrontational politics of Westminster.

Wallace summed it up:

> *I don't accept the lowest common denominator argument – I would prefer to describe it as the highest common factors garnished with some distinctive features attributable to one party or the other.*[26]

It is hard to separate voter attitudes to the coalition from approval, or disapproval, of devolution itself. In 1999, levels of optimism were unrealistically high. Between sixty and seventy per cent of voters believed devolution would improve education, the economy and health.[27] Whilst seventy per cent believed that the new parliament would give Scotland a stronger voice. By 2002, this figure had gone down to just thirty-five per cent and voter turnout levels also went down nine per cent between 1999 and 2003.

I am not convinced that we can interpret these figures as dissatisfaction with the coalition. Confidence in politics has declined across a range of institutions during the same period.

It is, however, fair to say that the enthusiasm and optimism over Scotland's own government is on the decline.

Away from policy areas the parliament has run effectively. The day-to-day relations under Dewar and Wallace depended on trust, but the mechanics they put in place have survived under the next generation of leaders. As Wallace acknowledges, it was a learning curve in the first parliament and both sides had lessons to learn. Labour had to learn to share power and the Liberal Democrats to have it:

> *As Ross Finnie used to remark to me in our first year in government, there isn't a book on a library shelf entitled 'how to run a coalition government' – although I think I might write one! Not just in the first year, but in all subsequent years, it has required patience, tenacity and sheer hard work, although experience probably means that the going gets a bit easier.*[28]

Despite the problems it seems to have been a genuine and effective partnership. The rock behind this remains the ability of Wallace and Dewar to give the coalition such a positive start. Would different characters have been able to develop the trust required to break the political mould in this way? I doubt it. To me it seems that trust was the key to success.

As David Whitton said:

The two leaders have to be able to look each other in the eye and say here is the deal and then stick to it. Then they need to cut each other some slack along the way and not get hung up on who claims credit for things.[29]

What is interesting is the impact that coalition has on the parties. By 2007, both partners suffered at the polls. Labour's problems can be explained in two words, Blair and Iraq. The Liberal Democrat position is more complex. For years the party has argued that participation in government will bring it much needed profile and credibility. For eight years they had shared power, introduced Liberal policies and had a raised media profile. None of this appears to have benefited them in the polls. Peter Lynch from the University of Stirling raised a similar point after the 2003 election where the party again won seventeen seats:

Four years of Liberal Democrat coalition produced no more votes or seats for the party itself. The Lib Dems have therefore seen extensive policy benefits from their role in government, but no actual electoral benefits.[30]

It is a disappointment for the Liberal Democrats and has left those advocates of partnership government scratching their heads to understand why. Some argue that the party lacked a distinctive big policy idea, like the abolition of tuition fees. Others have blamed the media's obsession with the rise of Alex Salmond's nationalists.

However, the failure to benefit from participating in government should not go unnoticed by Liberal Democrat leaders in Westminster.

The electoral system used in Scotland has had a fundamental impact on the political parties, media and voters. Clear single party government now looks unlikely with five political parties contesting most seats. Coalitions or minority rule are now the norm.

This means the Scottish public and media are now much more accepting of the fact that no party will win overall and coalition is the way forward.

I can't see a turning back, but I can see dissatisfaction growing if the SNP minority government ended up collapsing early and there was a period of instability or another early trip to the polls. Then the critics of PR and coalition government would find a stronger voice and the foundations laid so well by Dewar and Wallace could start to look shaky.

References

1.   Donald Dewar Speech, 1 July 1999

2.   Jim Wallace Interview, 13 February 2007

3.   David Whitton (Former Special Advisor to Donald Dewar) Interview, 27 February 2007

4.   David Laws MP Interview, 20 February 2007

5.   *Ibid.*

6.   *Ibid.*

7.   Jim Wallace Speech, Glasgow University, 2006

8.   David Laws/Jim Wallace Interview, February 2007

9.   David Laws MP Interview, 20 February 2007

10. Jim Wallace Speech, Glasgow University, 2006

11. Jim Wallace Interview, 13 February 2007

12. *Coalition Governance in Scotland and Wales*, Ben Seyd

13. Jim Wallace Interview, 13 February 2007

14. David Whitton (Former Special Advisor to Donald Dewar) Interview, 27 February 2007

15. Jim Wallace Interview, 13 February 2007

16. David Whitton (Former Special Advisor to Donald Dewar) Interview, 27 February 2007

17. *Ibid.*

18. *Coalition Governance in Scotland and Wales*, Ben Seyd

19. Scottish Social Attitude Survey of 2003

20. Douglas Fraser, political editor, *Sunday Herald*

21. Jack McConnell, *Sunday Herald*, 11 May 2003

22. 'Vote for Open Democracy', Neal Ascherson, 10 May

23. Robin Harper MSP Green Party, BBC Online, 8 May 2007

24. BBC, 16 May 2007

25. Damian Reece, *Daily Telegraph*, 10 May 2007

26. Jim Wallace Interview, 13 February 2007

27. 'Is Devolution at Risk?', Nicola McEwan, *Scottish Affairs Magazine*

28. Jim Wallace Interview, 13 February 2007

29. David Whitton (Former Special Advisor to Donald Dewar) Interview, 27 February 2007

30. 'Impact of the 2003 election on the Scottish Party system', Peter Lynch, University of Stirling, 6 May 2003

10

Entering No Man's Land

Entering No Man's Land

We could be entering no man's land at the next election.[1]

David Butler

Introduction

By the time the polls close at the next general election, candidates up and down the country are heading home to freshen up, check the exit polls and get ready for the count. It has been one of the hottest days of the year, with the spring sunshine causing voters to turn out in the largest numbers since 1997, and creating numerous sunburnt party activists exhausted from knocking up the voters and pushing final appeals through letter boxes. The election night teams at ITV and BBC now have their own election battle; to produce the quickest and most accurate exit poll. As they gather over the data, it's just not clear. News editors demand a line for the headlines and both broadcasters claim "it's too close to call". Everyone is in agreement that the heat of the day will be more than matched by events unfolding up and down the country as the ballot boxes are opened and begin to tell their story.

Of course, we just don't know yet when the next election will take place, or what the outcome will be, let alone what the weather will be like!

Predictions are dangerous things, but there is the strongest chance that the next election will be the closest we have seen since 1992. It begs so many questions:

- What will the electoral arithmetic be?

- What signs are there that we are heading for a hung parliament?

- What constitutional issues does this raise?

- And most interestingly of all, how do each of the three parties prepare and then respond to such a situation?

- Is Britain finally heading for a coalition government?

It's The Arithmetic, Stupid

The rest of this chapter is based on the assumption that the next election will produce a hung parliament. I am not predicting that for certain, but as David Butler told me the circumstances for no party winning an overall majority look more likely now than for years. The arrival of David Cameron and decline of Blair have created a situation where it's no longer laughable to predict a Conservative victory. Gordon Brown has inherited a Labour Party suffering from the same decline that Major inherited from Thatcher. The key question is if his premiership will be enough to squeeze out a fourth term for Labour. There are other factors to consider: Will the Liberal Democrats increase in strength, or fall away? What will be the impact of voter turnout, tactical voting and boundary changes? We also have to consider a peculiar bias to Labour in the electoral system. Put these together and you are left with a situation where the Conservatives can lead Labour in opinion polls by up to nine per cent and still be left with a hung parliament.

The Polls

The Conservative recovery in the opinion polls under Cameron has been remarkable. By 2006, and for the first six months of 2007, he had a clear lead over Labour with some polls showing the Conservatives up to ten points ahead.

The arrival of Brown reversed this situation and the polls showed just how unsettled the position remained between the parties. There is little connection between midterm polls and a general election. What they do show, however, is a trend. We know from past polling just how far ahead an opposition party has to be midterm if it is to go on and win the next election. Based on this analysis the news is less good for the Conservatives. Since the 1950s, opposition parties have tended to need a fifteen per cent midterm lead if they are to go on and win. In 1990, not even that was enough; Labour had a twenty per cent lead and went on to lose the election.

The recent Conservative lead, history would suggest, cannot be sustained through to an election and even if it were, as I will argue later, anything less than a ten per cent lead would not deliver an overall majority.

Even if the Conservatives were to start polling bigger leads there remains the danger that Labour might change leader again if Brown proves unable to cut the Tory lead. I think this is unlikely. In similar circumstances the Conservatives would have no hesitation in wielding the knife, but Labour's men in grey suits have never been very active. As Professor Paul Whiteley, an academic and expert in public opinion and polling at the University of Exeter, told me:

> Conservatives never have a problem with getting rid of a leader, but Labour have given Brown such dominance that it's unlikely the men in suits will knock at the door.[2]

It is, therefore, a fair assumption that Brown and Cameron will remain as leaders into the next election.

Although the current polling levels are likely to change, they are helpful in showing where the Conservatives need to be if they are on track to win an overall majority. In recent years various computer programmes have become more sophisticated at taking polling data and predicting election outcomes. At the time of writing this chapter most of these calculate that a hung parliament is at least a plausible outcome for the next election.

Boundary Changes

The polls though don't tell the whole picture. We need to look beyond them for further evidence. The current boundary review has been completed and the new seats will be fought at the next election. Various estimates have been made on the impact the changes will make, all showing that the review will favour the Conservatives. There are two types of affected seats; totally new ones, and those where the boundary has been changed significantly. Of the 13 new seats it is estimated that ten would be won by the Conservatives, two by the Liberal Democrats and one by Labour. If you then look at the seats which have changes made to them the Tories could expect to win a further 16/20 seats off Labour as these become marginal.

You then need to factor in the impact of abolishing nine seats at the next election. Six of these are Labour, two Tory and one is Liberal Democrat. Taken together, the impact for the Conservatives could be worth an almost guaranteed 15 seat advantage, rising up to 30, depending on how well they fight seats that become marginals under the review.

Voter Turnout

The fall in voter turnout has been analysed endlessly by others; my interest is the impact that differential turnout has on the parties' fortunes. It has long been known that Labour supporters are less likely to vote than others, but how strong is the impact in terms of seats. According to Martin Baxter at Electoral Calculus, a Labour voter is only 65 per cent as likely to vote as a Conservative or Liberal supporter. When you consider this impact across seats this favours the Conservatives. Opinion polls need to take this bias into account, which most now do. However, they adjust on a national basis. What they can't do is adjust this seat by seat. Many of the Labour seats have small electorates and it takes fewer votes to win those seats. Conservative seats often require more votes to win. The net impact of all of these factors, according to Baxter, is that despite less Labour supporters voting the seat, the size and impact of differential turnout actually means the polls understate the number of seats Labour will win.

Tactical Voting

As ever the marginal seats will be the battleground at the next election. Winning these can depend on the ability to squeeze the party in third place and get their supporters to vote tactically. In the elections of 1997 and 2001 there was strong evidence that Labour and Liberal Democrat voters worked out how to defeat Conservatives and would switch votes to try and oust them. It has been estimated that this may have cost the Conservatives around ten seats to the Liberal Democrats and a further 16 to Labour. This factor may disappear at the next election, as the Conservatives are no longer seen as the "nasty" party. The disappearance of tactical voting could significantly help the Conservatives regain seats lost last time.

The Bias

If you factor in the new boundary changes, turnout and tactical voting, what emerges is a bias between Labour and the Conservatives if the parties have equal support in the polls. The most significant work in this area has been undertaken by Lewis Baston and Simon Henry – they call this "The Gap" and argue that if the parties poll equally it would mean 90 extra seats for

Labour over the Conservatives, equivalent to 4.9 per cent support. In their research they acknowledge that if tactical voting were to disappear the impact could be more likely to see Labour ahead of the Conservatives by 60 seats, well short of a majority assuming a strong Liberal Democrat showing.

Watch Out For The 5% Lead

I have attempted to boil down all the various figures and analyses to give an indication of the various opinion poll ratings that we should be looking out for if the next election is to result in a hung parliament.

As I have argued, we cannot simply study the polls and transpose those percentage point leads into parliamentary majorities. It's a much more complex task. I have looked at the work carried out by experts in this field and accept that there is a significant factor that creates a bias to Labour. This would mean for Labour to have an overall majority they can be level with the Conservatives.

For the Conservatives to have an overall majority they need a poll lead of 9 per cent. In essence this means that anything in the range of a Conservative lead of 1–9 per cent will lead to a hung parliament. A Conservative lead of 5 per cent would probably be the point at which the Conservatives edge ahead in terms of seats, but still fall short of a majority.

The Constitutional Issues

Neither public opinion or constitutional arrangements are prepared for the problems that must arise when elections fail to produce clear decisions.[3]

David Butler's warning made in 1980 remains true today. Apart from the experiences in Scotland and Wales, Britain remains totally unprepared for a hung parliament.

The mainland European electoral systems create a situation where coalitions and party negotiations are the norm after elections. Handling the hours after polling day is set out in a constitution, or detailed process paper. The UK has no constitution and very little experience of what to do when the election is not decisive. We have no President to oversee the transfer between governments and our Speaker holds no role in this process. That leaves the monarch. Queen Victoria played a crucial role in the passage of events that led to the Aberdeen coalition in 1852. Although she was driven to disappear at times as she searched for a Prime Minister, it was her and Prince Albert's favour that politicians sought as they attempted to form a government. To a lesser extent, George V held a similar role in the 1930s when Ramsay MacDonald and Stanley Baldwin were both options to form a national unity government. The King's strong support for MacDonald often kept him from resigning and gave him much needed authority during a time of crisis. Today, the monarchy would not play such a role.

Since coming to the throne, Queen Elizabeth II has played an important private role as confidante to Prime Ministers via her weekly audience. As Head of State for over 50 years she has seen 14 elections and 11 Prime Ministers come and go. Most have spoken warmly of the advice and support she has given.

During this time there have been a number of occasions when a political vacuum has taken place. Early in her reign there was a battle to replace Anthony Eden after he resigned as Prime Minister in 1957. Then she consulted Winston Churchill and the Marquis of Salisbury about the options. When Macmillan was forced to retire due to ill health six years later, she was again called on to play a role in approving his successor.

However, the protocol for operating in a hung parliament is very vague. Firstly, there are no rules, just precedent. For today's monarch the closest written guidance comes from various constitutional academic studies. Rodney Brazier, in his book on constitutional practice, argues that the requirement is as follows:

> *The Queen should commission that person who appears best able to command the support of a stable majority in the House of Commons, or, failing such a person, that politician who seems able to form a government with a reasonable prospect of maintaining an administration in office.*[4]

This is vague and leaves open how the Queen should judge who to call on. Here though there is some recent precedent to help.

The most recent vacuum came in 1974, when Edward Heath failed to secure a clear majority after calling an election. Labour became the largest party with four more seats. Heath saw the Queen the day after the election to inform her he intended to try and form an administration.

Even though he had clearly lost his majority after the election and had fewer seats than Labour he was within his rights to do this.

The precedent that has emerged allows the sitting Prime Minister to have the first attempt at forming a government. This appears to be the established view according to Robert Blackburn's 'Monarchy and the Personal Prerogatives'. It is also the view put forward by the House of Commons Library in a note they prepared for me.

I think this is wrong. Logic would suggest that a different approach should be taken. The monarch should decide to call the party leader with the largest number of seats. It would better reflect the electorates' wishes than turning to an incumbent Prime Minister who may have twenty or so fewer seats than another party.

At this point I should explain that I regard seats, and not the popular vote, as the key issue. Whilst I acknowledge that votes would reflect the voters' verdict I believe that the formation of a government has to be based on the number of MPs that support it. I am arguing for a change in precedent to allow the leader with the largest number of seats to be allowed the first choice to form a government. I fear it would be a step too far to call for the leader of the party with more votes to take precedent.

Brazier argues that the monarch could decide to see each party leader in turn, starting with the largest in terms of seats:

> Such audiences would bear the advantage that the Queen would be following the electorates' choice as reflected in the seat given by it to the parties. No leader could feel piqued at not being consulted and the Queen would be informing herself personally of the leader's views.[5]

Of course all of this would take time. The British obsession with knowing who is Prime Minister within hours of the polls closing does not favour a long process.

As I argued earlier, in the chapter on Europe, there is no reason why Britain could not move to a constitutional model of having a caretaker government during and immediately after the election.

If it was known that the sitting government carried on for a ten-day period after polling day this would provide adequate time for any negotiations to take place. Frankly, it would also be a useful period for any incoming government, even with a large majority, to plan and prepare rather than the normal rushed Cabinet appointments. There is some precedent. In March 1979, after Callaghan was defeated on a no confidence vote he carried on up to the election and the Chancellor, Denis Healey, consulted the Conservatives on the content of April 13th budget. After all we suspended the House of Commons for three weeks during the election campaign and the country has not yet collapsed.

There is, in my view, a strong case for looking at the issue before the next election. There is no constitution to amend, but on other issues the monarchy and parliament have reacted to a changing world. The royal divorces, marriages and issue of funding the monarchy have all shown that the protocols can be changed. It would be a change that allows a monarch to better reflect her subjects' electoral wishes. However it is unlikely that the monarch would make a change at this point in her reign.

A Brown-led Labour government is also unlikely to make informal changes, as they would benefit from the incumbency protocol. In fact all three parties would be nervous of seeking any agreement on process in advance of an election for fear it showed they were even contemplating a close result.

The only other real issue for the monarch is the problem of an insecure minority government. If the outcome of any post-election result produces a government that battles on without any formal arrangement there may be a number of Commons defeats that could be interpreted as no confidence. In these circumstances the government may seek a very early election. Alternatively, if the minority government felt it was growing in electoral support it may seek a quick second election to try and secure a working majority. Harold Wilson was confident enough to call a second election in 1974 to try and increase his majority. In these circumstances it is unlikely the Queen would do anything other than rubber stamp a Prime Minister's request to dissolve parliament. However, the so-called "second dissolution" issue does raise some issues.

Brazier is perhaps a bit dramatic when he says:

> *The election of a hung parliament could set a constitutional time bomb ticking in that a resulting minority government might be defeated on a vote of confidence.*[6]

He does, however, raise one important point. If dissolution was sought after a no-confidence defeat, how could the Queen decide if the defeated government should be allowed to go to the polls, or be replaced by the opposition that may have created a coalition to come into power?

Let's take an example. If Labour were to form a minority government and last for four months until say, a budget vote, at that point the Liberals and Conservatives would combine to defend the budget. They are prepared to form a new administration together on the basis of a budget alternative on green issues. Meanwhile, Gordon Brown decides to resign and call an election. In these circumstances, so soon after an election, there are two options open; allow a general election, which could produce another indecisive result, or allow a Liberal/Conservative government. How would the Queen handle this position? Although dissolution has not been refused in over 100 years it remains the case that a monarch can decline a request for one, but the justification would need to be very clearly defined. Brazier argues that if the minority government is defeated on, say, the loyal address then the Prime Minister should resign and not seek a quick dissolution. The problem is that this becomes much greyer a few months into an administration. In these circumstances Brazier is less definite and makes a case that the issues could depend on a number of factors. Firstly, on how long the administration has been in office. Secondly, on how strong the claim of the alternative government is. This leaves the Queen in uncharted territory.

> *The Queen would be required to reconcile two conflicting constitutional principles, the one being that she must accept Ministerial advice [in my example Brown's call for a quick election] the other being that a person with a parliamentary majority behind him has the right to be Prime Minister [in this case Cameron led Liberal/Conservative arrangement].*[7]

If the Queen were prepared to refuse dissolution she would be avoiding a second quick election and allowing a perfectly acceptable alternative government to take office, but based on precedent it seems unlikely she would do this. Again, the incumbent Prime Minister seems to hold all the cards. In these circumstances the protocol would go against the wishes of the majority of MPs and helps the Prime Minister, even if he is in a minority and has lost a key vote. This seems indefensible, but under this monarch at least is unlikely to change.

Informal contact between the parties and Palace will already have begun and as the election gets closer it would make sense for all three party leaders to make contact with the Queen's new Private Secretary, Christopher Geidt. David Butler argues that good channels at an early stage will help avoid any unnecessary confusion in the hours after the polls close.

The role of Private Secretary has been around for over 150 years. It was established by Queen Victoria in 1861, perhaps as a result of the nightmare she had in finding a Prime Minister fit to govern during the 1850s! There is plenty of precedent for Private Secretaries acting as a conduit between political leaders and monarchs.

In his study of minority governments, David Butler discusses the merits of removing the sovereign from this process. He puts forward two alternatives: the Speaker, or an informateur (an elder statesman) would take on the role. These models are used in mainland Europe with some success.

I am of the firm conclusion that the current arrangement is unsatisfactory and a Speaker's conference should be established to review the problem. I can't think of a better reason for a written constitution, or an end to the link between parliament and the monarch. Whatever her private political views, there will surely be one non-voter in SW1 hoping for a clear election result.

Labour's Position

The enemy of liberalism?

The first half of Blair's premiership saw a range of policy issues that had much in common with the Liberal Democrats' own position. The constitutional issues were kept on the agenda by Ashdown and although his heart was not in it, Blair did deliver on devolution in Scotland and Wales, changed the voting system for European elections, introduced freedom of information and made steps towards House of Lords reform. This was a progressive agenda and could easily have formed the basis of a coalition, or pact, with the Liberals if it had been needed. Blair's final five years were just as busy on the legislative front, but could hardly be described as progressive and certainly not Liberal. It would have been unthinkable for a coalition with the Liberals to have overseen his centralisation agenda, let alone the range of criminal justice measures. Week after week his government traduced civil liberties and offended liberal thinking groups. The Home Affairs legislation alone illustrates the point. With one of the most anti-liberal Home Secretaries, David Blunkett's attacks on long held "liberal" policy agenda seemed deliberately designed to attract tabloid support and he would regularly attack the "Liberal chattering classes" on the *Today* programme. He introduced legislation on ID cards, undermined judges, attempted to abolish trial by jury and started locking up more and more people. On immigration he clamped down on support for asylum seekers and used a rhetoric that a right wing Home Secretary would find hard to better. After his resignation, I had hoped Charles Clarke would be a more progressive Home Secretary. In our early private meetings he seemed less confrontational and, certainly on prisons and offender management, I could see a Liberal trying to get out. Then the July 2004 bombs hit London and the Government's responses shifted over the weeks from measured, to confrontational. Within hours of the attack Clarke included myself, as the Liberal Shadow Home Secretary, and David Davis, the Conservative Shadow, in talks. The approach was to be consensual as we jointly considered measures which would make the job of police and security services easier without impacting on civil liberties. I can remember the moment that the consensus started to collapse. It was early August 2004, and most of the key players had gone on holiday. Blair was still in Downing

Street and decided to issue a shopping list of anti-terror measures. I'd received a call the night before from Home Office Minister, Hazel Blears, telling me it was coming and saying there was nothing controversial included. In fact the list was an outrageous attack on our criminal justice system, the most controversial of which was to hold suspects for 90 days without charge.

Iraq

The other big area of disagreement in this parliament was the conflict in Iraq. Charles Kennedy had been unconvinced over the evidence he had seen on weapons of mass destruction and the general threat posed by Iraq. The Liberal Democrats' opposition to war and the personal nature of the language between the two parties was a sign of just how distant the parties had grown since the cosy days of sitting round the Cabinet table as part of the Blair/Ashdown Joint Consultative Committee (JCC).

The reality behind the final Blair years is that the Liberal Democrats had very little in common with his government. This is best illustrated by the voting pattern of the two parties in Westminster. The chart below shows how the Liberals have voted less and less with Labour over the last parliament:

Year	Liberals Voting With Labour
2001/2	71%
2002/3	68%
2003/4	68%
2004/5	66%
2005/6	29%

On division between 2005-2006 parliament the Liberal Democrats voted with Labour on just 29 per cent, hardly the basis for a coalition.

On occasion after occasion the Liberals found that their partners in protecting Liberal values were the Conservatives. It was not easy working with Shadow Home Secretary David Davis, a pro-hanging right-winger, but he was, without question, determined to protect justice and freedom when he felt it was under attack.

It would have been unthinkable to have entered into any parliamentary pact, or arrangement, with this kind of Labour Party.

So why would the Liberals even consider it next time round? Is Brown more of a Liberal than Blair? Could the illiberal agenda be presented as part of the negotiations? Would the price of PR be big enough to put civil liberty issues as second best?

Finish The Project

Later on in this chapter, I will look at the case for completing the Ashdown/Blair project and argue that many of those associated with the 1995-1999 period are now those that influence Ming Campbell. But what of Labour? The Mandelson/Blair era is over; would there be any in a Brown-led government that see this as unfinished business?

Neal Lawson, author of *The Progressive Century*, thinks not. When I asked him about this he said:

> *There is nobody left in the Cabinet that believes in the Jenkins dream of the reunification of progressives.*[8]

Brown does not share the same big tent approach to politics that Blair started out with. He is by nature a tribal politician and although he has sought out to influence and bring on side the business and finance world, his instincts are not to work with others. He is as Lawson said:

> *Not yet the world's greatest purist.*[9]

In early summer of 2007, Westminster was taken by surprise when Brown offered Lord Ashdown the position of Northern Ireland Secretary. It was out of character and left most commentators concluding that Brown was up to trick work rather than a conversion to the politics of co-operation.

There is very little said about Brown's attitude towards the JCC set up between Labour and the Liberal Democrats in the late 1990s. He very rarely met Ashdown and there was no question of economic issues forming any of the joint working areas of the JCC. There was a joint meeting held between the Treasury teams, but it was not a significant development and little more than the regular briefing Ministers often have with opposite numbers. The *Ashdown Diaries* reveal few and mixed messages on Brown's position. In

December 1997, Ashdown held a meeting with Brown and asked him his opinion on the project:

> *Now, tell me bluntly, are you prepared to see us in government with you? Or is that something you would oppose?*[10]

According to Ashdown, Brown responded positively:

> *No, of course I want you to be in the project with us. It's the only sensible solution. And we need to get there as soon as we can.*[11]

A year later Ashdown felt Brown was behind a move to undermine Peter Mandelson and the project:

> *Brown is said to be behind this and there is a substantial move by Junior Ministers as well as Cabinet members, to use the opportunity to stamp out the Lib/Lab relationship and the whole project.*[12]

Most of the 2007 Brown Government were not around during the period of the JCC and those that were, such as Jack Straw, have never been big fans.

For the Liberal Democrats, completing the project or trying to establish a new progressive agenda with Labour may have strong emotional and practical appeal, but I see little evidence that in a post-Blair era the Labour Government have any attraction, or loyalty, to it.

Brown And Electoral Reform

Closely connected to the project and one of the major obstacles to its progression was the issue of electoral reform. It's always been a deal breaker and could be next time. Labour, and now New Labour, remains unconvinced. When Callaghan failed to put a whip on the key proportional representation vote during the Lib/Lab pact, he was not going back on a deal, but knew he could not persuade Labour MPs to vote for change even with a whip. The Cabinet was prepared to risk breaking up the pact and facing an election rather than introduce PR. It illustrates just how hostile the party is to change. Blair too faced considerable hostility in his Cabinet on the issue and even the eloquent arguments of Roy Jenkins could not convince them to change.

There is no evidence to suggest that Labour has undergone a conversion to PR at Westminster. Although they have introduced it for elections in Europe,

London, Scotland and Wales, the final frontier of Westminster remains a tough one for the party. The objections can hardly be on grounds of principle, as the system has worked well in the other places. The recent Scottish elections, and success of the SNP may be used as an argument against, but the SNP are not a minority party in Scotland and could have achieved impressive gains even under first-past-the-post.

The real objection, as it always has been, is that turkeys don't vote for an early Christmas. Both Callaghan and Blair did the sums and told their Liberal opposite numbers that to introduce PR would mean losing too many of their own seats. It takes a brave, or foolhardy, leader to tell backbenchers that he is going to create a system that will mean a large percentage will lose their jobs at the next election.

I have always felt that Labour would only shift on PR for Westminster when its back was right against the wall, but even then the Jurassic Park mentality would probably kick in and the change would be reluctant and delayed as long as possible.

Although Brown has shown no enthusiasm for reforming the voting system, he may be prepared to agree to a form of PR if his job depends on it. Neal Lawson believes this would be the case:

> I imagine Brown would not mind too much if his arm was twisted on election reform. If it was the price for doing a deal with Ming then AV is distinctly possible. And it has the added bonus of killing off the Conservatives.[13]

I can see the case for this. After all, AV would be easy to introduce, unlike other PR systems it does not require a referendum, or boundary changes and could be easy to introduce in time for the election in say 2013/2014. It would also act as an insurance policy for Brown, making it more likely he could continue in power as AV would help the left of centre parties.

There is another possibility that Brown will seek to surprise as Prime Minister and embrace a reforming agenda. His first months in office showed a surprising interest in constitutional reform. Lord Tyler, former Liberal Democrat Chief Whip, thinks Brown may be looking for a fresh new agenda.

Brown may be looking to create an agenda about reconnecting with people. It's possible reforming the electoral system could be part of that.[14]

This may in part explain his rather clumsy overtures to the Liberal Democrats in the days before he became leader, when he offered Ming Campbell discussions on joint working in certain areas.

I have hunted for more firm evidence of his thoughts on proportional representation. He made some interesting remarks at the Donald Dewar Memorial lecture in October 2006:

The fact is you cannot master the challenges ahead the old way with the old political and constitutional arrangements. It cannot be done by the old politics of a political class believing they were born to govern and a passive electorate. If today, each challenge can be met only by people as individuals and in communities working together with our great national institutions with elected politicians uniquely conscious of their position a servants of the British people in this process, then constitutional change is necessary and urgent.[15]

The last sentence could easily be a call to introduce a fairer voting system!

However, since becoming Prime Mister, Brown has said very little on the issue of proportional representation. In an interview with the *Independent* newspaper readers on 23rd July 2007, he said:

The issue of the voting system should not be based on the grounds of keeping one party or another out of power – it should be based on what is best for democracy in this country. And I believe strongly in the idea of a representative system with a strong geographical link of the MP to their constituency.

This is very similar to the stance he took in a speech in 1992 to Charter 88, the Constitutional reform group. He appears to favour an electoral system that maintains the constituency link.

Systems are widely varied and have had quite different consequences when they have been tried. The debate, in other words, must concentrate on mechanisms as well as ideas. In particular, I and many others want to ensure whatever system is adopted it maintains the close link between the constituency as a community and its representative.[16]

If Brown does set out to introduce a new reforming agenda, he could send the Liberal Democrats an important early message by indicating that electoral reform is on that agenda.

It seems that those around Brown are moving towards recommending the alternative vote system and believe that this would keep the constituency link and be relatively easy to introduce.

Despite these considerations, Brown is unlikely to get trapped on the issue before the next election, remembering the mess that Neil Kinnock got into during the 1992 election on the whole question of PR systems and hung parliament. This will remain an issue to be discussed in very private circles.

Labour's Options

If we assume that the next election produces a hung parliament, there are numerous calculations that could be made. For the sake of examining the most likely let's predict two outcomes:

- Firstly, Labour has the largest number of seats, but not a majority.

- Secondly, they are the second party in terms of seats and the Conservatives are just short of a majority.

In the first outcome, the following routes would be open to Brown:

1. Form an administration seeking no arrangement with other parties and hope to battle on and assume the opposition forces can't unite against you.

2. Approach the Liberal Democrats to secure either a working arrangement, a pact, or full coalition.

In the second outcome, the following seem realistic options for Brown:

1. Immediately resign as Prime Minister and throw the problem to the other parties.

2. As sitting Prime Minister, Brown would be within his rights to seek out an arrangement with the Liberal Democrats to form an administration.

3. Form a minority administration and force the other parties to combine to defeat him.

The first outcome is by far the easiest situation for Labour. Having the largest number of seats gives Brown a powerful position. Although he will have been seen to lose seats it's not necessarily the case that he will have lost the election. If he were to go to the polls with a large opinion poll lead and see it reduced by polling day then his position is weaker. If, however, he claws back from a predicted defeat to Cameron to edge ahead in seat terms he will have considerable authority. David Butler argues that winning and losing is more than just seats.

> Whether a party is seen to have won or lost an election is a psychic judgement, a complicated assessment based on the cause of the appeal to the country, the nature of the campaign argument and the extent of party gains and losses in seats and votes.[17]

Butler is right that the impression is important but the key, however, is not votes, or perception of winning or losing, but is all down to seats and in this scenario he would have the most.

It will be very tempting in these circumstances to just battle on. It's business as usual. You can almost hear him saying 'last week I was Prime Minister, the electorate have decided to give Labour the largest number of seats, so this week I will continue to be Prime Minister'.

His second option would be to create a firmer basis for staying in office. If he calculates that the Liberals are unlikely to want to vote him out, or cause a second election, he may try to form a friendly association with them, involving regular meetings, issue by issue understandings, with ministerial briefs for Liberal shadow spokesmen. The exact nature of any arrangement will depend to a large extent on the shortfall in seats Labour has. The more he is short of a majority, the greater the depth of arrangement he needs with the Liberals. I will examine later the option of a more formal arrangement.

Brown's options are much tougher under the second scenario where he has fewer seats. In these circumstances resignation must be the honourable thing to do. He will clearly have lost his working majority and be the second party in parliament. Even if he were to win the popular vote, he is still "defeated". Although he is not required to resign and protocol allows him to have first shot at staying in power, I think it is unlikely he will try. Edward Heath attempted to do it in 1974 and it turned out to be as Wilson said a 'long dirty weekend' as Heath struggled to find a deal. It looked shabby and I doubt Brown will find it very dignified.

However, he may have planned for this position and have an informal arrangement with the Liberal Democrats up his sleeve for such a situation. In which case he could quickly trigger that plan. I will look later at what this kind of deal would involve.

A third, but unlikely, plan is that he just carried on as Prime Minister, from a very weak position and calls the opposition's bluff. This is risky, ignores the electorate's wishes and must surely be doomed to long-term failure. It could work however if the Conservatives decided to leave him struggling and wounded for a couple of years before triggering a new election. That depends on the Cameron strategy, which I turn to next.

The New Conservatives?

The Conservatives had tended to play no part in post-war coalitions in this country. Apart from Edward Heath's brief attempt to work with Jeremy Thorpe, the significant arrangements have been between Labour and Liberals in 1977 and more recently in Scotland and Wales.

Could all that change at the next election? After over a decade without power, the Conservatives will be desperate to get back in, but at what price?

Their options depend on the number of seats gained in a hung parliament. It boils down to four likely positions:

- Attempt to govern alone as the party with the largest number of seats – perhaps triggering a second election fairly soon after.

- Secure a long-term arrangement with the Liberal Democrats to maintain a government from the basis of holding the largest number of seats.

- Attempt to displace Brown as Prime Minister even if he holds most seats by combining with minor parties – either to form an administration, or push for an early no confidence vote and second election.

- Allow Brown to govern alone and hope he runs out of steam.

If there is a hung parliament this will be seen as a victory for Cameron, irrespective of the number of seats he wins. The position he inherited from Michael Howard was much improved from the 2001 election, but Cameron will still have been given an enormous mountain to climb. Reducing Brown to a minority position will give him moral authority.

Whereas I think it is near impossible for Brown to govern from second position in the Commons, there is a case to be made for Cameron. He can argue that the electorate have rejected Labour and the clear signal from the country is a move towards the Conservatives.

I think this same authority will make it unlikely for him to seek support if the Conservatives have the largest number of seats. In this position he could form a minority administration and challenge Labour and the Liberals to defy the electorate's wishes and vote him out. A weakened Brown and nervous Liberal Democrats may judge triggering a no confidence vote as unwise.

Cameron could govern as Wilson did in 1974 for a few months and then seek a second election to try and secure a stronger majority.

If, however, he finds himself in second place, is there any possibility of working with the Liberals to oust Labour?

In a speech on 23rd March 2007, he called for a Liberal-Conservative consensus:

> Gordon Brown and the philosophy which drives him will only be detected if Liberal and Conservative supporters rally behind an alternative government-in-waiting. I believe that we need a new Liberal-Conservative consensus in our country.[18]

He then went on to describe what he saw as a split in the Liberal ranks, between "Orange Book" and "Brown Book" Liberals. A group of Liberal MPs got together to write the Orange Book, which was designed to create new Liberal thinking on a range of issues. The media simplified this to suggest that senior Liberals were paving the way towards a blue/orange alliance. It's true that many Conservative MPs could have supported chapters in the Orange Book, but it was genuinely written to set out a Liberal agenda. As I will argue later there is no doubt the Liberals are divided on the question of supporting the Conservatives. Even if Cameron was offering a superb deal it's questionable whether the Liberal leadership could get it passed amongst MPs let alone activists.

There is further evidence that Cameron is serious about his overtures toward the Liberal Democrats. In April 2007, he offered Campbell the chance to put forward a joint Tory/Liberal candidate to run as Mayor of London. Although the move was initiated by the potential candidate, Greg Dyke, it is interesting that the Tory leader did not reject it out of hand; it is even more telling that the Liberal leader did, within hours.

There is some common policy ground that could bring the parties together. There was a period of joint working on the environment where both parties campaigned in 2006 for a Climate Change Bill and, as I touched on earlier, much agreement on Civil Liberty issues. The Conservatives' decision to abandon ID cards is quite an important symbol of change. There are, however, some areas of conflict with the Liberal Democrats. On energy policy the Conservatives have said that nuclear power should be a last resort, the party favour replacing Trident and support tuition fees. Europe would remain a difficult area. It is also hard to find many Conservatives interested in electoral reform and this could again be the downfall of any arrangement.

Cameron has not said a great deal on the issue of electoral reform. In a number of speeches on constitutional reform he has spoken of modernising select committees, more free votes in parliament and greater cross-party working, but the words 'electoral reform' are notably absent. However, in May 2006, he made these remarks on the Power Inquiry into reforming government:

> One of the few proposals in the Power Inquiry Report I don't agree with is the idea of moving to a system of PR. And I say that as the leader of a party that would be a major beneficiary of such a change. One of the reasons I'm in favour of first-past-the-post is because the link between an MP and his or her constituency is a vital one.[19]

Of course the AV system of PR would keep the constituency link open, perhaps that might be a compromise route for the Tory leader.

In his remarks Cameron is right to point out that the Conservatives could benefit from a reform in the voting system. First-past-the-post is no longer the friend of the Conservatives. At the 2005 election in England the

Conservatives polled 50,000 more votes than Labour, but were 92 seats behind!

Whatever the current view, if the Conservatives find themselves 9 per cent ahead in popular vote and still without a working majority it might make the case for changing the system a lot easier.

As the Conservatives continue to re-invent themselves, they remain in need of endorsements from public symbols that the change is real. That's why Zac Goldsmith on green issues and Bob Geldolf on Third World poverty are important for the party. Could the Liberal Democrats offer the ultimate endorsement that the Conservatives can be trusted on public services? You can certainly see how a blue/orange alliance would be in keeping with Cameron's softer image.

There is a slight possibility that the margin between forming a government is so slim that the Conservatives may bypass the Liberal leadership and try to identify a dozen Liberal MPs to work with them. Technically this is possible and I can imagine some being tempted by office, but it would be virtually like defecting and would create a split in the party which would probably cost the individuals involved their seats next time round.

The other option open to the Conservatives if Brown has the largest number of seats is to sit tight and let him run a minority government. This was the opinion put forward by Michael Portillo when I spoke to him.

He believes the Tories should be patient and let Labour run a minority government and fail. This, Portillo believes, will result in a bigger Tory majority at the election after next. He also thinks:

> Waiting a few more years will allow Cameron to mature and work out ideas – it will not be a bad thing.[20]

Portillo went on to say:

> There will be a hung parliament with Labour as the biggest party. Cameron should let Brown go on governing and guarantee he will not defeat him for two years so that Brown will not have to do a deal with the Liberal Democrats on PR.[21]

It is an interesting theory, but seems based on the assumption that the Tories must do all they can to stop PR. It does not allow for the fact that Brown may now see an AV system as a benefit to his party's fortunes and want to introduce it anyway.

I am not convinced. If Cameron sees a chance to take office I can't see him sitting back and waiting. It's too risky to wait and see in politics – events come along that send the best laid plans awry.

The Liberal Devil Dilemma

When I asked Paddy Ashdown what he would do if there was a hung parliament at the next election, he was reluctant to say anything that could be seen to interfere with Campbell's leadership, but then made a remarkable statement:

> *I would not sup with God unless PR was on the menu, I would sup with the Devil if it was.*[22]

I take that as a clear message that Labour can forget it unless PR is part of any deal, but that Ashdown would work with the Tories if it was. It's an interesting dilemma.

The opportunity presented by a hung parliament is enormous, but so are the dangers. Do you risk supporting a failed government if Labour loses, or risk splitting your party by supporting the Conservatives? Is doing nothing a realistic opportunity? Can PR finally be gained? For the two main parties a hung parliament is an aberration in the normal pattern of two-party politics. For the Liberal Democrats it could be make or break.

In previous chapters I have looked at the attempts of Thorpe, Steel and Ashdown to make the most of co-operation to further the party. None has achieved the ultimate prize of PR and the Liberal Democrats remain a third force in a two party system. Now the baton has fallen to Ming Campbell. Can he deliver where others have failed?

Ming Campbell's Approach To Co-operation

The Liberal Democrats have the knack of getting the right leader for the right time. When the party was virtually a statistical error in the opinion polls it needed the dynamic, clear-headed Ashdown to drive it to success.

Kennedy's more relaxed style was the perfect way to deal with the control style of Blair. If the party is to face an uncertain election and tough negotiations, then in Campbell it has the right balance of experience, calmness and toughness, to steer it through the dangerous waters of a hung parliament.

Campbell is trusted on both sides of the party. He has promoted Nick Clegg and Edward Davey from the more economic Liberal wing, but given left-leaning MP Steve Webb the job of drawing up the party manifesto. By bringing in the younger, new generation of MPs he has also effectively moved the debate on from some of the divisions that existed under Kennedy between those that were somewhat lazily described as left and right.

He remains close to Ashdown and many of those he has in his inner circle came from the project era. Archy Kirkwood, Paul Tyler, Don Foster and Nick Harvey are all old veterans of the Ashdown/Blair talks. Away from Westminster he has sought the advice of Neil Sherlock, a project enthusiast and co-author of *A Progressive Century*, a book devoted to creating an alliance of progressive Liberals and Labour to block the Conservatives from coming into power. This ex-project group regard the Ashdown era as unfinished business and their political instincts remain close to Labour. Some of the links created during the pre- and post-1997 discussions remain and there is a comfort zone in contemplating working with Labour again.

Like Brown, he is a Scottish MP and I have a sense that if a post-election deal is done, it will have been on the basis of friendships and discussions made on the Edinburgh social circuit, rather than Westminster-based suppers. Both men will have the Scottish Parliament experience to draw on. Documents on how the Holyrood deals between the two parties were prepared have already been sent to Liberal Democrat Chief Whip, Paul Burstow.

Some MPs have suggested to me that these discussions are already very advanced and a deal is all but agreed. They point to the Lib Dems reluctance to back the SNP in Scotland as a sign of even closer Labour/Liberal relations. I have found no real evidence to suggest this and remain of the view that Campbell, although sympathetic to Brown, will keep his options open.

I think this view is reflected in the events that took place in the middle of June 2007, when these informal discussions hit the headlines. It emerged that Campbell had met, at Brown's request, to discuss the possibility of Liberal Democrats joining his first Labour Cabinet. The request was declined by Campbell, but not until it emerged that Brown's target had been Lord Ashdown. Campbell was prepared to talk, listen, but not damage his party's independence in advance of the general election.

However, Campbell's relations with Cameron are not as close. He has made more personal attacks on him than Brown and gone out of his way to dismiss talk of a deal with the Conservatives. In a speech in March 2007 he said of Cameron:

> *He does not understand the contradiction between these two*
> *philosophies. Being Liberal is about more than sound bites and photo*
> *opportunities. It's about policies, not posturing. Deeds not words.*[23]

In April 2007, he quickly dismissed an offer to fight the Mayor of London contest with a joint Tory candidate. Agreeing to meet Cameron he quickly and publicly rejected the offer hours later.

Wherever his sympathy may lie, one thing I am convinced of is that he is also without question a Liberal. Drawing on his legal skills he always spoke passionately about defending the criminal justice system against the Blunkett and Clarke reforms.

Campbell is, however, his own man and will draw on his own beliefs and experiences. He is a popular figure in the Commons. The respect shown to him after his battle with cancer and the votes he received when he ran for Speaker are testament to that. He values this enormously and is not by nature confrontational in his day-to-day meetings, or his Commons performances. I don't think he would care much for hand-to-hand warfare in a hung parliament and his instincts would be to seek agreement when he could.

Campbell is by nature fairly cautious. He is not going to want to risk ridicule in any negotiations and will rightly be anxious about how to handle the wider party. Any Liberal leader will tell you that one of the hardest parts of the job is managing the numerous party structures. As the most democratic party there are endless policy and strategy hurdles to negotiate and the question of what to do after the next election has already started being debated within the party. Campbell may even find that whatever he eventually decides after the election, he will need to face a special party meeting to get approval. Much as David Steel did in January 1978 after the pact nearly collapsed over PR, the fate of the country's government could once again rest in the hands of a thousand or so Liberal activists! That is a difficult prospect, as David Butler observes:

> *Most elected politicians will, in the last resort, make a deal with almost anyone – ordinary party workers being further from power are more likely to be absolutists and uncompromising.*[24]

Despite the dangers, Campbell will make some attempt to consult and take comfort from the successful consultation the party put in place following negotiations in Scotland even if replicating that on a larger scale will be difficult.

Despite these difficult hurdles, Campbell is a determined individual and his moment in history will not be lost on him. As Ashdown said:

> *The truth is that every Liberal Democrat leader is given this opportunity, each of us has a different hand to play in different circumstances, I think Ming will have it more powerfully than any of us.*[25]

Campbell was described by some as a caretaker leader; what better way to end his career and shut up his critics than to be the first Liberal leader since the war to deliver his party into power sharing and deliver PR. The question is which route will he take?

The Liberal Democrat options in a hung parliament are numerous. If we assume that the party remains with a seat range from forty to seventy it is going to have the seats to deliver power to either of the main parties.

Self evidently the Liberals can only form an arrangement with either Conservatives, or Labour. The critical point is whether that arrangement is designed to secure government for the party with the largest seats, or block it and put the second and third parties into power. There is a very big difference.

I believe the Liberals should make it clear that they will first seek to work with the party that has the largest number of seats, irrespective of popular vote. If that is rejected, or agreement could not be reached then they would open discussions with the second largest party. The party should also make it clear that PR has to be on the agenda with a whipped vote to take place in parliament within 18 months. This should be a clear statement in advance of the election. This has the merit of transparency, it avoids looking shifty and puts the decision in the electorate's hands; it also follows the model used in Scotland.

Once you establish this principle the Liberal Democrats are in practice agreeing to work with either Labour or Conservatives, depending on who wins the election. Equidistance is back on the agenda and according to Professor Whiteley:

> If equidistance is back and it's real that means opening up the possibility of talking to Conservatives, or at least Cameron's Conservatives.[26]

Indeed times have moved on. There is less to divide the two major parties as the manifestoes of all parties grow closer and closer. As Tom McNally said to me on the prospects next time round:

> The stark ideological differences between state ownership, big fix spending, cutting public services and privatisation have all disappeared. It would be difficult to judge what party is on the left or right in the old terms.[27]

Working With Labour

Working with a Labour government which has the largest number of seats is by far the easiest option for the Liberal Democrats. As I pointed out earlier, much of the necessary chemistry is in place. Brown could, I believe, be persuaded to back a form of PR. There would need to be a serious discussion over anti-terrorism legislation and ID cards.

However, although Labour will have the largest number of seats, the position would be made difficult if the Tories were considerably ahead in the popular vote. In these situations although seats matter so does public opinion. Clare Short thinks a deal could be difficult:

> To prop up Labour after it had lost the election would feel wrong even if it did have the largest number of seats.[28]

I think it would be even harder to deliberately seek to stop the Conservatives if they had the largest number of seats. In such a circumstance the party would be helping a defeated Brown to stay in government. It would look as if the Liberals were trying to block the wishes of the electorate. I think that could damage the party and drag them down into the dying days of a final Labour government that would hang on to power much as Major did from 1992-1997 and as happened to the Liberals in 1977 during the Lib/Lab pact.

To support Labour in such terms would be 'hazardous'. Andrew Rawnsley sums up the problem:

> It would be highly hazardous to sustain Labour in power. The Liberal Democrats would have spent the election campaign telling the country that Labour was clapped out. Could they then turn round and offer life support to Gordon Brown as Prime Minister? That would be extremely difficult if Labour was regarded as a rejected government which had lost its moral authority.[29]

Tom McNally tends to agree that the maths is critical when it comes to supporting Labour. If they remain the largest party that is one thing, but:

> If a Conservative Party ended up just a few short of absolute majority and Labour had lost 70 seats, I think it would be extremely difficult to support them and you would be punished by the electorate for going against those wishes.[30]

Neal Lawson was even clearer:

> The Liberals will find it difficult to keep in power a Labour government that had lost its legitimacy.[31]

He does, however, acknowledge that the Liberals could still turn to Brown, if the Conservatives with the largest number of seats rejected a discussion with Campbell. On this option he says:

> If Ming goes to Brown after he has tried Cameron it looks less shabby when Cameron has said no.[32]

However, Liberal Democrat MPs and activists are fiercely independent in their outlook; one only has to look at the outcry that took place when Brown offered Ashdown a job. Working with Labour would certainly be easier for party activists to accept. The majority of the Parliamentary Party feel more comfortable with Labour, although under Blair as each week passed they became less and less sympathetic. Some, however, are more hostile. A cluster of MPs are very nervous at the electoral and philosophical dangers of keeping Labour in power. They argue that their seats depend on safe Tory voters who will be alienated by any deal. They point to the voters' desire for change and fear being blamed for helping keep the status quo. They also argue that Labour and Liberalism just don't mix.

These MPs have tended to keep quiet about their concerns, but would a deal with Labour test their loyalty to the limit?

I very much doubt it. For them as long as PR was negotiated they would be prepared to sit it out and hope the party could grow under a new electoral system.

Would It Be Possible To Work With The Conservatives?

The assumption made by most Liberal activists is that they have more in common with Labour. They feel very let down by them over Iraq and civil liberties, but generally don't regard them as the real enemy. That is still reserved for the Conservatives. This hostility may have been justified during the Thatcher, Major, Duncan Smith period, but is Cameron any worse than Brown? The attitude one holds towards another party is coloured by its history, but should be based on its today not its yesterday. Labour today is centralist and illiberal. The Conservatives today defend civil liberties and are developing a more progressive agenda on social issues. The last four years have seen Conservatives and Liberal MPs in the same lobby on liberal issues such as holding suspects without charge and ID cards.

Cameron's Conservatives have held out the olive branch to a number of Liberal MPs, most notably David Laws, one of the party's brightest MPs, who has admitted that he was asked to defect in 2005. Others, such as Jeremy Browne and, the biggest prize of all, Nick Clegg, must also be in their sights. These MPs and a cluster of others would have little difficulty working with Conservatives in a hung parliament. They don't, however, represent a majority of the Parliamentary Party. I believe that any blue/orange combination after the election, even with PR to soften the blow, would result in a couple of Liberal MPs declining to take the Whip. It would be too much for them to work with the old enemy.

Frankly though, the MPs would be the least of the leadership's problems. Such a deal would cause outcry amongst rank and file activists. As Andrew Rawnsley wrote:

> Going into coalition with the Conservatives would be hugely contentious. Liberal activists tend to be more left wing than their leadership, ... a deal with David Cameron would split the Liberal Democrats.[33]

There is no doubt that the Conservatives are moving into the centre ground and attempting to capture Liberal territory. This shift, if genuine and sustained, makes the prospect of an arrangement with the Liberals more acceptable. As Clare Short said to me:

> If the Conservatives do fight the next election on the centre ground it then changes what is feasible for the Liberal Democrats after the election.[34]

The current hostility to such an arrangement could weaken if Cameron is prepared to walk the talk on the environment, reform and civil liberties.

Do Nothing

The third option is to decide that the party will play no part in pacts or coalitions. The do nothing approach was adopted by Charles Kennedy who dealt with the hung parliament issue by declaring the party would remain an independent force judging each issue and vote on its merits. This stance has the advantage of avoiding the issue and sounds rather principled. It worked for Kennedy, but was never tested by the journalists as there was never any serious question of the Liberals holding the balance of power.

Is it a credible option for the next election? Although the pre-election message would be clear, it would come under enormous pressure. Freelancing MPs would break ranks and under media scrutiny what looks rather principled could turn into foolhardy arrogance. Professor Paul Whiteley does not think it would work in practice:

> It's not realistic to vote on each issue as it comes. First you have the problem of the Queen's speech and secondly one of those issues will come up and turn into a no-confidence vote. Frankly you end up lacking political credibility if you say you won't work with others.[35]

The Queen's speech is a problem for the 'do-nothing' approach. It's the parliamentary endorsement of a new government programme and bluntly at this point you have to put up, or shut up. Even if this was overcome within months the main opposition will have found a case to force a no confidence vote forcing the Liberals into backing one side. Whilst it sounds a good sound bite two years away from an election, the staying independent route is just not an option for a party that wants to be taken seriously. Lawson agrees:

> *You can't just sit on your hands if you have a chance to gain seats in Cabinet and direct policy influence for your party. You have to take it and accept that the dangers are far outweighed by not taking your chance.*[36]

It could be possible to formally agree to support the minority government issue by issue without any deal. This could give the government of the day confidence that you won't defend them on a no confidence vote. I just can't see the advantage in this. The Liberals helped Labour in 1924 along these lines and ended up losing votes and seats as a result. It seems to me that the one lesson of this period is that it is terribly dangerous to support a minority government and yet not participate in it; you get all the blame for the things that the people don't like and no credit.

How A Coalition Could Work

Any successful coalition can't be put together in the days after an election. It requires more time. The problem is that before the election discussions can leak, and after the election the British public don't want to wait weeks for a solution. As David Butler told me:

> *The problem with forming a coalition in this country is that the public want removal vans in Downing Street on Friday and want to know what's going on, but rushed decisions are often bad decisions.*[37]

What's required are informal and very discreet discussions to start at a very early stage.

Tom McNally's advice is:

> *to have the policy and pipework in place and then see what the electorate decide.*[38]

The big fear for the politicians is that this information can leak out and start to dominate the media's coverage of the party. It is always a danger for the Liberal Democrats that they are viewed in relation to the other parties. Nevertheless it would be foolhardy not to prepare. Those preparations must be even handed; if a leak exposes that discussions are with just one party it would be more damaging than a revelation about discussions with all sides. Campbell has started that process and instructed his Chief Whip, Paul Burstow, to prepare various options for him. At an MPs away day outside Henley in March 2007, the party had an initial discussion on the options. The leadership's public message view is that 'it would be surprising if the leader had not asked for various options to be looked into'. This is a sensible approach.

However, the subject has already cost a senior member of staff his job. During the Spring Party Conference a muddled press briefing caused a string of headlines suggesting that PR would not be a condition of any deal. In fact Campbell was listing a set of priorities for a Brown government, but journalists looked at this as a possible deal wish list and saw PR was not included. It was much ado about nothing, but Head of Press, Mark Littlewood, resigned over the issue a week later. It was a warning that the entire issue of hung parliaments is fraught with danger.

Between now and the election the party needs a clear, thought out message. David Butler puts it in these terms:

> *Each of the parties will need a clearly thought out strategy that can be Paxman'd when the polls show we are heading for a hung parliament.*[39]

The lesson from the pre-election period in Scotland is that a firm set of rules and language must be used at all times. Any sense of weakness or public rejection is a disaster.

This could be tested to the limits if the Conservatives judge that it's worth raising a possible Liberal/Labour pact as one of their campaign messages. Major used this to great effect in the 1992 campaign. Cameron would put pressure on the Liberals to rule a deal with Labour out, or tie the party up on details over PR systems.

Professor Paul Whiteley argues that:

Brown and Cameron will make great play of saying that we need strong government.[40]

Both will dismiss talk of hung parliaments. The Liberal Democrats must avoid at all costs the sense that they are campaigning for one. Even if you agree with Clare Short's position,[41] campaigning with a view to a hung parliament is politically speaking near impossible to deliver.

As Roy Jenkins said:

hung parliaments depend largely upon accidents outside our control – the relationship which the other parties bear to each other – and is therefore not an effective call to action.[42]

After the special Liberal Assembly held during the Callaghan/Steel pact in 1978, the party issued a position paper on hung parliaments. There were three key points:

- Firstly, Liberals would adopt an even-handed approach 'being prepared in principle to consider agreements or arrangements with either Tory or Labour Parliamentary Parties'.

- Secondly, in the event of a hung parliament 'we are prepared in the first instance to enter into discussions with the party gaining the most votes at the elections'.

- Thirdly, the agreement would 'certainly include a cast iron commitment to introduce PR for Westminster and endorsement of the agreement by the parliamentary Labour Party or 1922 Committee as appropriate'.

I think this wording goes a long way to setting the type of condition the party should work towards thirty years later. I would make a few alterations. Such a statement could be issued months before an election, or immediately after the outcome is known.

Possible Draft Agreement

I would argue the following pre-conditions for any agreement:

1. The Liberal Democrats will firstly seek agreement with the party which has the largest number of seats in parliament.

2. A whipped vote on PR to take place within 18 months.

3. Any agreement will last for 18 months.

4. A detailed partnership agreement to be drawn up and made public within two weeks of the election and before the Queen's speech.

5. The Liberal Democrats will be allocated ministerial posts in proportion to the number of seats compared to the government.

Any agreement also has to cover personnel. The Liberal Democrats will need a combination of Cabinet and Junior Ministerial posts. Based on a ratio with the largest party and assuming the Liberals have between 40-70 seats they could expect between ⅕ and ¼ of Ministerial posts. This could mean around 20-25 of the Liberal Parliamentary Party in some official post. It would put enormous pressure on the party and careful thought would be needed on how to allocate these positions.

In Europe there are two models the minority party are given; a whole government department to run, or spread evenly with a number of Junior Ministers to provide a check and balance across government. I think the latter works best and allows real influence. It also avoids the danger that an unexpected event in the one department you run can damage the party's reputation.

There is also the question of what Campbell should do as leader. Does he remain outside of government to protect the identity of the party? (A position Ashdown claimed he would take.) Or, should he take a senior position in government? I am of little doubt that he should be at the heart of government as the symbol of an agreement, if not as Foreign Secretary then as Deputy Prime Minister.

The period of the agreement is also important. British Parliamentary sessions are long and full of hazards. A full parliament agreement would be hard to sustain. By-elections could change the seat dynamics, events come along which create coalition tensions and it does not allow the junior partner the option of reviewing and then seeking a better deal. The European coalitions seem to suffer beyond two years as the partnership agreement gets stale and lacks direction. An 18 month agreement with the option to continue under renegotiation keeps the right level of tension. It would also force the government to deliver and not delay on any policy promises such as PR.

The Question Of PR And Policy

Could the party get PR? I am sure a speaker's conference on Jenkins Mark II would be on offer. That's not enough. The party must ask for a parliamentary vote and legislation in time for the next election. This must come with two conditions. Firstly, the vote must be whipped by the government. In 1977, Callaghan did not Whip his MPs and the vote was lost. Secondly, a timescale should be put in place so the vote is completed within 18 months. The coalition should be signed for a similar period, allowing the option of voting down the government if PR is not delivered.

The attitude of the two major parties may be shifting on PR. As I argued earlier, Brown's desire to demonstrate a reforming agenda and his survival instincts appear to be moving him in the direction of an AV system. If the Conservatives end up with an eight point lead in the vote and still have less seats, the overwhelming sense of injustice might push them towards electoral reform.

The Liberal Democrats will want more than electoral reform from any deal. The list of key demands in any talks could include abolishing ID cards and other civil liberty related issues. However, the party has yet to set out distinctive new policies that could be on the shopping list.

What's Best for Britain

I have been a member of the SDP, then the Liberal Democrats, for over 25 years and I would dearly love to see my party form a government. Given that it is not on the cards at the next election, what would I prefer to see happen? A hung parliament could lead to a coalition and in turn the Liberal Democrats could gain influence and electoral reform. That would be good for the Liberal Democrats, but is coalition right for the country?

I am left with the conclusion that by the next election Britain will be ready for change, not the uncertainty caused by a hung parliament.

That leaves the question of what best represents a government of change. If Labour wins a fourth term under Brown, the omens are not good. Third term governments tend to do badly, look at Macmillan in the sixties, Thatcher in the eighties and Blair this century. Fourth terms do even worse: Major's government from 1992-1997 was a disaster, but did at least have the benefit of allowing the Labour Party more time to reform. I had always felt that Brown's leadership might be enough to squeeze out a fourth term but it would be clouded by a lack of direction and end up hanging on to power as he oversaw the dying days of New Labour. However, the change from Blair to Brown has surprised me, and in its early days the shape and style of government looks very different. It could now be that a Brown election victory with a clear majority would be a government of substance rather than a footnote to the Blair years.

The Conservatives have made great progress since their triple election defeats and are close to being ready to form a government. They are in a much stronger position than the Labour Party under Kinnock in 1992. If they can add detail to the policy positions starting to emerge, a case can be made for Cameron representing a new start after the next election.

However, the polls don't suggest that either party will have a comfortable majority. So if we are to face a hung parliament the Liberal Democrats will be left as kingmakers. They should grasp the opportunity and deal with the party that has the largest number of seats. I believe it would be possible to work with the Conservatives as they are currently the more liberal of the two major parties, but if Brown continues to surprise and embrace constitutional change and move away from illiberal home affairs legislation then an arrangement could be agreed with him.

Whatever happens, it will require strong leadership and nerve from the Liberal leader, but despite the risks there is the best chance in a generation to achieve electoral reform.

References

1. David Butler Interview, 27 March 2007

2. Professor Whiteley Interview, 21 March 2007

3. *Minority Governments*, David Butler

4. *Constitutional Practice*, Rodney Brazier

5. *Ibid.*

6. *Ibid.*

7. *Ibid.*

8. Neal Lawson Interview, 16 April 2007

9. *Ibid.*

10. *The Ashdown Diaries: 1997-1999, Volume 2,* Paddy Ashdown

11. *Ibid.*

12. *Ibid.*

13. Neal Lawson Interview, 16 April 2007

14. Paul Tyler Interview, 24 April 2007

15. Donald Dewar Memorial Lecture, 12 October 2006

16. Gordon Brown speech to Charter 88 – 9 March 1992

17. *Minority Governments,* David Butler

18. *Independent,* 24 March 2007

19. Speech by David Cameron, 6 May 2006

20. Michael Portillo Interview, 3 May 2007

21. *Ibid.*

22. Paddy Ashdown Interview, 6 March 2007

23. *Independent,* March 2007

24. *Minority Governments,* David Butler

25. Paddy Ashdown Interview, 6 March 2007

26. Professor Whiteley Interview, 21 March 2007

27. Tom McNally Interview, 29 January 2007

28. Clare Short Interview, 1 May 2007

29. *Observer*, 4 March 2007

30. Tom McNally Interview, 29 January 2007

31. Neal Lawson Interview, 16 April 2007

32. *Ibid.*

33. *Observer*, 4 March 2007

34. Clare Short Interview, 1 May 2007

35. Professor Whiteley Interview, 21 March 2007

36. Neal Lawson Interview, 16 April 2007

37. David Butler Interview, 27 March 2007

38. Tom McNally Interview, 29 January 2007

39. David Butler Interview, 27 March 2007

40. Professor Whiteley Interview, 21 March 2007

41. Clare Short MP resigned as the Labour Whip in September 2006 calling for a hung parliament at the next election.

42. Roy Jenkins quoted from *A Progressive Century: The Future of the Centre-Left in Britain*, Neal Lawson & Neil Sherlock

11

Was Disraeli Right?

Was Disraeli Right?

Those who hanker after what a coalition government might theoretically deliver will never be satisfied.[1]

When I started this book I was fairly confident I could challenge Disraeli's assertion that 'England does not love coalitions'. I have spent 18 years of my life as an elected politician, both at local and national level, and have always found the moments when parties work together to be the most rewarding and fruitful. As an advocate of changing the electoral system I have spent hours arguing on doorsteps and in TV studios that it would deliver a more consensual and less confrontational approach to government which would be better for our country. Now, after eight months of delving into history, visiting coalitions around Europe, and interviewing those involved in more recent electoral alliances, I am faced with a tough choice. I could argue that you have to judge coalitions on a case by case basis, but the conclusion I have drawn is that Britain is best governed by a strong single party with a strong opposition. I can see little evidence that coalitions, or pacts, deliver good government. I tend to agree with David Butler when he concluded:

Coalitions may be necessary, they may solve particular problems, they may save particular parties, but they are seldom ideal.[2]

A quick review of the chapters in this book highlights the problems.

The coalition that went on to defeat Disraeli in 1852 was an administration of enormous talent, but it was a coalition of egos. The collective skills of Palmerston, Gladstone, Russell and Aberdeen did not result in a great all-reforming government. Gladstone's budget was the only real success. The coalition tried to run the Crimean War by committee with disastrous consequences and the obvious realignment of politics to create a Liberal Party was delayed by the cult of personality over party. What makes its failing worse is that this coalition did not inherit a crisis. The early Victorian era was one of prosperity and security, in fact the only instability was the political turmoil.

The First World War coalitions were characterised by internal fighting and a failure by politicians to provide the military with the speed of decision-making required. Asquith's coalition was far too slow to adapt to the pressures of war. By establishing the War Committee the Lloyd George coalition was more successful and did at least create a genuine partnership with the Conservatives, it did however result in dividing the Liberal Party.

The decade from 1922-1932 shows the danger for political parties in pacts and coalitions. Both the Labour and Liberal parties were punished by the voters for either failing in minority government, or triggering elections. Ramsay MacDonald ended up as a hate figure after leading Labour to its first victory and then going on to head up a Conservative dominated coalition. This period of three-party politics and inconclusive elections was a minefield for politicians; few came out of it unscathed.

The national unity government created by MacDonald and Baldwin was another illustration of where compromise failed to give clear direction. The 1930s depression and economic crisis needed firm leadership and a clear economic recovery plan. Instead, between them the partners in government delivered indecision and inertia.

The Second World War is perhaps the only true example of a successful coalition. Churchill combined strong leadership with a determination to make his government one of genuine unity. However, the start of the war under Chamberlain's leadership had more in common with the failings of Asquith.

Between 1945 and 1974, Britain had its longest period of clear parliamentary majorities. Then the close election of 1974 saw Edward Heath and Jeremy Thorpe spend what Harold Wilson described as a 'long dirty weekend' trying to form a government. It showed that however close an election might be, coalitons can only work if the arithmetic adds up. On this occasion the combined seats of Conservatives and Liberals were still not enough to form a workable majority. With an eye to the next election, it also showed that the party with the least seats in Westminster has little moral authority to form a government. Although Heath, as sitting Prime Minister, was within his rights to try and establish a government he had clearly lost the election. It makes a nonsense of the convention the Queen would have to follow at the next election.

The coalition that was then formed after the 1918 coupon election has gone down in history as one of the most unpopular governments ever. Although it has become a scapegoat for post-war difficulties, it still presided over a period of unemployment, industrial unrest and political corruption.

In the same chapter I wrote about the pact created between Callaghan and Steel. There are several lessons to be learnt, not least of which is the importance of chemistry between leaders. I doubt if Wilson, Thorpe or Healey could have pulled together a pact in such difficult circumstances. They had an easy relationship and built the kind of trust that is essential for any arrangement to work. The 1977 pact carries with it two warnings. Firstly, the Liberals found themselves getting dragged down by the unpopularity of their larger partner and were not thanked for propping up an unpopular government. Secondly, it is very hard to negotiate a deal midway through a parliament. It was rushed and Steel rightly argues that both sides had little authority to create a programme for government which might have included proportional representation. Instead it was a mishmash of measures that did little to further the cause of Liberal values.

My chapter on Europe details practical ideas on the mechanics of formulating and then maintaining coalitions which I will not repeat. I do, however, draw two key lessons we can learn. In mainland Europe after a close election there is often a referee to help manage the uncertainty and a system of caretaker government to allow time for the negotiations to take place. Britain has neither. Our sovereign has no real power to help broker a deal and the removal vans turn up at Downing Street the day after the election leaving no time for discussions to take place. If Britain is to have closer elections in the future this will have to change.

I was disappointed with the quality of government that I observed in Italy, Austria and Germany. All seemed to have kicked difficult political issues into the long grass and wasted the opportunity to use consensus as a way of developing forward thinking policy.

That said the politicians were charming, the negotiation process worked, and a combination of alcohol and friendship helped create a climate of trust. In a strange way these coalitions all seem to work for their country.

Closer to home I found the coalition in Scotland harder to evaluate. Eight years of Liberal/Labour coalition had been built on a firm trust between Jim Wallace and Donald Dewar. It delivered policy success to the Liberals on tuition fees and health care. The experiment of devolved government and coalition worked, but in 2007, the electorate rejected the Lib/Lab coalition approach and the jury is out on how the Scottish Nationalists will survive as a minority government. I see little evidence that holding senior posts in government and introducing Liberal policy has helped the Liberal Democrats north of the border. They were squeezed out of the 2007 election campaign as if they did not exist.

I named my chapter on the Blair/Ashdown talks 'The Coalition That Never Was'. It struck me that there was a unique opportunity around 1997 to create a progressive new political movement. After eighteen years of Conservative government the parties on the left shared common objectives and it could have been a reforming coalition based on shared values, not just shared needs. It was not to be. We learnt that unless the old established parties are forced to, their instincts are to govern alone and keep the electoral system unreformed.

In my final chapter I set out the key challenges for the political parties if we end up with a hung parliament at the next election. I argue that we need to set out in advance an agreed protocol to deal with this situation. This should require the sovereign to call first on the leader with the party that has the larger number of seats to offer them the chance to form a government. At the same time the sitting Prime Minister should be allowed to continue to run a caretaker government until the issue is resolved.

With the next election in mind, there are some practical lessons that can be learnt if any coalition is to succeed:

1. Establish the principle of a caretaker government to allow time for talks to take place post-election.

2. A political referee is needed to oversee this process in the absence of a president, or monarch with constitutional powers to act.

3. Coalition partners need to consult party members to establish support outside Westminster.

4. Policy working parties should negotiate towards a shared policy coalition agreement.

5. The junior partner should take ministerial posts across government, not just in one department.

6. Day-to-day management of the agreement requires a close relationship and trust between its leaders and a network of bilateral meetings and protocols to deal with "events".

7. The coalition agreement should be time limited to ensure the larger party delivers on its promises within an agreed timescale.

8. Arrangements work best if negotiated at the start of a parliament rather than midterm.

9. Partnership agreement documents can quickly run out of steam and need updating.

10. Events can throw coalitions into turmoil. Processes are needed to resolve these.

11. Trust between the leaders is critical.

12. Coalition between parties that share common values work better than those forced on a narrow set of self-interest policies.

Dangers For Small Fish

The role of a junior coalition partner is one of the hardest to get right. What can seem like an enormous opportunity can quickly turn into a nightmare. The dangers are numerous, as David Butler points out:

> *Coalitions between two unequal parties can turn out to be like the relationship between the tiger and the young lady of Riga. The electorate may soon prove unable to distinguish between the parties. The lesser fry may quickly lose their identity, and with that their goodwill and electoral base.*[3]

There seem to be two problems. The first is the swallowing up and loss of identity that Butler refers to. I see evidence of this in Scotland. The Liberal Democrats should have expected to gain in stature and seats after power sharing. In fact they have not benefited and are now the fourth largest party in Scotland with less seats. The second is that the party identity remains strong, but is associated with failure. This caused a problem for the Liberals in the dying days of the Callaghan Labour government. Although the pact had ended before the winter of discontent, the Liberals were dragged into the downfall.

As David Steel told me:

We were lambasted for simply keeping in office a government which had outstayed its welcome.[4]

The minor parties in the National Government of 1931 were both swamped by the Conservatives. Although both the Labour and Liberal parties secured high offices of state they did not benefit at the polls. The Labour Party divided and faced a decade without power. The Liberals also split and were never again to reach three figures in parliamentary seats.

Paddy Ashdown had the toughest hand as he attempted to share power from a position of weakness, despite securing the largest number of Liberal MPs for decades; his 46 were dwarfed by Labour's thumping majority in 1997. In these circumstances the Liberals did well to negotiate PR for the European election and devolved assemblies in Scotland and Wales. Achieving this for Westminster was just a step too far.

On paper at least, David Steel had an easier task in delivering PR from a Labour government on the ropes facing a vote of no confidence in 1977. Again it proved elusive, as Callaghan was unable to deliver the votes in his own party, many of whom would rather have lost power than agree to electoral reform.

The opportunity for Liberals to share power and gain electoral reform doesn't come along very often. In the last century there have been a handful of chances to use the position of kingmaker to obtain a change in the voting system – all have failed.

If the Liberals are to gain PR then they will need to be very focussed on their approach. I believe the shape of any coalition should be based upon seeking agreement with the party with the largest number of seats. Any deal must include a whipped vote on PR within 18 months and ministerial posts based on a percentage of seats the party have won.

Leaving the coalition is not easy for the parties involved. Charles Kennedy was anxious about avoiding a big announcement when he wanted to abandon the Joint Cabinet Committee with Labour. David Steel pushed hard for the Lib/Lab pact to end before the election, allowing a cooling-off period.

In Scotland the relations between Labour and the Liberals worsened the closer the election got towards the end of 2006. The 1856 coalition ended in acrimony as partners fell out, setting back the establishment of a Liberal Party by years. When Asquith's coalition was replaced by Lloyd George in the First World War it created a total split in the Liberals. David Butler points to the inevitability of strains during coalitions:

> *A coalition is like an incomes policy, easier to establish in a moment of crisis than to escape from gracefully. As time passes the strains are likely to grow and when the hour comes for it to end, the status quo proves impossible to re-establish. Mere participation in a coalition must change each party's image.*[5]

In most cases that image is often worse for the parties involved and particularly so for the third party. And there is a warning for the politicians; the reputations of leaders involved in these coalitions have not been enhanced by their involvement.

The Lowest Common Denominator

I now turn to the critical issue. Are coalitions good for the country?

There is no fixed formula to judge the success of any government. Each one finds itself facing a set of circumstances unique to its time. Coalitions often occur at difficult times and it's all too easy to forget this when assessing their success.

The association of crisis and coalition comes in three main forms: economic, military, or political. In the first two of these the coalition has a clear objective – recovery or victory. The political crisis is more complex. It either arrives as a result of a period of political realignment, such as the period after Peel split the Conservatives, or when the electorate creates a hung parliament, as in the mid 1970s. In these circumstances the coalition objectives are harder to define.

Whatever their differences some common themes emerge. Most coalitions try to play on the appeal of unity.

> *The attraction of the idea of National Government is that it appeals to such praise worthy qualities as kindliness, sacrifice, service and altruism.*[6]

Searle's point is that National Government sounds good. The image of politicians pulling together has popular appeal. Whenever a controversial or complex issue takes place, it is tempting for politicians to churn out phrases like "above party politics", "we need to work together", or "it's time for a cross-party approach". This appeal to work together is common throughout periods of political instability. In 1921, Lloyd George's Attorney General, Gordon Hewart, made this call:

> *Away with faction, away with sectionalism, away with all the self centred demands of groups and inscribe upon your banner the welfare of the whole people.*[7]

Of course there are times to work together. When the bombings took place in London over the summer of 2005, I took part in cross-party talks for months as my party's Home Affairs spokesman.

However, we must not be seduced by the attractions of political unity. Sometimes it is an easier option than a single party having the vision and courage to take a tough decision alone.

My general point is that the image and rhetoric of National Government is often stronger than the reality, or at least as Kenneth Morgan says open to question:

> *One man's national vanity is another's opportunism. One man's petty partisanship, is another's principled independence.*[8]

It is tempting to dodge difficult challenges under the label of national unity. Some politicians also feel more comfortable without the cut and thrust of party debate.

Robert Peel was an example of a politician who preferred the role of national leader to party politician.

> *His allegiance was to an older concept than party loyalty, it was to the service of the state.*[9]

Years later MacDonald used the same justification for putting the country ahead of his Labour Party when he formed a coalition that put up candidates against his old party. Similarly, Lloyd George found the restraints of party difficult and his most successful period was as the leader of a coalition in the First World War. Interestingly when Blair and Ashdown were working together both defied their parties and felt comfortable together as neither were natural leaders of their parties. As Ashdown said to me:

The difficulty with both of us and why we had difficulty carrying our parties was because neither of us are of our party – we are both outsiders.[10]

There is a draw to politicians to create the impression they are above the knock about of party politics. Looking statesmanlike and acting in the national interest is sought after by Prime Ministers.

The problem with this, however, is the way we generate political ideas in this country. Our system is based on conflicting, or opposing, ideas, which compete to win the argument. The consensual approach dampens this creative tension and I am not convinced this helps deliver good policy. The Grand Coalition in Germany requires all parties and voters to be winners, this means difficult decisions which can create losers are fudged.

Deep down the electorate understand that sometimes sacrifices are needed. Tough choices on tax, the environment and delivering health care often require unpopular decisions. I would have felt that a coalition government might have the courage to do this without fear of political attack. The evidence suggests the contrary. Often it is a self-confident government with a healthy majority that tackles the issue head on, whilst it's the coalition governments that can't agree amongst themselves on the measures that would be needed.

There is, I think, also a slight contradiction in the electorate on this issue. Many voters say they don't like the Punch and Judy confrontation style of politics. They warm to the idea of consensus, but equally want strong leadership. They don't want to be troubled with big conflicting arguments, but then one of the reasons put forward for the recent decline in voter turnout is that the public can't see much difference between the parties. Perhaps in a strange way we already have a three-party coalition in Britain. After all most parties are a combination of opinions and to appeal to the electorate have to be very broad based. The big ideological differences have disappeared and the difference between New Labour and Cameron's Conservatives is not easily explained. Blair's legacy may have been to turn the political parties into a twenty-first century coalition of the centre.

Listening To The Voters

One argument for coalition governments is the ability to combine parties to better reflect the voters' wishes. In Britain, governments have large majorities with the support of just 40 per cent of the vote. In 2005, Tony Blair won a clear majority with just over a third of the votes cast. If taken as a percentage of those able to vote it was just 21 per cent. A parliamentary arrangement between Labour and the Liberal Democrats after the last election would have meant at least over 50 per cent of the electorates' wishes would have been reflected in government.

David Butler makes this valid point:

> *They may have that special virtue of adding legitimacy to government action, a party that although possessed of a parliamentary majority, has been backed by only 40 per cent of votes has less moral authority for imposing unpopular measures on the country than a united group of parties which between them received the support of 60 per cent.*[11]

However, there is a problem with this agreement. Creating a coalition to represent 60 per cent of the votes may add up but it assumes that the voters are happy with the combination that takes place. A Lib Dem voter might be aggrieved if his vote is then used to put a Labour/Liberal alliance in place. The problem with coalitions is that the electorates' votes are taken by the politician and then used after the election to assist in private deals. In Italy the parties now make clear who their preferred coalition partners are before the election. This is easier to achieve under a PR system, but under the British electoral system the voters have no real way of influencing the coalition formations.

Without coalitions, governments will always rule despite more people voting against them. However, this simple fact does not seem to trouble the British voters. They view coalitions with suspicion, based on deals made in smoke filled rooms that then deliver weak governments.

In 2006, the former Labour Cabinet Minister, Clare Short resigned the party Whip and said she would campaign for a hung parliament at the next election. She argues that coalition or minority governments are a stronger method of running the country:

> *Large majority government is actually often ego out of central government with no checks and balances. However, if you have a*

*minority government you have to assemble on agreement, make the
case and listen to people not just make a policy with the flick of a
wrist.*[12]

She is scathing of the impact that large majorities have:

*The Thatcher government was arrogant, smashing up institutions but
then we got Blair who was even worse in my view with his
exaggerated majority.*[13]

Others have attacked governments with big majorities. Famously, Francis
Pym in the Thatcher government was given a dressing down after he went
on television and said he felt a large Conservative majority would be
undesirable.

An argument can be made that a minority or coalition government is more
accountable in parliament as every issue has to be debated and the argument
won. I have certainly experienced some of the best parliamentary debates
when there has been a non-whipped vote or, as in the case of terrorism
legislation in 2005, there was a large Labour rebellion and knife-edge vote.
In these circumstances you feel parliamentary democracy works. However,
the consequence of some European coalitions is that these controversial
issues never get debated and if they are it is done behind the scenes, not with
the benefit of full parliamentary scrutiny.

I don't accept that large majorities produce bad government. There is ample
evidence that some of our most needed reforms have been as a result of
parties having a clear mandate and confidence to drive forward a clearly
thought out programme.

However, for this to work there is a need for a strong opposition to challenge
the government and make it justify the agenda for change.

Two-party politics work if there is a tension, but not total war.[14]

Two-party politics can work if this fusion brings with it the right checks
and balances. This involves not just good opposition, but a second chamber
or separate form of scrutiny. In an attack on coalition government after the
Scottish election in May 2007, Simon Jenkins recommended this model:

A constitution that empowers a stable cabinet subject to an external check – a separately elected assembly – is preferable to one that internalises that check with a rolling coalition, where it is vulnerable to the whim of minority parties.[15]

I am not convinced that minority coalition governments can deliver a philosophically united programme or provide strong enough leadership. The track record is not good. The 1850 coalition created an unnecessary war and failed on domestic policy. The First World War lurched from one coalition to another with near disastrous consequences. The 1930 National Government never resolved the economic crisis and dodged difficult choices. The Lib/Lab pact although successful in stabilising the economy was in the business of survival and did not provide a new beginning. The Joint Cabinet Committee created by Ashdown and Blair made some constitutional reforms but still ducked electoral reform at Westminster. The German Grand Coalition led by Angela Merkel has parked necessary health reform and has become a "do nothing" government. The Italian governments keep collapsing with minority parties holding them to ransom, leaving domestic policy at the whim of church groups or pensioner parties. The 1856 and 1931 coalitions and many in mainland Europe suffer from policy by committee.

There is one obvious exception to this. The Second World War coalition, led by Churchill, is in A.J.P. Taylor's words a success:

It was the only genuine National Government in British history since it was in the unique position of commanding the almost unanimous allegiance of both parliament and the country.[16]

Perhaps this indicates one of the keys to success. If a coalition government can have a strong leader it stands a greater chance of success. Aberdeen, MacDonald, Asquith and Chamberlain were not able to give the leadership that was needed. Lloyd George and to a greater extent Churchill could, and this goes some way to explaining why their coalitions go down as the most successful.

Coalitions then have a role to play and allow the business of government to continue during difficult times. They can also bring short-term advantages to political parties if handled correctly. But given the alternative between a majority government and coalition, I conclude that it is ideal government if one is elected with a clear mandate, based on a set of understood values, with a strong leader. This must be matched with a healthy system of opposition and parliamentary scrutiny.

However, I have come to learn that in politics, as in life, things are often far from ideal. It's full of surprises and uncertainties. So if at the next election we end up with a hung parliament I'll watch with interest to see how the key players take their chances.

I wish them well, but one thing is for sure it will make or break them.

References

1. *Country Before Party: Coalition and the Idea of 'National Government' in Modern Britain*, G. R. Searle

2. *Coalitions in British Politics*, David Butler

3. *Ibid.*

4. David Steel Interview, 27 February 2007

5. *Coalitions in British Politics*, David Butler

6. *Country Before Party: Coalition and the Idea of 'National Government' in Modern Britain*, G. R. Searle

7. *Ibid.*

8. Kenneth O. Morgan, from *Coalitions in British Politics*, David Butler

9. *A United Kingdom*, David Owen

10. Paddy Ashdown Interview, 6 March 2007

11. *Coalition in British Government*, David Butler

12. Clare Short Interview, 1 May 2007

13. *Ibid.*

14. *Country Before Party: Coalition and the Idea of 'National Government' in Modern Britain*, G. R. Searle

15. Simon Jenkins, *The Guardian*, May 2007

16. A.J.P. Taylor in *Coalitions in British Politics*, David Butler

Appendices

Appendix

References

Books

Ashdown Diaries Volume One, The, Paddy Ashdown (Penguin Press, 2000)

Ashdown Diaries Volume Two, The, Paddy Ashdown (Penguin Press, 2001)

Aspects of British Political History 1914-1995, Stephen J Lee (Routledge, 1996)

Austria 1945-1995: Fifty Years of the Second Republic, Kurt Richard Luther and Peter Pulzer (London, Ashgate, 1998)

Baldwin: The Unexpected Prime Minister, H Montgomery Hyde (Hart-Davis, 1973)

Baldwin, Roy Jenkins (Collins, 1987)

Baldwin Papers: A Conservative Statesman 1908-1947, 1st Earl Baldwin of Bewdley, 1st Earl, Philip Williamson *et al* (Cambridge University Press, 2004)

Benjamin Disraeli Letters 1852-1856, Earl Beaconsfield, Mary Millar *et al* (University of Toronto Press, 1998)

Blair, Anthony Seldon (Free Press, 2005)

British General Election of 1931, The, Andrew Thorpe (Clarendon Press, 1991)

British Politics and the Great War: Coalition and Conflict, 1915-18, John Turner (Yale University Press, 1992)

Cabinets in Western Europe, Jean Blondel and Ferdinand Muller-Rommel (Palgrave Macmillan, 1989)

Callaghan: A Life, Kenneth O. Morgan (Oxford University Press, 1997)

Charles Kennedy: A Tragic Flaw, Greg Hurst (Politico's, 2006)

'Chips': The Diaries of Sir Henry Channon, Sir Henry Channon & Robert Rhode James (ed.), (Weidenfeld & Nicolson, 1967)

Churchill, The End of Glory, John Charmley (Harcourt, 1993)

Churchill: A Biography, Roy Jenkins (Macmillan, 2001)

Churchill Coalition 1940-1945, The, J.M. Lee (Batsford Academic and Educational Ltd, 1980)

Churchill Coalition and Wartime Politics 1940-1945, The, Kevin Jefferys (Manchester University Press, 1991)

Coalition Diaries and Letters of H.A.L. Fisher, 1916-1918: The Historian in Lloyd George's Cabinet, The, Volume 1, H. A. L. Fisher

Coalition Diaries and Letters of H.A.L. Fisher, 1919-1920: The Historian in Lloyd George's Cabinet, The, Volume 2, H. A. L. Fisher (Edwin Mellen Press, 2006)

Coalition Government in Britain: Lessons from overseas, Ben Seyd (Constitution Unit, 2002)

Coalition Governance in Scotland and Wales, Ben Seyd (Constitution Unit, 2004)

Coalition Governments in Western Europe, Wolfgang C Müller and Kaare Strom (Oxford University Press, 2003)

Coalitions in British Politics, David Butler (Macmillan, 1978)

Consensus and Disunity: The Lloyd George Coalition Government 1918-1922, Kenneth O. Morgan (Oxford University Press, 1986)

Conservative Party from Peel to Churchill, The, Robert Blake (Collins, 1972)

Conservative Party from Peel to Thatcher, The, Robert Blake (Fontana, 1985)

Constitutional Practice: The Foundations of British Government, Rodney Brazier (Oxford University Press, 1999)

Country Before Party: Coalition and the Idea of 'National Government' in Modern Britain, 1885-1987, G. R. Searle (Longman, 1995)

Disraeli, Lord Robert Blake (Prion Books, 1998)

Disraeli, Sarah Bradford (Stein and Day, 1983)

Disraeli and Gladstone, D C Somervell (Faber and Faber, 1925)

Edward Heath: A Biography, John Campbell (Pimlico, 1993)

Edward Heath, Prime Minister, Margaret Laing (Third Press, 1972)

England in the Nineteenth Century: 1815-1914, David Thomson (Penguin, 1950)

Fascists and Conservatives: Radical Right and the Establishment in Twentieth Century Europe, Martin Blinkhorn (Routledge, 1990)

Fateful Years: Memoirs, 1931-1945, The, Hugh Dalton (Muller, 1957)

Gladstone, Roy Jenkins (Macmillan, 1995)

History of the Labour Party from 1914, A, G. D. H. Cole (Routledge, 1948)

House Divided, A, David Steel (Weidenfeld and Nicolson, 1980)

In My Own Time, Jeremy Thorpe (Politico's, 1999)

Jo Grimond: Towards the Sound of Gunfire, Michael McManus (Birlinn, 2001)

Kinnock, Martin Westlake (Little, Brown, 2001)

Labour in Power? A Study of the Labour Government 1974-1979, David Coates (Longman, 1980)

Last Years of Liberal England, 1900-1914, The, K W W Aikin (Collins, 1972)

Letters of Sidney and Beatrice Webb, The, Norman MacKenzie (Cambridge University Press, 1978)

Life and Times of Ernest Bevin, Vol. II Minister of Labour 1940-1945, The, Alan Bullock (Heinemann, 1967)

Life at the Centre, A, Roy Jenkins (Macmillan, 1991)

Life of Neville Chamberlain, The, Keith Feiling (Macmillan, 1946)

Life of Ramsay MacDonald 1866/1919, The, Lord Elton (Collins, 1939)

Lord Aberdeen: A Political Biography, Muriel E. Chamberlain (Longman, 1983)

Lord Palmerston, Jasper Ridley (Anchor Press, 1970)

Men and Power 1917-1918, Lord Beaverbrook (Hutchinson, 1956)

Michael Foot: A Life, Kenneth O. Morgan (HarperPress, 2007)

Minority Governments, David Butler

Multiparty Government, Michael Laver (Oxford University Press, 1990)

National Crisis and National Government: British Politics, the Economy and Empire, 1926-1932, Philip Williamson (Cambridge University Press, 2002)

Orange Book, The, David Laws & Paul Marshall (Profile, 2004)

Parties and Democracy: Coalition Formation and Government Functioning in Twenty States, Ian Budge and Hans Keman (Oxford University Press, 1993)

Passing of the Whigs 1832-1886, The, Donald Southgate (Macmillan, 1962)

Penhaligon, Annette Penhaligon (Bloomsbury, 1989)

Political Diary of Hugh Dalton 1918-1940, The, Ben Pimlott (ed.) (Jonathan Cape, 1986)

Political Parties in the New Europe: Political and Analytical Challenges, Kurt Richard Luther and Ferdinand Müller-Rommel (Oxford University Press, 2002)

Political Parties of the World, Bogdan Szajkowski (John Harper Publishing, 2005)

Politics in Industrial Society: The Experience of the British system since 1911, Keith Middlemas (Andre Deutsch, 1979)

Progressive Century: The Future of the Centre-Left in Britain, The, Neal Lawson & Neil Sherlock (Palgrave Macmillan, 2001)

Ramsay MacDonald, David Marquand (Jonathan Cape, 1977)

Ramsay MacDonald's Political Writings, Ramsay MacDonald and Bernard Barker (St. Martin's Press, 1972)

Road to 1945: British Politics and the Second World War, The, Paul Addison (Jonathan Cape, 1975)

Short History of the Liberal Party, 1900-1997, A, Chris Cook (Macmillan, 1998)

Stability and Choice: Review of Single Party and Coalition Government, Ian Budge (Charter 88, 1998)

Stanley Baldwin, G. M. Young (Greenwood Press, 1979)

Time and Chance, James Callaghan (Collins, 1987)

Time of My Life, The, Denis Healey (Michael Joseph, 1989)

Victorian People: A Reassessment of Persons and Themes, 1851-67, Asa Briggs (Penguin, 1970)

War Speeches of Churchill, The, Charles Eade (Cassell, 1951)

Wilson, Philip Ziegler (Weidenfeld and Nicolson, 1993)

Winston S. Churchill: The Stricken World 1916-1922, Vol. IV, Martin Gilbert (Houghton Mifflin, 1975)

Manuscript sources

Asquith Papers

Lloyd George Papers

Personal and Literary Papers of Herbert, First Viscount Samuel, Herbert Samuel

Printed sources

Primary sources

Hansard Reports

The Times Archives

The Observer Archives

Secondary sources

Books

Against Goliath, David Steel (Weidenfeld and Nicolson, 1989)

Age of Balfour and Baldwin, 1902-1940, The, John Ramsden (Longman, 1978)

As It Seemed To Me: Political Memoirs, John Cole (Weidenfeld and Nicolson, 1995)

Asquith, Roy Jenkins (Collins, 1986)

Disraeli, Derby and the Conservative Party: Journals and Memoirs of Edward Henry, Lord Stanley, 1849-1869, John Vincent (Harvester Press, 1978)

Downfall of the Liberal Party 1914-1935, The, Trevor Wilson (Collins, 1966)

Empire at Bay: The Leo Amery Diaries, The, 1929-1945, Leo Amery (Hutchinson, 1987)

Four and a Half Years: A personal diary from June 1914 to January 1919, volume II, Christopher Addison (Hutchinson, 1934)

Governing Together: The Extent & Limits of Joint Decision Making in Western European Cabinets, Jean Blondel & Ferdinand Müller-Rommel (St. Martin's Press, 1993)

Lloyd George and Churchill: Rivals for Greatness, Richard Toye (Macmillan, 2007)

Memories and Reflections, Herbert Asquith (London, 1928)

Memoirs of an Ex Minister, Volume 1, James Howard Harris Malmesbury (Adamant Media Corporation, 2001)

Political Lives, Hugo Young (Oxford University Press, 2001)

Politicians and the Slump: The Labour Government of 1929-1931, Robert Skidelsky (Penguin, 1971)

Politicians and the War 1914-1916, Lord Beaverbrook (Lane, 1932)

Politicians At War July 1914 to May 1915: A Prologue to the Triumph of Lloyd George, Cameron Hazlehurst (Jonathan Cape, 1971)

Riddell Diaries 1908-1923, The, Lord Riddell (Athlone Press, 1986)

Sir Robert Peel: The life of Sir Robert Peel after 1830, Norman Gash (Longman, 1972)

Stanley Baldwin: Conservative Leadership and National Government Values, Phillip Williamson & Stanley Baldwin (Cambridge University Press, 1999)

Strategy of the Lloyd George Coalition, David French (Clarendon Press, 1995)

War and the State, Kathleen Burk (Allen and Unwin, 1982)

Papers

'Asquith, Bonar Law and the First Coalition', Martin Pugh, *The Historical Journal*, 17 (1974)

'Asquith's Predicament, 1914-1918', Barry McGill, *Journal of Modern History*, 39 (1967)

'Lloyd George's Premiership: a Study in "Prime Ministerial Government"', Kenneth O. Morgan, *The Historical Journal*, XIII (1970)

'Lloyd George's Timing of the 1918 Election', Barry McGill, *Journal of British Studies*, 14 (1974)

'Political Change in Britain, August 1914 to December 1916: Lloyd George Replaces Asquith: the Issues Underlying the Drama', Michael Fry, *The Historical Journal*, 31 (1988)

Interviewees

Ashdown, Lord Paddy, 6 March 2007

Butler, David, 27 March 2007

Gerlich, Professor Peter, 23 January 2007

Ghibaldan, Sam, 27 February 2007

Kennedy, Charles, 9 May 2007

Khol, Andreas, 23 January 2007

Laws, David MP, 20 February 2007

Lawson, Neal, 16 April 2007

Morgan, Lord Kenneth, 26 March 2007

McNally, Lord Tom, 29 January 2007

Pera, Marcello, 8 February 2007

Portillo, Michael, 3 May 2007

Scholz, Olaf, 15 March 2007

Short, Clare MP, 2 May 2007

Siegele, Ludwig, February 2007

Steel, Lord David, 27 February 2007

Stuart, Gisela MP, 7 May 2007

Thorpe, Jeremy, 2 May 2007

Tyler, Lord Paul, 24 April 2007

Wallace, Jim MSP, 13 February 2007

Walston, Professor James, 8 February 2007

Whiteley, Professor Paul, 12 March 2007

Whitton, David, 27 February 2007

Worcester, Bob, 27 February 2007

Index